Journal of College Student Development

THE JOURNAL OF ACPA – COLLEGE STUDENT EDUCATORS INTERNATIONAL VOL 64 / NO 2 • MAR–APR 2023

EDITOR

Vasti Torres
Indiana University

EXECUTIVE ASSOCIATE EDITOR

Research in Brief / Translational Educational Research
Jason C. Garvey
The University of Vermont

ASSOCIATE EDITORS

International Research
Ebelia Hernández
Rutgers, The State University of New Jersey

Book Reviews
Leilani Kupo
University of Nevada, Reno

Assistants to the Editor

Larry Locke, Publication Coordinator

Dr. Tracy Skipper, Copy Editor

Membership and Subscriptions

JCSD is a benefit of ACPA membership. Information concerning application for membership in ACPA and individual or library subscriptions to the *Journal of College Student Development* may be obtained from:
ACPA – College Student Educators International, One Dupont Circle, NW, Washington, DC 20036-1188, telephone 202-835-2272, www.myacpa.org

Member Address Change / Claims

Notice of change of address should be sent at least five weeks in advance to ACPA at the above address. Undelivered copies resulting from an address change will not be replaced but may be purchased at the single-issue price; addressees should notify the post office that they will guarantee second class postage. Member claims should be made through ACPA. Other claims for undelivered copies must be made within four months of publication by calling Johns Hopkins University Press at 800-548-1784.

Microfilm

Available from University Microfilms, Inc.
P.O. Box 1346
Ann Arbor, MI 48106-1346

Indexing

Education Index, Higher Education Abstracts, Current Index to Journals in Education, Educational Administration Abstracts, Current Contents, Psychological Abstracts, Social and Behavioral Sciences, Social Sciences Citation Index, Social Work Research & Abstracts, Research Alert, Social SciSearch, ERIH PLUS.

Submissions

Manuscripts submitted for publication should meet the requirements of *JCSD*'s "Guidelines for Authors," found at http://www.myacpa.org/Journal-College-Student-Development

Authors should submit manuscripts electronically via http://www.editorialmanager.com/jcsd

Ownership / Postal Information

The *Journal of College Student Development* (ISSN 0897-5264) is published bimonthly by the ACPA—College Student Educators International, One Dupont Circle, NW, Suite 300, Washington, DC 20036-1110, and is distributed by the Johns Hopkins University Press.

Periodicals postage paid at Washington, DC 20090-7501, and at additional mailing offices.

POSTMASTER: Send address changes to *Journal of College Student Development*, ACPA – College Student Educators International, One Dupont Circle, NW, Suite 300, Washington, DC 20036-1110.

Front cover photograph provided by Indiana University Bloomington, which acknowledges and honors the Miami, Delaware, Potawatomi, and Shawnee peoples on whose ancestral homelands and resources Indiana University Bloomington is built.

ISSN 0897-5264

Journal of College Student Development

THE JOURNAL OF ACPA – COLLEGE STUDENT EDUCATORS INTERNATIONAL   VOL 64 / NO 2 • MAR–APR 2023

TABLE OF CONTENTS

International Research

Dr. Ebelia Hernandez, ASSOCIATE EDITOR

Research in Brief

Jason C. Garvey, EXECUTIVE ASSOCIATE EDITOR

Translational Education Research
Dr. Jason C. Garvey, ASSOCIATE EDITOR

Dr. Sherry Watt, ASSOCIATE EDITOR

ACPA – College Student Educators International

Individual and Systemic Impacts of Hegemonic Masculinity on College Men Sexual Violence Peer Educators

Daniel Tillapaugh

In this article, I explore the individual and systemic impact of hegemonic masculinity on college men serving as peer educators in sexual violence prevention programs. This ethnographic study was completed during the 2017–2018 academic year at a public university in the Southwest. Following an organization in the midst of a great deal of transition, I observed how hegemonic masculinity, particularly by way of male/men privilege and cisheteropatriarchy, was entrenched, actualized through curriculum, and occasionally resisted and critiqued. Through this article, I outline how the program allowed college men participants opportunities for further self-awareness around hegemonic masculinity, yet the program's systemic outcomes did not always play out in expected ways. Implications for future practice and research are discussed.

Hegemonic masculinity has a significant effect on the lives of college men (Davis & Wagner, 2005; Edwards & Jones, 2009; Kimmel, 2008; Tillapaugh & McGowan, 2019). Defined by Connell (2005), hegemonic masculinity represents societal practices that normalize the privileging of men in a dominant position without merit and justifies women being placed in subordinate roles. In their work, Davis and Wagner (2005) argued that "men are simultaneously privileged and harmed by their experiences of power" (p. 34), particularly given that upholding and reinforcing hegemonic masculinity can create multiple negative life outcomes for men. Such outcomes can include restrictive emotionality, restrained affectionate behaviors toward other men, an obsessive focus on achievement and success, and socialized power and control (O'Neil et al., 1986). For many working in student affairs, promoting opportunities for college men to become engaged in social justice work, including having men engaged in sexual violence prevention work on campus, can serve as an important developmental experience in disrupting hegemonic masculinity.

Sexual violence prevention work in higher education is critical given that college students with any gender identity are at increased risk of violence compared to their non-student peers. College women aged 18 to 24 are three times as likely to experience sexual violence; men in college are 78% more likely to be raped or sexually assaulted than their non-student peers (Sinozich & Langton, 2014). In a study that looked at the rates of violence among transgender college students compared to their cisgender peers, Griner et al. (2020) found that transgender students were at significantly greater risk for sexual victimization. Relatedly when looking at the perpetrators of this violence, men are disproportionately victimizing others (Black et al., 2011). The earlier discussion of hegemonic masculinity and its influence on men's development in our society makes clear that sexual violence is often weaponized as a tool of dominance and power over others (Harris & Linder, 2017; Linder et al., 2020). As a result, it is important for higher education administrators to understand the ways that hegemonic masculinity may create tensions and possibilities for college men

Daniel Tillapaugh (https://orcid.org/0000-0002-7349-9557) is Associate Professor of Counselor Education at California Lutheran University.

who are engaged as peer educators in sexual violence prevention programs in colleges and universities.

The purpose of this ethnographic study was to understand the ways hegemonic masculinity is seen organizationally, as well as individually, among college men who serve as sexual violence prevention (SVP) peer educators. Two research questions underpin this study:

1. How does hegemonic masculinity mediate the experiences of college men who serve as SVP peer educators?
2. How do college men who are engaged as SVP peer educators confront, navigate, resist, or push back against these gender norms?

This particular manuscript highlights some observed contradictions of hegemonic masculine norms that existed within the group's organizational culture and individual members' experiences.

LITERATURE REVIEW

For a number of years, health and wellness offices in higher education in the United States have used peer education programs for topics such as SVP, alcohol and drug use/misuse, and mental health and well-being (American College Health Association, 2007). College peer educators are often more successful than professional staff members in connecting with their audiences and providing key information for healthier outcomes around personal health and wellness (White et al., 2009). Wawrzynski et al. (2011) noted that college peer educators often are able to leverage the commonalities they have with other students to talk openly and more comfortably about personal health and wellness topics, particularly given that many peer educators serve as role models to other students. Given that men are overwhelmingly the perpetrators of sexual violence (Harris &

Linder, 2017; Linder, 2018; Rennison, 2002), it stands to reason that peer-to-peer education programs facilitated by college men for college men may have a significant impact on addressing rape culture and sexism on campus (Barone et al., 2007).

Over the past two decades, SVP efforts have proliferated globally, especially those designed to educate young boys and men about rape culture (Casey et al., 2018). In particular, there has been a strong focus on the creation of same-gender programs (i.e., all-men groups) to involve men as allies in SVP (Barone et al., 2007; Casey, 2010; McMahon & Dick, 2011; Pease, 2008; Piccigallo et al., 2012). Given this attention, some colleges and universities have established all-men programs to engage in SVP and bystander intervention around violence and rape culture on campus (McMahon & Dick, 2011; Piccigallo et al., 2012). Other institutions have also implemented bystander intervention training as a part of student leader development initiatives to help paraprofessionals engage with their peers to eradicate rape culture and harassment (Banyard et al., 2009). While these efforts aim to create social change around sexual violence, it is unclear whether these programs adequately produce the desired programmatic outcomes.

As SVP efforts become more commonplace in US colleges and universities, more men have found ways to engage in these efforts through services and programs such as Walk a Mile in Her Shoes (Linder & Johnson, 2015; Nicolazzo, 2015). However, as Nicolazzo (2015) and Linder and Johnson (2015) articulated, these programs can be essentialized by college men to be seen as "good men" and allies. They may often reinforce the notion that heterosexual cisgender women need to be saved from sexual violence rather than truly problematizing gender and rape culture. Linder and Johnson's study was informed by college women and their experiences with and perceptions of men engaged in ally work, not men themselves, which further emphasizes the importance of the present study.

Hegemonic Masculinity and College Men

The literature on college men's development has often linked hegemonic masculinity to the socialization of boys and young men in Western society (Edwards & Jones, 2009; Edwards, 2022; Harper & Harris, 2009; Kimmel, 2008; Tillapaugh & McGowan, 2019). Many scholars studying college men and masculinities (see Edwards & Jones, 2009; Edwards, 2022; Harper & Harris, 2009; Tillapaugh & McGowan, 2019) have posited that higher education institutions themselves, given their policies, structures, institutional agents, and socialized cultural practices and rituals, reinforce hegemonic masculinity as a tool of dominance and power. Hegemonic masculinity has also been used as a theoretical framework in higher education scholarship to explore college men's alcohol consumption (Radimer & Rowan-Kenyon, 2019), models of college men's development (Edwards & Jones, 2009; Harris & Edwards, 2010), and SVP peer education programs (Barone et al., 2007).

Linking theory and practice around hegemonic masculinity and its impacts on college students, some college educators have attempted to create spaces for men to engage with one another about masculinity, including SVP and response efforts (Barone et al., 2007; Berkowitz, 2011; Piccigallo et al., 2012). In many cases, SVP programs are spaces where men can talk with other men about hegemonic masculinity and its negative life outcomes, the eradication of rape culture in higher education, and ways that college men can engage in bystander intervention with peers around sexual violence (Barone et al., 2007; Berkowitz, 2011; Katz, 2009). Scholars studying all-men programs have offered mixed messages about their efficacy. Among the 26 participants of an all-men SVP program, researchers found that the men's "knowledge related to sexual assault, their empathy for sexual assault survivors and motivation to engage in the prevention of sexual violence increased" (Piccigallo et al., 2012, p. 508). Barone et al. (2007) found that participants in an all-men SVP program employed more strategies around bystander intervention regarding sexism and rejected hegemonic masculine values and ideals. Yet, other scholars (see Berkowitz, 2011; Kimmel, 2008) have raised concern about all-men spaces given that there is often a tension experienced by college men where they articulate their discomfort around other men's toxic or hegemonic masculinity while still desiring approval and validation of their manhood from those same men.

CONCEPTUAL FRAMEWORK

When examining gender in much of Western society, hegemonic masculinity is deeply embedded in systemic power through patriarchy and dominant power structures (Connell, 2005). Connell (2005) noted that multiple masculinities exist and are embedded in the political, economic, and power structures that mediate our daily lives. In highlighting hegemonic masculinity, Connell proposed four specific positions of masculinities that are experienced within society: (a) hegemony, (b) subordination, (c) complicity, and (d) marginalization. Hegemonic masculinity is understood as the ideal type of masculinity within a particular culture (Connell, 2005). Subordination is the consequence and experience of men who fail to adhere to hegemonic ideals, such as gay men or men from other marginalized communities (Connell, 2005). Complicity, which is experienced by most men, occurs when men adhere to and accept hegemonic masculinity because they earn and maintain dominant power, thereby avoiding subordination (Connell, 2005). Lastly, marginalization is experienced by men with multiple minoritized social locations and actively enacted by those holding power through hegemonic masculinity (Connell, 2005). Each of these positions serves as an interlocking system by which "the configuration of gendered practice which embodies the currently accepted answer to the problem of the legitimacy of patriarchy, which guarantees (or is taken to guarantee) the dominant position of men and the subordination of women" (p. 77) and other gender and sexual minorities.

Within higher education, hegemonic masculinity is replicated and reinforced through practices that center young men who prove their manhood by being emotionally restrictive, engaging in and being willing to receive violence from other men, being competitive and seeking control, and seeking promiscuous and high-risk behaviors (Kimmel, 2008; O'Neil et al., 1986). Scholars focusing on college men (see Edwards & Jones, 2009; Kimmel, 2008; Tillapaugh & McGowan, 2019) have argued that the socialization of hegemonic masculinity is internalized, reinforced, and enforced through peer-to-peer relationships and cultural practices within various student cultures/organizations/spaces on campus. Therefore, these practices may be performative on an individual basis but also structured through policies, procedures, and practices that serve as rites or traditions on college and university campuses (i.e., homecoming king and queen elections, fraternity life). Given that hegemonic masculinity is culturally embedded in society, this conceptual framework serves as a lens for this particular study of men who serve as SVP peer educators on their university campus and for exploring how contradictions of hegemonic masculinity mediate their experiences in this group.

STUDY DESIGN

For this ethnographic study, I embedded myself within Southwest University's (SU;

a pseudonym) Men Against Sexual Assault (MASA) student organization for the 2017–2018 academic year. Located in the US Southwest, SU is a large public state university with more than 75% of the student population identifying as students of color, one of the most racially diverse campuses in the state. MASA was started in 2014 as a men-only peer education group focused on discussions of masculinity and on educating other predominantly men-only student organizations, such as fraternities and men's athletic teams, about toxic masculinity and ending rape culture.

The group itself was going through substantial transition and member turnover throughout my time embedded with MASA. At the conclusion of the academic year prior to the study, the majority of MASA participants graduated, leaving only a handful of remaining members. While the group regularly attempted to recruit additional members, those efforts were not successful. Throughout the academic year, there were fewer than 10 regular student participants in the group, with multiple other prospective attendees showing up for one (or two at most) meetings and then not returning (see Table 1). Throughout this article, I use pseudonyms for all participants. Among the core group of regular attendees, the lack of accountability for participation and attendance led to irregular involvement, even for members of the executive board. While the student participants themselves were racially diverse (4 Latino, 3 White, 1 Black, 1 Asian American), the professional staff facilitators were all White. Participants were often recruited directly by the group facilitators or through tabling events on campus, with members being required to table a minimum of 5 hours a semester. Yet, participants themselves openly complained about tabling and often avoided participating if they could. Additionally, public health majors taking certain classes were required to participate in peer education programs. Therefore, some participants were

Table 1.
Participants' Demographics

Name	Role in MASA	Undergrad, faculty, and/or staff	Gender	Race/ethnicity
Narek	Facilitator (Fall 2017)	Staff	Man	White/Armenian
Sean	Creator of MASA	Faculty	Man	White
Jeff	Member (Fall 2017)/ Facilitator (Spring 2018)	Undergrad & Staff	Man	Black
Jeremy	Co-Facilitator (Spring 2018)	Staff	Man	White
David	Treasurer	Undergrad	Man	Asian-American
Carolina	President	Undergrad	Woman	Latina
Karla	Secretary & Student Intern (Fall 2017)	Undergrad	Woman	Latina
Gosdan	Member	Undergrad	Man	White/Armenian
Vinny	Member & Student Intern (Fall 2017)	Undergrad	Man	Latino
Mike	Member	Undergrad	Man	White
Vanessa	Member	Undergrad	Woman	White
Juan	Prospective Member	Undergrad	Man	Latino

required to be involved for academic credit; typically, these were the students regularly in attendance because their academic unit required them to be present. Other participants were paid student interns through the campus's counseling center, which supported the program.

As a researcher, I approached my work through a lens of critical constructivism (Kincheloe, 2008), which focuses on the mutuality formed between researchers and participants and allows for "a thicker, more detailed, more complex understanding of the social, political, economic, cultural, psychological, and pedagogical world" (Kincheloe, 2008, p. 3). Critical constructivism draws on both constructivist and critical theory paradigms, allowing individuals to examine socially constructed concepts while investigating how systems of power and oppression mediate that social construction (Kincheloe, 2008). This approach was particularly useful given Kincheloe's (2008) argument that critical constructivist perspectives "pushes

interpretation to new levels, moving beyond what is visible to the ethnographic eye to the exposure of concealed motives that move events and shape everyday lives" (p. 22).

I used an ethnographic approach to study how hegemonic masculinity played a role individually and collectively among the college men who were SVP peer educators. Ethnography is useful for research that examines a particular group and its cultural norms and artifacts by having the researcher engaged in a sustained, prolonged stay within the group or organization (Mertler, 2019). Ethnographic research is grounded in interpretive interactionism (Denzin, 1989). This, along with my orientation as a critical constructivist, meant I worked to center the importance of establishing trust and meaningful relationships between myself as the researcher and participants in constructing a shared reality (Lykes, 1989). This approach to ethnographic research is grounded in other studies exploring student sub-groups and populations in higher education (see Magolda, 2003, 2016; Nicolazzo, 2016).

As a part of the data collection, I relied on two main ethnographic tools: observations (Wolcott, 1994) and ethnographic interviews (Heyl, 2007). Over the academic year, I attended weekly training meetings during the fall and spring semesters, as well as public presentations on campus as a privileged observer (Mertler, 2019). Being a privileged observer meant that I was an active participant in the MASA group meetings, engaging in dialogue and participating in the curriculum, yet I was also engaged as a researcher taking observation fieldnotes and documenting aspects of the site and organizational life of MASA. Additionally, I interviewed, both formally and informally, participants of the peer education program as well as the leaders of the program. To better understand the organization and its culture, I also reviewed multiple written documents about MASA, including the program curriculum, the slide decks used for peer education training, the organization's website and member handbook documents, as well as online articles in the student newspaper. These documents were essential in providing greater context while collecting and analyzing the data.

Throughout data collection, I kept a thorough ethnographic fieldwork journal with entries that outlined the date, time, and location of my observations of MASA training meetings and presentations. Within these entries, I indicated the names of individuals with whom I interacted and detailed my observations and participation. Additionally, I actively wrote analytic memos throughout my time embedded within the MASA program. Following group meetings or presentations, I reflected on critical questions or reflections I had and used these to later raise a question or invite the participant or facilitator to share their perspectives of that session and dialogue to find mutual meaning and understanding.

During the fall semester, I formally interviewed Jeff, Gosdan, Vinny, and Mike, who each agreed to meet with me one-on-one. In the spring semester, I formally interviewed Jeff and Mike again (Vinny graduated in December 2017; Gosdan decided not to continue his involvement in the group after Narek left his position in December). All interviews used a semi-structured interview protocol and explored participants' views on masculinity, their perceptions of sexual violence education on campus, and their work within MASA. I audiotaped these formal interviews, had them professionally transcribed, and shared the transcripts with each participant to engage in member checking. Each interview lasted between 40 to 90 minutes.

After each interview, I asked the participants to respond to 10 journal prompts as a form of triangulation. Acknowledging that some participants might share more detail or information in writing than in a face-to-face interview, I wanted to provide an opportunity for further dialogue. Sample questions included "How would you explain hegemonic masculinity to others who might not know what that means?" and "When you think about your role as an SVP peer educator, what have you learned most about yourself through that involvement?" Most of the participants' responses were very brief and often aligned with what they shared in the ethnographic interviews. Participants were compensated with a $25 Visa gift card for each semester that they completed the interview and journal prompt responses.

Simultaneous with data collection, I engaged in memo writing to analyze the data, and I often used these memos in dialogues and conversations with the participants to engage in collaborative meaning-making. Using Glaser's (1965) constant comparative method for data analysis, I attempted to find patterns and themes across the data and test whether and how those themes connected or diverged from one another. For instance, given the ways masculinity and gender role socialization played out within the group, I used memo writing to identify how patterns of observed behaviors or thoughts among the participants' interactions and discussions in MASA coalesced and to note ways that participants might shift their discussions or behaviors with me in a one-on-one interview. In this way, I began to reflect, analyze, and question certain patterns and tensions, and I often used these to track my observations and further data collection points with the MASA participants. When tensions arose, I often asked the participants for their insights into what I was observing to resolve questions or potential confusion, again as an act of collaborative meaning-making. In particular, I attempted to meet Wolcott's (1994) notion of rigorous subjectivity in my analysis, aiming for sensitivity, balance, and thoroughness given my own personal beliefs and opinions.

Positionality

I came to this work as a sexual violence survivor myself and as someone who has an ongoing commitment to eradicating sexual violence in all forms. I have had experience both as a practitioner and researcher in supporting men's development in colleges and universities. Yet, I also have a healthy skepticism for passive and active programming geared to college men around SVP, particularly given how much of the curriculum and programming can often over-rely on messages about certain victims (i.e., heterosexual cisgender women) and their need to protect themselves rather than addressing interventions for perpetrators of sexual violence. That being said, I believe in the potential of same-gender groups to provide young adults with opportunities for meaning-making. When done well and if facilitated in a critical and inclusive manner, I believe that all-men groups can be used as a powerful intervention for learning and transformation. As a queer, White, cisgender man, I also simultaneously worry about how SVP

work in all-men spaces can be challenging for peer educators if they have not been adequately trained or do not have the fortitude to respond to resistance from their audience members.

FINDINGS

In what follows, I focus on findings that center the contradictions I observed and discussed with participants of MASA around hegemonic masculinity. I have drawn on idioms I overheard throughout my time embedded in the MASA organization. These idioms are significant archetypical phrases often repeated by leaders and students involved in MASA and include the following: (a) "We don't want a politically correct conversation here"; (b) "I know we're being very heteronormative . . ."; (c) "Everyone has privilege, but we need to recognize it"; and (d) "We'll be an army taking on the world." More than just a stylistic choice, these phrases elucidate and enrich the analysis by pointing toward the study's major themes.

"We Don't Want a Politically Correct Conversation Here."

Over the course of the year observing the inner workings of MASA, the notion of political correctness or being political was often discussed in seemingly complex contradictions. MASA's mission itself was a political one, but those in charge—including the paid (mostly White) staff facilitators and the racially diverse student participants themselves—arguably did not always see it that way. On the program's website, the mission statement read, "The centerpiece of MASA is peer education for men, by men, through small-group discussion, workshops, and outreach events." Additionally, the group's description read, "MASA will be driven by male students from every aspect of the campus community, including fraternities, athletics, residential advising, and cultural organizations." When considering hegemonic masculinity, having men engaged as social agents attempting to disrupt systems of rape culture and engaging in peer education with other men is, in essence, a political act.

Very quickly during my time with the group, I learned of deep tensions regarding the necessarily political edge of the group. For instance, during the August training for the participants, Sean was present and facilitated a module. He shared, "We don't want a politically correct conversation here." Instead, he argued there was a "desire to engage in conversations across difference" and "a disconnect between politically correct ideas and people's actual thoughts and actions," particularly when discussing topics like rape and sexual assault. For the MASA participants (and to be clear, not all of the group identified as men), the exercises and activities presented asked them to contemplate issues of toxic masculinity and the ways men are socialized in society, signaling sexual violence as a sociopolitical happening. However, the participants, who were expected to eventually lead training and workshops for their peers, were often still struggling to understand these concepts.

For example, Sean facilitated a guided imagery exercise in early fall with the group. He asked the group to imagine what it would look like if rape did not exist in the world for 48 hours. The participants commented about how it may be more comfortable for everyone, inclusive of gender, to be in social settings where alcohol was being consumed and that individuals could be more open about their affections with others. However, the participants also spoke at length about the fear of rejection, their feelings of being "emotionally constipated" (i.e., not allowing oneself to feel one's feelings), and their fear of being the "evil weirdo" (i.e., crossing a line around consent with their partner). Naming these feelings and fears showed vulnerability but also was reflective of the challenges inherent in the men who were trying to understand how hegemonic masculinity played a role in their own daily experiences. In essence, the activity was helpful in allowing participants the opportunity to reflect on themselves individually, but it did not try to examine the larger systems at play around rape culture and sexual violence. By ignoring the systemic, there was a continued disconnection to the sociopolitical issues mediating participants' internalized hegemonic masculinity.

In trying to make sense of hegemonic masculinity, the discussions themselves were often messy and somewhat uncomfortable, given that participants used hegemonic tropes and metaphors as ways to make meaning around what they were learning in MASA. In the spring, as the group was talking about a breaking story from the #MeToo movement having to do with an actor sexually harassing a woman, Jeff, the new co-facilitator who was an undergraduate student himself, stated:

> It seems as though he had one idea, and she had a different idea. They eat and drink. She comes back to his place. He tells her to come sit on the counter, and she does, but she didn't really want to do it. He starts taking off his clothes and her clothes. She said that she didn't want to have sex. He stopped. And then he tried again later.

He continued, "I see it sort of like you're boxing. You're sparring with someone, and they told you to stop. And then later, they hit you again." This notion of discussing gender-based violence with a different example of violence highlights the ways in which hegemonic masculinity gets reinforced and internalized. Jeff's statements were similar to those of other men in the group, particularly when discussing issues of how rape and sexual violence happen on and off campus. This type of discussion reinforced an open desire to create a space within the organization that was not "politically correct," but by doing so, it reinforced hegemonic masculinity through its ideology.

In the spring semester, there also seemed to be an increased emphasis on a desire by the non-profit counseling agency that helped staff MASA to avoid any political stances. In an April meeting, the agency's staff members, who were present to support Jeff in his role, circulated a document about the organization's guidelines. One bullet point read, "Don't make it political/Don't take a definitive stance." Another read, "We're trying to create a rape-free environment. That's as far as we should go. MASA is a controversial group, so we need to be careful." During this particular meeting, very few students were present. In fact, out of the attendees there, only two were unpaid student participants. All of the others were either staff members from the agency or Jeff, who was paid by the agency as the part-time facilitator. These guidelines were being presented to the students as "talking points" to create "standardized messages about MASA" to be used at tabling events or campus workshops. Yet, it was somewhat alarming that, as an organization that supposedly was "student-driven" and meant to eradicate rape culture on campus, the staff were the ones presenting these talking points and attempting to be apolitical in the organization's approach—which, to be clear, is a decidedly political choice. As Jeremy, one of the staff members, stated, "We're new, and we're trying to build our reputation. We're trying to not be political."

However, to be an organization attempting to create a societal change in sexual violence on campus by having men trained to have conversations with other men means the group has a specific and directed political orientation. The meeting also served as a clear example of hegemonic masculinity functioning on the systems that seep into the individual. Additionally, the fact that the professional staff facilitators of the student organization, who largely all identified as White, were the ones promoting this viewpoint of MASA as apolitical demonstrated the linking of hegemony masculinity and Whiteness

(both being forms of dominance). One of the tools of hegemony is silence. Under the guise of value-neutral politics, the larger organization was maintaining patriarchy, White supremacy, and the status quo. This stance, perhaps linked with a concerned understanding of MASA's dwindling/unsteady membership numbers, seemed to imply the future direction of MASA may look different than its original purpose.

"I Know We're Being Very Heteronormative."

Throughout MASA's training sessions and regular member meetings, a constant refrain heard from facilitators and guest lecturers was: "I know we're being very heteronormative, but . . ." Throughout the MASA curriculum, the clear focus was that men were the perpetrators of sexual violence and women were the victims. Sometimes the aforementioned phrase was used to reinforce the point that men were not always the perpetrators and women were not always the victims, but there would rarely be any follow-up in depth to that statement. In the fall, Narek often used the aforementioned refrain, "I know we're being very heteronormative here . . .," and would glance my way, almost apologetically. Yet, his discussion would end there. Instead of having a full discussion of what heteronormativity meant and how that often resulted in homophobia and heterosexism, Narek's comment was typically used to close a conversation rather than serve as an invitation to explore how these issues played a role in rape culture and sexual violence on campus.

This notion of heteronormativity was not limited to just those who were regularly a part of MASA meetings, however. One of the guest lecturers, a SU staff member who served as a campus care advocate, made a presentation that was quite inclusive of gender, representing a shift from the regular heteronormative discussions of the group. However, one PowerPoint slide centered on victim blaming read: "This statement plays off the idea that people can't control their sexual urges and that a women's attire has made the offender powerless to resist his or her urge to take her." In this case, the statement centered only women as survivors of sexual violence but did open up the possibility that perpetrators could be a man or a woman. However, the example also reinforced a binary of man/woman and erased transgender, gender-queer, or gender non-conforming individuals or even cisgender men as survivors. The advocate herself acknowledged this by saying, "I know I'm being very binary in my talk. I apologize, but it's just for brevity's sake." Yet this example raises an important issue. The discussions in MASA about sexual violence were not just heteronormative; they were cisheteronormative, reifying the gender binary and heterosexual sexual and affectional behaviors. Additionally, this lack of inclusion around gender and sexuality may also have been a major reason why few queer participants found MASA to be a space where they wanted to spend time or affiliate.

These patterns occurred repeatedly. Staff members from the counseling agency led discussions and noted aloud in the meetings, ". . . again, binary terms," but then kept using them and upholding them throughout. These statements seemingly served as a recognition of self-awareness, but the continued use of such essentialist language maintained a false sense that talking about sexual violence outside of cisheteronormative experiences was not necessary or important.

This pattern was particularly salient at a new member open house held in the middle of the fall semester. Narek was leading a presentation for prospective members, and throughout the session, much of the information shared about the organization and its mission presented a cisheterosexist perspective. For example, a PowerPoint slide on rape culture focused on "affecting women's lives" as if rape culture does not affect men or gender non-conforming

individuals. When discussing sexual violence statistics where all the data points were exclusively focused on heterosexual relationships, Narek commented, "This is very heterocentric [sic]." It was also cisgender-focused. Jeremy's statement at a Greek 101 event was another example of erasure: "We understand that there are more genders than man/woman, but we're asking you to think in the binary because that's how most talk about it." Such statements fundamentally represent a subordinated sense of hegemonic masculinity, reinforcing dominant privilege to anyone present. These cisheteronormative values were deeply embedded in the lifeblood of MASA's culture as well as in the members' and facilitators' language around this topic.

At the same time, this issue of cisheteronormativity seemed not to have a negative effect on queer individuals in MASA. For example, Vinny, a gay cisgender man, shared how prior to college, "socialization played a huge part in my life because I had to act as masculine as I could in order to keep other guys from treating me badly." He shared that MASA actually helped him become more comfortable around masculinity, saying, "I think the other members in the program have shown me that masculinity doesn't necessarily mean fitting under one category and that guys are capable of expressing emotion and kindness." That being said, Vinny's involvement in the group ended when he graduated at the end of the fall semester. No other openly queer or trans individuals participated in the group for the remainder of the year, and even Vinny's participation in the group was mediated because he was a paid student intern for the organization. As an employee, he may have been resistant to speak openly and honestly about any concerns he had about the staff facilitation of the program, particularly around issues of cisheteronormativity. These concerns also connect to the next theme, which centers around issues of identity privilege.

"Everyone Has Privilege, But We Need to Recognize It."

While cisheteronormativity was certainly a major aspect of privilege that was not always named or recognized within the group, male privilege was also another topic that had contradictions within MASA. On paper and in promotional materials, MASA was named as an organization where men would be trained as SVP peer educators and then engage in primarily men-dominant spaces to help other men understand the connections between toxic masculinity and rape culture. When arriving for my first observation of MASA during their summer retreat prior to the start of the academic year, I waited for 20 minutes outside the classroom space that I was told to come to because when looking through the small window in the door, I saw a group of women and men engaged in a session. I ended up interrupting Narek, who was facilitating, and he waved me in and introduced me to the members. Yet, during my preliminary discussions with both Narek and Sean, I had never been told that women were a part of the MASA membership. Yet, in reality, the executive board and membership of MASA were comprised of men and women; half of the executive board, including the president and secretary, were women.

With women being core members of the program, the curriculum presented in the group still focused on men exclusively. In a one-on-one conversation with Narek, he shared that when the organization first started, MASA was a men-only group, but the toxic masculinity that emerged within the group was so difficult to manage that he and Sean felt as though having women involved might be helpful because then the men present would conduct themselves differently than they might in a men-only space. This admission suggested a concern about what happens when men, particularly straight men, come together. As Narek often noted in training sessions and meetings, "Statistically, men are the majority of perpetrators. Not all men are rapists, but we believe that a lot of this is due to the culture men are raised in, toxic masculinity, machismo, masculinity." Yet, this also brought forward concerns, often raised by the women of color involved in the organization, about a lack of understanding among the men participating in MASA about the privileges they possessed around their gender and sex.

At one meeting in October, Carolina, the MASA president, said, "Sometimes people don't even recognize their own privileges. Everyone has privilege, but we need to recognize it." In processing this with the group, the participants started to name the ways in which privilege played out differently for each of them. As an African American man, Jeff shared that he felt uncomfortable walking around campus at night, particularly when wearing a hoodie, because there had been times when women saw him and crossed the street because he perceived they saw him as threatening and dangerous. David, another participant who was Jeff's fraternity brother, acknowledged that the activities in which he had participated through MASA helped him realize his own male privilege, how "something like walking home I take for granted." The women in the group often were vital in pointing out ways in which their experiences on and off campus were different from their peers who were men. This labor by the women seemed to be just another example of how those from subordinated identities had to do extra work to inform and teach others with more dominant identities; therefore, even in a space like MASA, the women who were often rendered invisible through the curriculum were asked to do more work than their peers who were men. It also spoke to the fact that many of the men in the group continued to be unable to engage in this emotional labor when thinking about the complexities of gender and sexuality on their own.

The concept of male privilege was also central to a particularly unusual meeting at one point in the fall semester. Up to this point, the group had largely been gathered and facilitated by Narek. They had just finished several weeks in a row where at each of their 2-hour Friday night meetings, they were required to watch lengthy documentaries on men and masculinities; however, these films were never debriefed or processed. On this occasion, the only students present were executive board members and Juan, a prospective member. Narek tried to begin, and almost immediately, Carolina and Karla, the club's president and secretary, respectively, pushed back. Carolina was frustrated, saying, "I wish we talked more about masculinity." From there, Karla added her concerns that the group was not really student-led and that she wished participants were provided more direct training on how to talk about these important issues with others. Narek got defensive, responding, "I feel like I'm being audited by the guy in the back," referring to me taking notes, and then elaborated, "I wanted to have less ownership, not no ownership." Narek's responses seemed to be very performative of his own male privilege.

Similar to Narek, Jeremy, the co-facilitator who replaced Narek in the spring semester, also demonstrated a great deal of White male privilege through his words and actions. In his conversations, Jeremy often added "bro" at the end when speaking to the men of the group. "Bro," historically a term of endearment used among Black men, has been appropriated by White people (Abad-Santos, 2013). Jeremy's White male privilege was used in particular racialized and gendered ways that were reflective of others in the group. In general, the men who served as facilitators and leaders of the group took up a great deal of space at meetings, launching into monologues about masculinity rather than creating opportunities for dialogue within the group. Even group sessions that were meant to train student participants were largely dominated by the paid staff members who identified as men; they often questioned guest speakers or were the first to disclose stories or answers to posed questions. This domination of time and space by the men seemed to be in direct opposition to the idea that MASA was supposedly a student-centered, student-driven organization; this performativity of hegemonic masculine norms felt very much informed by male privilege.

Yet, there were glimpses of change and awareness of this privilege as the year progressed. In February, when preparing for the fraternity and sorority life new member orientation presentation, the group spent a great deal of time reviewing the PowerPoint slide deck and providing feedback to Jeff and Jeremy. One of the inherited slides read, "Think of a woman you care deeply for . . ." and that slide was to frame a discussion of how participants would feel about that woman potentially being assaulted. Through the conversation, participants verbalized how they thought they should use "person" in lieu of "woman." This was one of the first times where the group seemingly was thinking carefully about inclusivity around gender and sexuality. As Jeff stated, "It's about making it personal and tailoring it to them." This seemed to be an important step forward in Jeff being conscious of how to better support those with various gender and sexual identities attending MASA. At the same time, one critique of this approach to the presentation is that it still centers individuals present having to imagine someone being victimized, which could be potentially very triggering for individuals present at such a presentation who themselves may have experienced sexual violence. Therefore, this progressive step forward for the group signaled more awareness and consciousness for the participants in their future work.

"We'll Be an Army Taking on the World."

As a relatively new program (at the time of data collection, it was in its fourth year of existence), MASA still seemed to be finding its footing on campus, and this also seemed to present a few contradictions. Members came to the organization for various reasons. Some came because they had a personal connection to sexual violence. Jeff, in his discussions with me, disclosed that both his mother and stepmother had experienced sexual assault. When asked why he was interested in joining MASA, Juan, a prospective member, shared with the group, "That injustice [of sexual violence] angers me, and I want to use that anger to get me here and make change. I want to be a voice for women." That personal desire to make a difference is certainly commendable, but that reason of "being a voice for women" seemed to uphold rigid cisheteronormative views discussed earlier. Some of the men in the group seemingly felt as though men's voices were more likely to be heard on issues of sexual violence and rape culture than those of women. As such, there may be some internalized sexism being demonstrated by some of the men. This was clear by some of the comments of the men in various meetings when they tried to dismiss the women participants' comments about rape culture on campus or only use their own stories as a way to understand masculinity and rape culture instead of trying to understand the ways these issues happen systemically.

This lack of nuance around hegemonic masculinity also played out at times in the language used by members within MASA. At the open house for new members, Jeff remarked, "It's cool to be a part of this new wave [of members] coming through. It's growing . . . we'll be an army taking on the world." Narek, in response, said, "I think we're trying to challenge the perceptions of being an army; we should be a choir." The overriding message from MASA

members in presentations and tabling events on campus was that men at Southwest University should be "The Gentlemen of Today": supportive, fair, and emotionally expressive.

Yet, that often resulted in members engaging in code-switching based on who they were with. In conversations with Mike, one of the new members of MASA, he admitted that the way he acted and even the things he said at MASA meetings were different than what he said or did with his best friends. Likewise, Jeff noted how he was beginning to internalize what he was learning from his time with the MASA program and figuring out what that meant for his engagement with others. For him, the context of who he was with and what was being shared often resulted in different expressions and performances of his masculinity. All of the men I interviewed stated that they often shared things at MASA meetings they would never share with their best friends or family members. In essence, this code-switching served as a protective barrier to self-disclosure. MASA provided the men a space where they could share vulnerably. Their relationships outside the group may have been more rooted in traditionally hegemonic masculine norms, which restricted such behaviors.

For many of the members, while they actively wanted to change issues of rape culture on campus, they still were closely tied to wanting to be perceived by others as being masculine and being a "good man." However, that was a challenge when other men, particularly those who disagreed with MASA's message and mission, perceived the group members as potential gender traitors to manhood and hegemonic masculine expectations and roles. This was also significant given that many of the MASA members secretly disclosed to one another or to me during breaks in meetings that they never planned to give a public presentation on the topics of masculinity and sexual violence, a requirement of being involved and earning priority registration for classes. In fact, several of the members shared how they disliked having to table for the organization because of the ways in which some men on campus were not receptive to MASA's message at organization fairs. For example, in conversations with Mike, he mentioned that the emphasis of MASA should actually be less about presentations and tabling and more about what can happen through group meetings. Yet, group meetings were held in small groups and in private. While Mike felt as though the content of the group meetings was most significant to his growth as a member, it has to be understood that the private nature of engaging in conversations about masculinity allowed him to feel more comfortable than in a public view where his beliefs may be challenged by others or where he could be perceived as being less masculine for caring about such issues on campus. This speaks to a larger potential flaw in programs like MASA. Such programs demand that men become performative allies too early in the process, and then they are propped up as exemplars of men who are "woke" or "get it." This behavior, in and of itself, is rooted in hegemonic masculinity and being seen as a valiant hero. These contradictions were complex and deeply felt by many of the participants.

DISCUSSION

One of the complications of all-men group work is the inherent challenge that hegemonic masculine norms may be upheld and reified, even as the group attempts to challenge such norms through interpersonal interactions, curriculum, and programming. Male privilege plays a substantial factor in this work, with many men not believing there is a need for involvement and others believing that involvement with SVP work may lead to them being perceived as weak or soft, which aligns with previous research by

Casey (2010). Yet, as previous research (Piccigallo et al., 2012) and this study showed, many men are drawn to SVP work because of the personal nature of the issue. Many men are surrounded by family members and friends who are survivors of sexual violence. As such, they have a strong desire to be involved in prevention efforts and programming on campus (e.g., Juan and Jeff). However, it is vital that men engaged in these programs begin to interrogate their male privilege in order to avoid, as Juan once said, "being a voice for women" and instead align with women and other gender minorities to amplify their voices.

The subordination aspect of masculinity that Connell (2005) named was seen in the code-switching among the men within MASA. Whether it was the staff facilitators or the students themselves who identified as men, code-switching and posturing were often used as a way to navigate potential subordination, particularly from other men. Some participants avoided tabling events or did not want to participate in giving public presentations on campus partially because they were uneasy discussing the eradication of rape culture. The mere discussion of ending rape culture, by its very nature, might be perceived by some men, particularly those who tightly subscribed to hegemonic masculinity, as being traitorous of one's manhood. These challenges have been well documented as a potential problem with men engaged in SVP work (Casey, 2010; Pease, 2008).

Embedded within the curriculum and discussions of MASA was a dual role of Connell's (2005) notions of complicity and marginalization via hegemonic masculinity. Throughout the organization, the central value held by participants was that the group was working to eradicate rape culture, but really the focus was to help cisgender women not be victims of such violence on campus. There were rarely conversations about why men were the primary perpetrators of sexual violence and what the MASA participants could do to think about intervening around (potential) perpetrators themselves. By focusing on the survivors or victims, MASA was erasing the (potential) perpetrators, which supports hegemonic masculinity and, by extension, leaves rape culture intact.

Additionally, few discussions were centered on survivors who were transgender, gender non-conforming, or sexual or gender minorities. In fact, it was not until late spring when members of the group actually started to have any substantive discussions about their presentation materials being more inclusive of gender and sexual minorities. Even then, the information was still presented from a cisheteronormative perspective. The ongoing erasure of trans and gender non-conforming survivors in these conversations represents complicity with hegemonic masculinity (Connell, 2005) to reinforce a dominant and not fully accurate or complete story about who are survivors of sexual assault. As a result, MASA and its members often upheld rather than resisted or critiqued hegemonic norms related to sexual violence.

IMPLICATIONS

These findings have significant implications on the direct need to help college men unlearn hegemonic masculinity and problematize this concept, particularly as it relates to peer education around SVP. There is a distinct need for educators to spend greater time with college men examining gender roles and expectations. It was clear from ongoing conversations with the faculty and staff in charge of this program that hegemonic masculinity and its influence played out in both positive and negative ways among the members over the course of the program's history. While practice had moved away from a men-only peer education program, hegemonic masculinity created and replicated problematic norms and practices that reinforced the men involved as heroes, saviors, or the good

guys. These norms and practices also continued to perpetuate that men were needed to solve a systemic problem happening to women, which was an essentialized and inadequate way of understanding rape culture and sexual violence. Instead, MASA programs can potentially serve as a way to help educate men about cisheteropatriarchy as a first step toward solidarity work.

Failure to question and problematize hegemonic masculinity certainly cannot be seen as a positive outcome of such peer education programs, yet, in this case, this was a direct outcome. As a result, college student educators must be thoughtful about the messages surrounding SVP efforts. Even those who are most directly affiliated with SVP at SU used language in training presentations that reinforced a gender binary and negated their own self-awareness of sexual violence survivors beyond just women. If professionals continue to reinforce this type of gender and sexual erasure, how can we expect young men just beginning to learn the language and discourse of gender and SVP work to get this right?

In terms of future research, more direct research is needed to understand how to better support men-only programs and the ways in which college student educators may respond to eradicating sexual violence in higher education. Current efforts around having men as allies and engaging in bystander intervention does not seem to be wholly adequate, given the statistics involved in sexual violence in our institutions. As Linder et al. (2020) argued, "Rather than addressing power as the root of sexual violence, bystander intervention addresses the symptoms of the problem of abuse of power" (p. 1033). Educators also need additional research that is grounded in culturally relevant training around sexual violence. Currently, much of the SVP programming reinforces the false binary that cisgender women are the primary victims of sexual violence. However, when one disaggregates sexual violence statistics, it becomes clear gender and sexual minorities are increasingly at higher risk of assault or victimization. Additional research and praxis should explore how transphobia and heterosexism may be affecting the current efforts around SVP.

CONCLUSION

The participants of MASA came to their work for an array of reasons, but most cited knowing someone who survived sexual violence or harassment as motivation for their involvement. They wanted to be a part of a group that was attempting to make a change in their community. Yet, the reality is that this work really is messy, and part of the messiness is due to the ways in which hegemonic masculinity gets replicated, reinforced, and reified within the

organization. Throughout my year with this group, I attempted to listen carefully and consider the frequent contradictions that happened through language and interactions, varied by context and audience. Decoding these contradictions, which at the core were affected by hegemonic masculinity, itself is an imprecise and messy task, but one that needs continued attention. If we, as college educators, want to eradicate rape culture and sexual violence in higher education, we must continue decoding the contradictions that are inherent in our collective efforts in this work.

Correspondence concerning this article should be addressed to Daniel Tillapaugh, California Lutheran University; dtillapaugh@callutheran.edu

REFERENCES

Abad-Santos, A. (2013). How the bro became white. *The Atlantic*. Retrieved from https://www.theatlantic.com/culture/archive/2013/10/how-encino-man-changed-race-bros/310146/

American College Health Association. (2007). National college health assessment. *Journal of American College Health, 55*, 195–206. https://doi.org/10.3200/jach.55.4.195–206

Banyard, V. L., Moynihan, M. M., & Crossman, M. T. (2009). Reducing sexual violence on campus: The role of student leaders as empowered bystanders. *Journal of College Student Development, 50*(4), 446–457. https://doi.org/10.1353/csd.0.0083

Barone, R. P., Wolgemuth, J. R., & Linder, C. (2007). Preventing sexual assault through engaging college men. *Journal of College Student Development, 48*(5), 585–594. https://doi.org/10.1353/csd.2007.0045

Berkowitz, A. D. (2011). Using how college men feel about being men and "doing the right thing" to promote men's development. In J. A. Laker & T. Davis (Eds.), *Masculinities in higher education: Theoretical and practical considerations* (pp. 162–176). Routledge.

Black, M. C., Basile, K. C., Breiding, M. J., Smith, S. G., Walters, M. L., Merrick, M. T., Chen, J., & Stevens, M. R. (2011). *The National Intimate Partner and Sexual Violence Survey: 2010 Summary Report*. National Center for Injury Prevention and Control, Centers for Disease Control and Prevention.

Casey, E. (2010). Strategies for engaging men as anti-violence allies: Implications for ally movements. *Advances in Social Work, 11*(2), 267–282. https://doi.org/10.18060/580

Casey, E., Carlson, J., Two Bulls, S., & Yager, A. (2018). Gender transformative approaches to engaging men in gender-based violence prevention: A review and conceptual model. *Trauma,*

Violence, and Abuse, 19(2), 231–246. https://doi.org/10.1177/1524838016650191

Connell, R. W. (2005). *Masculinities*. Polity.

Davis, T. L., & Wagner, R. (2005). Increasing men's development of social justice attitudes and actions. In R. D. Reason, E. M. Broido, T. L. Davis, & N. J. Evans (Eds.), *Developing social justice allies* (New Directions for Student Services, No. 110; pp. 29–41). Jossey-Bass. https://doi.org/10.1002/ss.163

Denzin, N. K. (1989). *Interpretative interactionism*. SAGE.

Edwards, K. E. (2022). Becoming a man: A longitudinal study of men's gender identity development. *Journal of College Student Development, 63*(2), 185–199. https://doi.org/10.1353/csd.2022.0014

Edwards, K. E., & Jones, S. R. (2009). "Putting my man face on": A grounded theory of college men's gender identity development. *Journal of College Student Development, 50*, 210–228. https://doi.org/10.1353/csd.0.0063

Glaser, B. G. (1965). The constant comparative method of qualitative analysis. *Social Problems, 12*(4), 436–445. https://doi.org/10.2307/798843

Griner, S. B., Vamos, C. A., Thompson, E. L., Logan, R., Vázquez-Otero, C., & Daley, E. M. (2020). The intersection of gender identity and violence: Victimization experienced by transgender college students. *Journal of Interpersonal Violence, 35*(23–24), 5704–5725. https://doi.org/10.1177/0886260517723743.

Harper, S. R., & Harris, F., III (Eds.) (2009). *College men and masculinities: Theory, research, and implications for practice*. Wiley.

Harris, F., III, & Edwards, K. E. (2010). College men's experiences as men: Findings and implications from two grounded theory studies. *Journal of Student Affairs Research and Practice, 47*(1), 43–62. https://doi.org/10.2202/1949-6605.6085

Harris, J. C., & Linder, C. (Eds.) (2017). *Intersections of identity and sexual violence on campus: Centering minoritized students' experiences.* Stylus.

Heyl, B. S. (2007). Ethnographic interviewing. In P. Atkinson, S. Delamont, A. Coffey, J. Lofland, & L. Lofland (Eds.), *Handbook of ethnography* (pp. 369–383). SAGE.

Katz, J. (2009). Reconstructing masculinity in the locker room: The mentors in violence prevention project. In S. R. Harper & F. Harris III (Eds.), *College men and masculinities: Theory, research, and implications for practice* (pp. 541–552). Jossey-Bass.

Kimmel, M. (2008). *Guyland: The perilous world where boys become men.* HarperCollins.

Kincheloe, J. (2008). *Critical constructivism primer.* Peter Lang.

Linder, C. (2018). *Sexual violence on campus: Power-conscious approaches to awareness, prevention, and response.* Emerald Publishing.

Linder, C., Grimes, N., Williams, B. M., Lacy, M. C., & Parker, B. (2020). What do we know about campus sexual violence? A content analysis of 10 years of research. *The Review of Higher Education, 43*(4), 1017–1040. https://doi.org/10.1353/rhe.2020.0029

Linder, C., & Johnson, R. C. (2015). Exploring the complexities of men as allies in feminist movements. *Journal of Critical Thought and Praxis, 4*(1). Retrieved from https://lib.dr.iastate.edu/jctp/vol4/iss1

Lykes, M. B. (1989). Dialogue with Guatemalan Indian women: Critical perspectives on constructing collaborative research. In R. K. Unger (Ed.), *Representations: Social constructions of gender* (pp. 167–185). Baywood Publishing.

Magolda, P. M. (2003). Saying good-bye: An anthropological examination of a commencement ritual. *Journal of College Student Development, 44*(6), 779–796. https://doi.org/10.1353/csd.2003.0073

Magolda, P. M. (2016). *The lives of campus custodians: Insights into corporatization and civic disengagement in the academy.* Stylus.

McMahon, S., & Dick, A. (2011). "Being in a room with like-minded men": An exploratory study of men's participation in a bystander intervention program to prevent intimate partner violence. *Journal of Men's Studies, 19*(1), 3–18. https://doi.org/10.3149/jms.1901.3

Mertler, C. A. (2019). Introduction to educational research (2nd ed.). SAGE.

Nicolazzo, Z. (2015). "I'm man enough; are you?": The queer (im)possibilities of Walk A Mile In Her Shoes. *Journal of Critical Scholarship on Higher Education and Student Affairs, 2*(1), 18–30.

Nicolazzo, Z. (2016). "Just go in looking good": The resistance, resilience, and kinship-building of trans* college students. *Journal of College Student Development, 57*(5), 538–556. https://doi.org/10.1353/csd.2016.0057

O'Neil, J. M., Helms, B. J., Gable, R. K., David, L., & Wrightsman, L. S. (1986). Gender-Role Conflict Scale: College men's fear of femininity. *Sex Roles, 14*(5–6), 335–350. https://doi.org/10.1007/bf00287583

Pease, B. (2008). Engaging men in men's violence prevention: Exploring the tensions, dilemmas, and possibilities. *Australian Domestic & Family Violence Clearinghouse, 17*, 1–20.

Piccigallo, J. R., Lilley, T. G., & Miller, S. L. (2012). "It's cool to care about sexual violence:" Men's experiences with sexual assault prevention. *Men and Masculinities, 15*(5), 507–525. https://doi.org/10.1177/1097184x12458590

Radimer, S., & Rowan-Kenyon, H. (2019). Undergraduate men's alcohol consumption: Masculine norms, ethnic identity, and social dominance orientation. *Journal of College Student Development, 60*(1), 1–16. https://doi.org/10.1353/csd.2019.0000

Rennison, C. M. (2002). *National crime victimization survey, criminal victimization 2001: Criminal changes 2000–2001 with trends 1993–2001* (NCJ 187007). U.S. Government Printing Office.

Sinozich, S., & Langton, L. (2014). *Rape and sexual victimization among college-aged females, 1995–2013* [NCJ 248471]. U.S. Department of Justice, Office of Justice Programs, Bureau of Justice Statistics.

Tillapaugh, D., & McGowan, B. L. (2019). *Men and masculinities: Theoretical foundations and promising practices for supporting college men's development.* Stylus.

Wawrzynski, M. R., LoConte, C. L., & Straker, E. J. (2011). Learning outcomes for peer educators: The National Survey on Peer Education. *New Directions for Student Services, 133*, 17–27. https://doi.org/10.1002/ss.381

White, S., Park, Y., Israel, T., & Cordero, E. (2009). Longitudinal evaluation of peer health education on a college campus: Impact on health behaviors. *Journal of American College Health, 57*, 497–505. https://doi.org/10.3200/jach.57.5.497-506

Wolcott, H. E. (1994). *Transforming qualitative data: Descriptions, analysis, and interpretation.* SAGE.

Environmental Influences on Disabled Students' Cocurricular Involvement

Nancy J. Evans   Ellen M. Broido   Jody A. Kunk-Czaplicki   Val M. Erwin
Charlie E. Varland

Involvement of students in the cocurriculum is critical to the development of desired outcomes in college. However, the literature on disabled college students centers academic experiences, largely overlooking cocurricular experiences. In this study, we explored the cocurricular involvement of disabled students, examining factors that created barriers for their involvement, how students responded to barriers, factors that made involvement possible, and those that encouraged involvement. Grounded in a critical realist approach to disability, augmented by environmental theories, and employing a descriptive-interpretive design, we used both individual interviews and focus groups to obtain data from 33 disabled students at a midwestern, comprehensive, land-grant university. We found that (a) other people's behaviors and attitudes created more barriers to disabled students' involvement than did physical or organizational factors; (b) participants reported a wide variety of emotional and behavioral responses to the barriers; (c) accessible physical design, flexible organizational policies, and assistance from others made involvement possible; (d) universally designed elements of the physical and organizational environment as well as active support from staff and peers encouraged involvement; and (e) barriers to and encouragers of involvement varied by impairment. We offer implications for further research and practice.

Involvement is positioned in the higher education literature as critical to the development of desired outcomes of college (Mayhew et al., 2016). Involvement in student organizations, sports and recreation, leadership, and other cocurricular activities, as well as out-of-class interaction with peers, have a strong positive relationship with sense of belonging (Strayhorn, 2019); acceptance of socio-cultural differences (Dugan & Komives, 2010); and persistence, retention, and graduation (Mayhew et al., 2016). However, the literature on disabled college students centers academic experiences, largely omitting cocurricular involvement. Kimball et al. (2017) stated that it is important to provide disabled students[1] with encouragement and assistance to be involved with campus life as well as academics to ensure they have well-rounded college experiences.

We address this gap in the literature by answering four research questions: (a) What environmental barriers limited or prevented the

---

[1] We use the term *disabled students* because disabled scholars use identity-first language to show that disability is part of their identity (Linton, 1998). According to Linton (1998), because of pervasive discrimination and devaluing of disabled people, using the word *disability* and delineating between disabled and nondisabled, brings awareness of ableism.

Nancy J. Evans is Professor Emerita of Higher Education and Student Affairs at Iowa State University. Ellen M. Broido is Professor of Higher Education and Student Affairs at Bowling Green State University. Jody A. Kunk-Czaplicki is adjunct instructor of Higher Education and Student Affairs at Bowling Green State University and postdoctoral scholar in the Flora Stone Mather College for Women at Case Western Reserve University. Val Erwin is a doctoral student of Higher Education Administration at Bowling Green State University. Charlie E. Varland is Director of Leadership and Student Involvement at Boise State University.

Journal of College Student Development

cocurricular involvement of disabled students? (b) How did participants respond to the barriers they encountered? (c) What environmental factors made involvement possible? and (d) What environmental factors encouraged involvement?

THEORETICAL FRAMEWORKS

We used a critical realist (CR) approach to disability (Shakespeare, 2014) as the primary framework for this study, expanding its conception of the environment to include Porteous's (1977) and Ellen's (1982) models of specific ways environments influence behavior. CR has been used both by researchers studying disability (e.g., Mooney, 2016) and those studying organizational dynamics (e.g., Belfrage & Hauf, 2017), making it a good fit for this study. CR presumes that reality exists independent of observation or interpretation and that multiple causal mechanisms are at play simultaneously and may interact with each other while recognizing that reality can only be interpreted in context. It "aims at producing critical knowledge to enable social emancipation" (Belfrage & Hauf, 2017, p. 254). Applied to disability, CR recognizes the physical realities of disabled bodyminds and the ways those bodyminds interact with structural and social systems as well as physical environments (Shakespeare, 2014). Structural, social, and physical systems often enact ableism; that is, physical and social environments create barriers for people who function in atypical ways. Thus, CR sees both ableism and impairment as creating disability (Shakespeare, 2014).

Much disability research has been based on the medical and functional limitations models (Evans et al., 2017). As such, researchers have investigated the effects of specific impairments on disabled individuals and ways to "fix" these impairments to enable people to adjust to and be successful in environments (e.g., college campuses). By contrast, a CR understanding of disability implies that involvement is influenced by both environment and impairment (Shakespeare, 2014). By using the CR framework, our study focuses on environmental factors related to student cocurricular involvement.

Other theories grounding our study explain the environment's influence on behavior. Porteous (1977) and Ellen (1982) described environmental determinism, possibilism, and probabilism as ways geography and climate influence behavior. Porteous argued that environments could make behaviors impossible or required (determinism), possible (possibilism), or probable (probabilism). Moos (1979) described campus environments as made up of physical, human aggregate, organizational, and social climate aspects, a model expanded upon by Strange and Banning (2001), who renamed *social climate* as *perceived environment*. While Moos and Strange and Banning considered the human aggregate (i.e., the collective characteristics of the people in an environment) a key aspect of campus environments, the participants in this study talked about the influence of multiple individuals rather than human aggregates. We explore this dynamic in the discussion section of this paper. Given how participants in this study described the influence of members of the campus community, we refer to people or human aspects of the environment rather than human aggregates.

LITERATURE REVIEW

Initially, Astin (1984) defined involvement as the time and energy a student commits to their academic experience. However, Mayhew et al. (2016) argued that involvement extends beyond academic experiences and is influenced by the broader environment. Harper and Quaye (2015) specifically called on institutions to create environments that support the engagement of all students, especially those historically and currently minoritized in higher education.

Membership and formal leadership in student organizations is positively associated with the development of leadership capacity (Dugan & Komives, 2007). Culturally focused organizations provide support and encourage involvement in other campus activities (Hurtado et al., 1999). For example, Latina/o-based fraternities and sororities engender a greater sense of belonging in members and increase peer support and motivation (Moreno & Sanchez, 2013). Participation of students of color in peer networks, along with culturally focused campus spaces and student organizations, promotes positive outcomes (Museus et al., 2018).

Research on disabled students' involvement is limited. Mamiseishvili and Koch (2011) found that socially engaged first-year disabled students were almost 10% more likely to persist to the next college year than uninvolved disabled students. Physically disabled students who participated in a student organization that educated about ableism and created accessible experiences felt socially integrated with nondisabled members (Bialka et al., 2017). Vaccaro and Newman (2016) concluded that involvement fosters a sense of belonging for minoritized (including disabled) students. Learning-disabled students reported that involvement in peer social networks and student organizations was important to their success (Kimball et al., 2017). Kimball et al. (2017) cautioned, though, that "disability is an intersectional identity" (p. 72); each disabled student requires different types of involvement to enable success. Additional study of the degree of and factors influencing involvement is warranted.

Dolmage (2017) described the ableist nature of education, illustrating assumptions of able-bodiedness in the way universities conceptualize time. Universities expect members to navigate bureaucracies and function in narrowly defined ways and on institutionally defined timelines. Existing research illustrates these points. Many disabled students experience time costs that limit their engagement in cocurricular activities (Fox et al., 2022; Kimball et al., 2017; Reed & Kennett, 2017). Fox et al. (2022) pointed out time-consuming barriers, including "gaining access to accommodations, . . . scheduling appointments, [and] waiting for appropriate course material formats" (p. 8). Kimball et al. (2017) found that time management was an ongoing concern for learning-disabled participants. Their participants also noted that money and time both affected whether they became involved on campus. Katzman and Kinsella (2018) added that negotiating physical spaces, along with time spent on self-care and medical appointments, limits the time available for cocurricular involvement. Dolmage advocated for *crip time* (i.e., recognition of the ways that disability and ableism consume time that are not experienced by nondisabled people). Crip time includes not expecting people to attend events for their duration and allowing additional time for bodies and minds that move slowly, must deal with ableism, or must address assistive device failure. Current research, while important, does not fully address the barriers to, or encouragement for, disabled students' involvement (Kimball & Thoma, 2019), nor does it use CR principles, such as crip time, as a basis for addressing that gap.

METHODOLOGY

We used a critical realist paradigm to explain how disabled students make meaning of their cocurricular involvement and the factors that influence it. Critical realism (CR) has a realist ontology and a constructivist epistemology (Fletcher, 2017). Critical realism, as both a paradigm and a theoretical framework, has often been used in studies of disability (Shakespeare, 2014) and enables an understanding of disabled students' involvement by emphasizing bodies, ableism, and their interaction. We used a descriptive-interpretive methodology (Elliott

& Timulak, 2021), an umbrella approach inclusive of forms of grounded theory and phenomenology, as well as thematic analysis and other traditional qualitative approaches. It is characterized by

> exploratory research questions . . . verbally reported experiences . . . systemic analysis . . . representing their meaning; cluster[ing] of similar experiences . . . critically aware of and disclosing the researcher's interests . . . prior expectations and organizing conceptual framework . . . [and] integrating categories into . . . [a] coherent story or model. (p. 5)

Data were collected at a midwestern, comprehensive, land-grant research university enrolling approximately 30,000 students (pseudonym Midwestern Land Grant University, MLGU). MLGU is in a small city within a rural area. At the time data were collected, 56% of undergraduate students identified as men and 44% as women; about 8% of the students were students of color. MLGU offered a range of activities and other involvement opportunities typically seen at large, rural, residential universities. Most students lived on campus; intercollegiate and intramural sports and fraternity and sorority involvement (approximately 10% of the undergraduate population) played a significant role in campus life. The university's disability resource office (DRO) provided accommodations to qualified students, outreach to faculty, and support to about 1,000 disabled students.

Researcher Positionality

The first author designed and supervised the study; she and five MLGU higher education graduate students collected the data. This team included disabled and nondisabled members, all well-versed in disability and social justice theory. All were white; three identified as cisgender men and three as cisgender women. Differences in interviewing experience and personal experience with a specific disability influenced the

data collected. For instance, team members who shared a disability with participants sometimes were triggered by an experience mentioned or quickly understood participants' stories about their disabilities.

Two members of the data collection team continued to the analysis and writing phase, and three new researchers joined the team; these five are the authors of this paper. This group consisted of two higher education faculty members (one of whom is retired) and three higher education doctoral students, one of whom also is a professional in student involvement and leadership. All are knowledgeable about disability. Three members of the team had worked at MLGU. Of this group, four identify as disabled, white, cisgender women, and one identifies as a nondisabled, white, cisgender man. The varied professional experiences of team members allowed greater insight during data analysis into the dynamics described by participants.

Data Collection

Following Seidman (1998), the data collection team conducted in-depth individual interviews focusing on students' perceptions of their involvement during college. They used purposeful sampling to select 10 students who had been enrolled for at least one year, used DRO accommodations, and identified as having at least one of the following types of impairment: learning (LD), ADHD, psychological (PSY), mobility (MI), or sensory (SI) (including d/Deaf and Hard of Hearing – DHH, and visual – VI). Team members conducted two or three 60- to 90-minute face-to-face interviews with two students in each impairment category. Interview topics included diagnosis, participation in campus activities and events, and socialization. Interviews were audiotaped and transcribed. Participants verified transcripts via email.

During the data collection phase, team members met and reflected on how their experiences influenced or informed the study (e.g., interviewers with experience as counselors were more likely to elicit feeling-focused responses) and challenged one another's assumptions regarding disability. They also helped each other improve interviewing techniques, such as alternative ways to ask questions, follow-up approaches, and staying on topic.

To confirm themes identified in interviews, the data collection team conducted five focus groups with 25 students (23 additional students plus 2 who had been individually interviewed). Six students participated in the LD focus group, seven in the ADHD group, three in the PSY group, four in the MI group, and five in the SI group. To triangulate the data, questions for focus groups addressed themes arising in the individual interviews (Krueger, 1994). Each focus group lasted approximately 45 minutes. Conversations were recorded and transcribed.

Data Analysis

The authors of this article used Dedoose to code the interview and focus group transcripts and to facilitate analysis, focusing on participants' cocurricular involvement during college. Each author read all transcripts, highlighted text relevant to the research questions, assigned a code to the text, and organized similar codes hierarchically. We wrote memos to track all analytical decisions, such as why we grouped codes or to ask clarifying questions. Next, we collectively examined all coding and adjusted the codes to ensure consistency. We strengthened dependability by reviewing all analytical decisions. Finally, we combined related codes by reviewing all text within each code, identified themes from the coded data, and organized them by how prevalent and influential they were on participants' involvement. Using this deductive process, we identified patterns. While analyzing data, we met weekly to discuss and reconcile conflicting analyses, particularly addressing ways our disability identities and experience influenced analyses, such as how

we were triggered by barriers the interviewees experienced. To track important discussions and decisions during data analysis, we kept an audit log that we often referenced to support consistent data interpretation.

FINDINGS

Participants discussed engagement in most types of involvement at MLGU, with some variance by impairment type. Participants with ADHD and LD reported extensive participation, especially in fraternities/sororities. Participants with sensory disabilities, mobility impairments, and psychological disabilities reported infrequent involvement. Participants with mobility impairments were performers or spectators in cultural (especially musical) events.

Just over half of the participants in the study indicated that they had held at least one leadership position on campus. All LD participants were actively involved in leadership; most held numerous positions in fraternities and sororities, residence hall councils, and student organizations. Participants with other types of impairments less frequently held leadership roles, and those who did were involved in only one activity. Some participants with LD and ADD who wanted to hold organizational leadership positions were blocked from doing so by MLGU's GPA requirement, lack of accommodations, and peers who did not believe the participant could effectively perform the duties of the position.

Environmental Barriers

Regardless of impairment type, participants faced ableist physical, organizational, and human barriers that limited their involvement.

Physical Barriers. Only mobility-impaired participants mentioned physical barriers to their involvement. The most often referenced barriers were lack of accessibility, segregated access, and inadequate snow removal. Courtney (MI), a

STEM major and wheelchair user, was interested in joining a science club, "but a lot of their activities are like canoeing and hiking . . . and it would be interesting to be in that club, but I wouldn't be able to participate in a lot of the activities." Segregated seating at sports events and musical and theatrical performances discouraged the involvement of mobility-impaired participants. Jessica (MI) stated that there was no wheelchair seating at swim meets. Instead, she had to watch the meet from a second-floor window. She said, "You don't get the whole feeling of what's going on because you're on a . . . separate floor from where the pool is." The lack of snow removal was particularly challenging for mobility-impaired participants. Courtney (MI) described being unable to get to events because "sidewalks that were never cleared, that's just a safety hazard. I fell [once], and luckily nothing happened."

Organizational Barriers. Organizational barriers originated in student groups or in the institution as a whole. Many MI or SI participants said that they lacked information about campus accessibility. For instance, DHH participants explained that their involvement often depended on interpreter availability, while MI participants noted that knowing whether buildings, rooms, and bathrooms were accessible determined if they attended events. Transportation issues also created barriers for MI and SI participants. Jessica (MI), a wheelchair user, explained, "I've had major problems with lifts breaking down, being stuck on a bus for hours," while Lilith (VI) stated, "I don't drive, and I don't have transportation, so I'm pretty limited in what I do."

Participants reported that inappropriate application of policy, lack of flexibility, and lack of accommodations created barriers that limited their involvement. For example, an usher told Jessica (MI) that she could only sit in the student section, which was up a flight of stairs. Kate (DHH) stated, "I probably would have been in a leadership position in my sorority if I had accommodations, but I didn't," an example of lack of accommodation precluding involvement.

Human Barriers. People created numerous obstacles to disabled students' involvement. Participants described more human than organizational or physical barriers. They described intentional ableism: others discounting disability, patronization, purposeful ignorance, and stigmatization.

Only participants with non-apparent disabilities reported that other people did not understand disability, believe the participant was disabled and/or needed accommodation, or take disability seriously. Kelli (PSY) explained, "Sometimes I feel like I have to justify myself to somebody. Like why I have to leave or why I need to pace for a while." Patronization involved people assuming a disabled person could not do something or did not understand something. According to Jessica (MI), "It just makes me frustrate[d] that they talk to me like I'm an idiot." Purposeful ignorance occurred when others made no effort to learn about disabilities or accommodations. Andy (DHH) explained how others misunderstood her accommodations: "If I [felt] that maybe they could come to understand what that's about, I wouldn't sense the hostility . . ., and so I would feel like becoming more involved." Participants experienced disability stigma when others made them feel undesired or avoided them. Almost all participants who mentioned stigma had a psychological disability or ADHD. Julia (ADHD) shared, "A lot of time we don't pay attention, we space out; they laugh at me and my friends because they don't understand, and to me, that's a huge deterrent in getting involved."

Participants also relayed that other peoples' thoughtlessness and discouragement were barriers. Thoughtlessness occurred when someone failed or forgot to consider the disabled person's access needs. When Courtney (MI) practiced with the college band, "they would always forget to unlock the [accessible] door." Participants also experienced discouragement from parents and peers. Max (LD) reflected, "A lot of time, you try to step into a leadership position or do more. People tell you that you can't do it or don't think you're the best person for the job." After James (ADHD) disclosed to a fraternity brother, "he actually didn't think it was a real disability. So, I figure a lot of people handle it like that, 'You're just using that as an excuse.'"

Response to Barriers

Feelings About Lack of Access. Unsurprisingly, barriers to involvement elicited strong behavioral and emotional responses; the latter were particularly common in participants with mobility impairments. The most common emotional responses to barriers to access were anger, irritation, and frustration, caused by the actions of others or the general situation. These responses were reported only by participants with mobility and psychological impairments. Courtney (MI), a wheelchair user, relayed a hypothetical conversation with a staff member about a broken elevator, saying, "This is something that I really need. . . . I can't function completely if [I] don't have this . . . Could you take a little time out of your day to [fix] it?" Kelli (PSY) was frustrated by the limited attention given to psychological disabilities. She explained, "You see all over these ribbons that they have for breast cancer and for AIDS, and they have all of the awareness campaigns. You don't see that for mental illness. You don't see anything." While limited to only a few participants, feelings of anger, irritation, and frustration were powerful and arose multiple times in each of their interviews.

Not wanting to burden others was a reaction expressed only by participants with mobility impairments. Courtney (MI) worried, "I don't want people to look at me every time I

. . . come in and ask for help, to be: 'She's asking for help again' or be annoyed that every time I come in, I'm too pushy."

Also unique to MI participants were feelings of being left out or missing out because their access to involvement was segregated from their peers. Jessica (MI) described being separated from other students when the wheelchair-accessible seating was at the back of a concert hall: "You feel like you're kinda not part of what's going on . . . I kind of feel left out . . . I feel like I don't fit in . . . like [I'm] not in the group." Courtney (MI) participated in a student organization trip where the bus was inaccessible. She said, "I didn't really get to socialize as well, and in that way, I maybe felt a little alienated."

Behaviors. A pervasive response to encountering barriers was to disengage physically or emotionally from the situation or the larger campus or to limit one's participation. Disengagement could be proactive or reactive, permanent or temporary. Sometimes participants disengaged because they needed to prioritize academics or had other time constraints. However, most often, disengagement was a response to encounters with peers' ableism or inability to access a space. Jamal (PSY) said, "Well, I didn't feel comfortable here. I didn't like to leave my dorm. I didn't like to walk on campus. I got extremely nervous, and it was just hell, complete hell." James (ADHD) withdrew to his room when his fraternity partied. Disengagement was the most common response to encountering barriers of any sort, although no participants with sensory impairments described reducing their involvement or withdrawing when encountering barriers.

Participants from the MI, LD, VI, and DHH groups spoke of persisting in involvement despite the presence of barriers. Courtney (MI) was confident that inaccessibility would not stop her: "If I can't go over to somebody's house because the bathroom isn't accessible, that's not going to stop me from going over there; I might just shorten my time there." Problem-solving enabled persistence. Participants made otherwise inaccessible cocurricular environments accessible, usually by working with their peers. Kay (DHH) said, "I have to communicate with my friends, and we have to figure out a way it will work out."

Making Involvement Possible

Although environmental barriers may have limited cocurricular involvement, physical, organizational, and human aspects of the environment could create the potential for involvement.

Physical Environments. Participants with mobility impairments noted that physical accessibility helped make their involvement possible. Ramps, clear visibility at sporting events, and renovating outdated building entrances were critical in making the physical environment accessible and permitting full participation. Some participants noted that when physical improvements were more permanent, their experience improved. For example, before MLGU improved their sporting event bleachers, Jessica (MI) could not see the game because disabled seating was on the ground behind the goalposts. With a permanent relocation of disabled seating, Jessica noted, "[N]ow it's better cuz you sit up higher, and you can see over all those people that are walking down below, and you can see the game perfect[ly]."

Assistive listening devices were key to the involvement of participants who were d/Deaf or hard of hearing. Andy (DHH) noted how important this technology is for her participation: "I can compensate for that [with] . . . assistive listening devices. So there really haven't been situations where [my deafness] alone has prevented me from getting involved."

Organizational Environments. Participants noted two ways that some student organizations and the institution made their involvement possible: easily available information and permanent professional staff. When organizations made information easily available, participants were able to join them and participate. Alina (LD) described how essential information was to her involvement.

> [The vice president of the organization] pulled out . . . this card. And it had like his name on it as the vice president, and the president, and the advisor. And on the other side of the card, it had like the dates of all their meetings and the room and everything. I was like, "Wow, that's really organized. They got business cards made." And so, I thought that was pretty cool. And so, I started going to the meetings.

Other participants noted emails, websites, bulletin boards, and consistent weekly announcements as important organizational elements that made their involvement possible.

Participants described specialized staff as particularly important to their involvement. DRO staff were skilled professionals who helped by providing specific information about types and details of cocurricular activities, interpreting for events, removing (or advocating for a removal of) barriers, and providing support. Renee (LD) noted that weekly meetings in the DRO helped her get involved: "We would meet and, you know, discuss, sometimes plan things. They'd have a little program for us or just a talk every Friday." To Kay (DHH), available interpreters were important: "They make sure that we can participate and go to whatever we want. . . . If we didn't have full-time staff interpreters, it would be an entirely different story because it would be almost impossible to find an interpreter."

Human Environments. By accepting participants, providing help when needed, and delivering psychological support, people helped make involvement possible. Helpful peers, as well as staff and faculty, assisted in three main ways. Participants felt accepted when others showed genuine interest in them and were open to difference, created a comfortable space for sharing, and created opportunities for more than a minimum level of involvement. Kelli (PSY) described how she felt accepted by a student group: "They understand that sometimes I freak out, and sometimes I need to leave. They understand that this is real and that I have all of these things going on."

Assistance took many forms, including carrying participants up flights of stairs, pushing participants up a ramp, explaining participants' needs to others, summarizing inaudible conversations, anticipating participants' needs, and taking the extra step to provide accommodations before participants had to ask. Finally, participants noted that psychological support made their involvement possible, especially when trusted others believed in them.

Environmental Encouragers

Similar aspects of the environment (e.g., physical, organizational, and human aspects) made involvement possible and probable. However, involvement became probable and was encouraged by ease of use, predictability, and explicit invitation.

Physical Environment. Participants observed that when the physical environment was universally designed, they felt encouraged to participate. For example, Lilith (VI) noted that a universally designed physical environment helped her fully enjoy theatrical events: "They reserve certain spots for people with vision difficulties. . . . All of my tickets this year are 4th row or better. . . . [For] the first time in a very, very long time, I could actually see the people that were on stage."

Organizational Environment. While many participants, across all impairment types, noted that planning is a critical element of successful involvement, participants also pointed out ways universities could design policies and organizational practices that would reduce the extent of planning (or the time between planning and doing) participants were required to do.

Such changes would increase the likelihood they would get involved. For example, Kay (DHH) described how having full-time staff interpreters available for students at any time allowed her to more easily stay involved; she explained: "Because it's easier to say, 'Oh, today I need an interpreter' at the last minute." Alina (LD) described how she stayed involved when she observed that the student organization had predictable meeting schedules and counted on her to attend. The institution nurtured involvement by employing specialized, full-time staff who supported disabled students; organizations encouraged involvement when they had consistent practices.

Human Environment. Although physically accessible spaces and the university's commitment to full-time professional staff encouraged involvement, participants described individuals, especially friends and peers, as having more influence on their involvement. Individuals encouraged involvement by making informal accommodations for participants and inviting them to get or stay involved. When participants felt accepted by peers and knew that other disabled students would be present, they stated that they were more likely to participate in activities.

Participants noted that many friends and peers made sure that events, activities, organizations, and spaces were accessible to them. Kelsey (DHH) shared that her peers and friends consistently made informal accommodations for her, helping her stay involved. "When we're . . . with a group of people . . . a lot of my friends will . . . let me know what's going on and make sure that I'm kept up to date with everything, and so then it's not so bad for me."

When peer groups made efforts to invite or include them, participants felt particularly encouraged to try out an activity, to stay involved, or to increase involvement in a leadership capacity. Kelli (PSY) mentioned how people in an organization reached out to her to invite her to participate: "That encouragement meant that I felt safe to try it out, and I ended up going to a couple of meetings." Courtney (MI) noted, "That extra encourage[ment] . . . just kind of gives me like an extra little boost of energy and makes me really feel like this is something that I really should be doing." Paco (LD) observed that when he was a leader for a Bible study, he was encouraged to stay involved due to the expectations of his peers: "The guys that come are relying on me to be prepared for what we're going to talk about."

Students from all impairment types noted how important others' acceptance of them was to their involvement. Kelli (PSY) explained that others' acceptance of her impairment/disability made her feel valued and seen: "I think that [the student organization is] more open to difference. . . . They don't really care if I [need] to take care of myself . . . it is more of an accepting environment." Courtney (MI) noted that when her peers nominated her for a leadership position, she felt that they accepted her into the organization and believed in her ability. "I mean, for a freshman being the president of an organization, although it was small, was kind of a real shocker." She also felt particularly accepted when the former president reached out to her to help with the transition.

Across all impairments, participants were encouraged to get involved or continue their involvement when they knew other disabled students would be present. Alina (LD) described how she felt when she knew another learning-disabled person also participated in the same organization: "I don't feel like I'm the only one in the sorority anyway. It's just nice to know that there's somebody else that struggles like I do."

DISCUSSION

Using the theoretical frameworks of environmental theories and critical realism, we summarize and then discuss our findings as they relate to prior research. We next draw from our findings to suggest modifications to Moos's (1979) theory and to involvement theories.

This study answered four research questions, each of which addressed environmental factors that affect the cocurricular involvement of disabled students. We found that environmental barriers that limited or prevented the cocurricular involvement of disabled students included other people's behaviors and attitudes, which created more barriers to disabled students' involvement than did physical or organizational factors. Participants' responses to barriers included anger, feeling left out, not wanting to burden others, and disengaging from or persisting in involvement. Environmental factors making involvement possible included accessible physical design, flexible organizational policies, and availability of trained professionals. Universally designed physical and organizational environments, as well as active support from staff and peers, encouraged participants' involvement. In the next sections, we explain how these findings support, extend, and challenge some aspects of prior research.

Determinism

Some participants in this study experienced barriers in MLGU's human, physical, and organizational environments as deterministic, preventing their cocurricular involvement (e.g., GPA requirements excluded some participants from leadership roles; inaccessible seating prevented some participants from attending sporting events), a finding that parallels those of Fox et al. (2022). Ableism in the MLGU environment manifested in the behaviors of participants' peers and institutional agents, in organizational dynamics, and in the physical environment. While some barriers arose directly from their impairment (a topic we will address in a later paper), participants located most disabling influences in the campus environment.

This finding aligns with critical realism's framing of disability as a result of the interaction of physical and social environments with impairment (Shakespeare, 2014).

Barriers created by other people were more of a concern for participants than those in the organizational or physical environment. Our data suggest that when spaces are not universally designed, individuals often create (or occasionally remove) barriers to access. For example, Max (LD) experienced an access barrier because his fraternity brothers thought he was unsuited for leadership roles because of his disability. Participants described strong negative emotions when others prohibited or limited their involvement by discounting disability, patronizing and stigmatizing them, or displaying purposeful ignorance. These findings suggest that nondisabled individuals at MLGU may lack knowledge about disabilities and hold stereotypes and negative attitudes about disabled persons.

Major organizational barriers, especially for mobility- and sensory-impaired participants, prevented them from getting involved; lack of information about accessibility, transportation barriers, absence of accommodations, and inflexible or inappropriately applied policies made involvement more difficult. Participants with non-apparent disabilities had difficulty staying involved or becoming a leader because of inflexible policies and ableist organizational practices. These organizational barriers often reflected a lack of awareness of crip time—that is, the need for "a flexible approach to normative time frames" (Price, 2014, p. 62).

Physical barriers, including lack of accessibility and accommodations and segregated access, were major obstacles for participants with mobility and sensory impairments. These concerns all point to MLGU's physical spaces being designed for nondisabled individuals. Little effort appears to have been made to move the university toward universal design.

We conclude that determinism was evident in all aspects of the environment and strongly inhibited disabled students' cocurricular involvement. Additionally, participants encountered barriers not mentioned in the more general college involvement literature, particularly experiencing ableism, organizations' inflexible expectations of members and leaders, and participants' expectations of what involvement entailed. These dynamics reflect normative perceptions of time, a common manifestation of ableism (Dolmage, 2017).

Possibilism

Despite the barriers they encountered, other aspects of the environment made disabled students' involvement at least possible. Environmental possibilism describes an environment that allows for but does not require or make probable certain behaviors (Ellen, 1982; Porteous, 1977). Possibilism explained many influences of the campus environment on participants' involvement, extending this concept to a previously unstudied population.

We found availability of professional staff and being provided with adequate information enabled involvement by participants with all impairment types. We also found, unsurprisingly, that the absence of many of the barriers discussed above made involvement possible. Participants supported Evans et al.'s (2017) call for accommodations to support involvement. Physically accessible spaces were crucial to those with mobility and sensory impairments to enable even minimal cocurricular involvement. The presence of specialized and skilled professional staff made involvement possible for these participants because they knew where to go for assistance and psychological support. Participants with PSY, LD, or ADHD described help from others, notably psychological support, as a minimum requirement for cocurricular involvement. Assistance and psychological support may serve as prerequisites for the sense of belonging that Vaccaro et al. (2015) and Vaccaro and Newman (2016) reported as a consequence of disabled students' involvement.

Probabilism

Finally, our participants described multiple environmental influences that actively encouraged or fostered their involvement, making it probable (Ellen, 1982; Porteous, 1977). A physical space that was universally designed encouraged full participation by participants with MI and SI. Organizations that had consistent and predictable schedules encouraged involvement by participants with LD and ADHD. The human environment had the most influence on participants' involvement. Personal support and assistance from permanent, specialized, and skilled professional staff encouraged participation. Participants felt most welcomed when peers, friends, and leaders in student organizations created informal accommodations, invited them to participate, and genuinely accepted them. As Bialka et al. (2017) found, the presence of other disabled students, especially those with similar impairments, nurtured participants' involvement.

Disabled participants made widely varying recommendations for environmental changes to support their involvement, with notable patterns by impairment type. Most participants with LD expressed little desire for university support for involvement. Participants with ADHD and PSY desired more flexible forms of involvement, particularly forms that required less time, a finding congruent with Fox et al.'s (2022) conclusion that time costs related to disability were significant barriers to disabled students' involvement. Participants with SI and MI recommended that student organizations make their meetings and activities accessible to all students and let students know the accessible route to meeting spaces, aligning with Katzman and Kinsella's (2018) argument that finding accessible routes takes additional time. In contrast

to earlier research (Katzman & Kinsella, 2018; Kimball et al., 2017), our participants did not cite time needed for medical appointments or explicitly address time needed to manage personal care attendants as barriers to involvement.

Modification of Moos's Theory

As noted earlier, our data suggest that individual interactions were a stronger environmental influence than human aggregate influences, particularly when it came to creating informal accommodations. This finding contrasts with Strange and Banning's (2001) argument that the "collective characteristics of environmental inhabitants, whether demographic . . . or psychological" (p. 36) are the primary human influence in the environment. We hypothesize that because disability awareness was not a part of the campus culture, individual actions were more significant than the human aggregate in creating or preventing access to involvement opportunities. As individuals, however, they did not have a collective influence on campus culture, as would a human aggregate.

Expanding Involvement Theory

Our findings confirm many aspects of traditional involvement theory while challenging and complicating other aspects. Our findings support those of Bialka et al. (2017), who found that disabled students can feel inclusion and support through student organization involvement when their nondisabled peers prioritize accessible experiences. The experiences of our participants also confirmed the findings of Vaccaro et al. (2015) and Vaccaro and Newman (2016), showing that involvement enhanced their sense of belonging.

Astin's (1984) developmental theory of involvement makes two key assumptions that are challenged by the findings of this study. The first assumption is that more involvement is inherently better (e.g., Astin, 1984). While Bowman and Trolian (2017) conclusively demonstrated that there is a curvilinear relationship between cocurricular involvement and most desired college outcomes (that is, involvement is good up to a point when its benefits level off and then decrease), the diminishing benefits of higher levels of involvement have not been noted as a specific finding in prior qualitative studies. For some participants in our study, involvement itself diminished the time and energy available for other pursuits (a finding that echoes that of Fox et al., 2022). These findings support Bowman and Trolian's quantitative findings and challenge Astin's arguments. For many of our participants, there was a ceiling to the benefits of cocurricular involvement. We note that environmental pressures to increase involvement can have detrimental effects on some students and question the premise of involvement theory that more is inherently better.

A second assumption of involvement theory is that different forms of involvement compete for a finite amount of time (Astin, 1984). Our findings indicate that time spent managing one's impairment can facilitate involvement (because one has addressed one's mental health issues, obtained needed medication, or had one's wheelchair repaired) while simultaneously decreasing the time available for involvement. For some participants (especially those with LD or ADHD), involvement made other forms of participation more feasible because the initial involvement created greater structure in their lives, leading them to be more efficient, which in turn made further involvement possible. For these students, involvement begets involvement. For others, spending time on disability management enabled involvement in their remaining time. Thus, Astin's (1984) assumption that time spent on non-cocurricular involvement diminishes the time available for cocurricular involvement does not hold for all students. His conceptualization of time reflects ableist assumptions that time spent negotiating

disability takes away from one's ability to be involved.

These challenges to traditional descriptions of student involvement are not necessarily unique to disabled students. We hypothesize that students working off-campus, adult students, commuting students, and students with family responsibilities may all encounter similar dynamics. In recognizing that involvement may look different for nontraditional student populations, it is critical to avoid a deficit framework (Pendakur et al., 2019) or to communicate to students that forms of involvement that differ from those of "traditional" students are inadequate or insufficient. Student affairs practitioners and researchers need to consider what involvement looks like and what constitutes "optimal" involvement for more than full-time, white, traditionally aged students (Pendakur et al., 2019). What may be unique to (some) disabled students is the dynamic in which some uses of time facilitate involvement rather than compete with it.

Delimitations and Limitations

We note two delimitations and four major limitations of the study. We completed this study at one institution and recruited students who were registered with MLGU's DRO and, therefore, were already accessing formal accommodations. Students at other universities and those not connected with disability services might have had different barriers.

The first limitation is the lack of information about participant demographics, particularly race. Because of the small number of people with apparent disabilities at MLGU, to encourage participation in the study and limit participants' identifiability, we did not systematically collect demographic data. Thus, we cannot address racial group patterns in involvement experiences. Research addressing the intersection of involvement, race, and disability status is imperative. Second, all the interviewers and analysts were white. This limitation was unrecognized during the design of the study, development of interview questions, and data analysis. Including researchers from different racial backgrounds may have led to different findings and conclusions. Also, due to the lag between data collection and analysis, we were unable to conduct member checks. We support the quality of our conclusions by providing extensive documentation of decision-making in the analysis process. Finally, data were collected by interviewers with varying levels of experience and comfort exploring emotion. We suspect that the concentration of information about the emotional response to barriers from participants with mobility impairments may be an artifact of that interviewer's willingness to explore those dynamics and that the interviewer and these participants shared the experience of mobility impairment.

IMPLICATIONS

Findings from this study suggest both theoretical and practical implications. Critical realism (Shakespeare, 2014), a theory that recognizes the influence of physical variables as well as structural and social systems on behavior, was a strong framework for understanding how ableism and other aspects of the campus environment affect the level of involvement of disabled students. The environmental theories of Porteous (1977) and Ellen (1982) showed great promise for use in campus settings by expanding understanding of the environment's influence on disabled students' ability to become involved on campus. The distinctions between possibilism and probabilism (Ellen, 1982; Porteous, 1977) have implications for creating inclusive climates for disabled students. Possibilism aligns with legal compliance and allowing access. Making cocurricular involvement possible is insufficient to fully engage disabled students in activities that foster success. Making

their participation probable requires strategies such as facilitating ease of use, strengthening predictability, and explicit invitation.

Our findings also have practical implications for those working with disabled college students. Participants mentioned that they experienced ableism enacted by people in the college environment more than physical or organizational ableism; thus, addressing individually enacted ableism, including discounting disability, patronization, stigmatization, and displaying purposeful ignorance, is critical. Administrators can enhance disabled students' cocurricular involvement by confronting ableist language and behaviors, explicitly supporting many different forms of participation, and listening to disabled students' experiences. It is also important for Disability Resource Office staff to support students in their cocurricular involvement as well as their academics. In addition, training should educate all student leaders about how to provide access, respond to disclosure, and reconfigure the expectations of leadership.

While other students and institutional agents presented the most barriers, physical and organizational barriers also frustrated participants, especially those with mobility impairments who desired to be involved in cocurricular activities. Accessible entrances should be clearly marked, websites should indicate room accessibility, and snow must be removed quickly and thoroughly. In addition, expanding campus transportation (e.g., routes, types of lifts, evening availability, and frequency) would enhance access for the entire university community.

As an institution, MLGU had the resources to address physical barriers. However, not all universities have prioritized these resources, and physical barriers still present significant obstacles to involvement on many campuses. Student activity fees might be allocated to increase access to spaces frequently housing events funded by those fees. University officials also might seek private and state funds to create physical access.

Student government advisors should educate students about the importance of creating access to support valued student outcomes. Additionally, disabled students should be included on all committees planning new and renovated physical spaces.

The findings of this study highlight the importance of universal design in both architecture and organizational practice. It is critical to address ableism apparent in organizational barriers, such as inflexible policies and the absence of accommodations. As a DHH participant articulated, involvement required that sign language interpreters be readily available, which often means that the university must hire them as full-time staff members.

Involvement would be enhanced if institutional administrators recognized that policies and practices designed using normative approaches (a manifestation of ableism) do not work for all disabled students or even all students (Dolmage, 2017). Our findings suggest that accommodation needs vary across disability type. GPA requirements and organizational expectations of extensive time commitments were barriers to the involvement of students with learning disabilities, psychological disabilities, or ADHD. Are those expectations always necessary? Often, GPA requirements are used to ensure students' academic standing is not jeopardized by their involvement; however, some participants in this study reported that involvement served to increase their grades. GPA requirements are also based on the ableist assumption that everyone can achieve a specific GPA, that success is defined by GPA, or that with more time to study, a student's GPA will increase. Because not everything can be universally designed and because accommodation forms vary, it is important to support the provision of informal accommodations by providing ally training for students and administrators that would include how to provide access at the moment it is needed.

Participants highlighted organizational efforts that helped make their involvement possible, particularly actions allowing spontaneous participation. Although participation may never be fully spontaneous for disabled students, organizational supports (e.g., readily available interpreters, predictable meeting schedules, captioning) may help facilitate disabled students' involvement by reducing the planning necessary or the time between planning and doing.

Campuses might modify involvement opportunities to support students with finite time, a redesign that could benefit many types of students, including commuters, adult learners, and disabled students. For example, meetings and events could be scheduled with an awareness of when public transportation ends and make clear when it is or is not necessary to attend events for their full duration. Often programming on residential campuses is held late in the evening on the presumption that the event is, therefore, more attractive to students; this may not always be true.

FUTURE RESEARCH

Our findings raised questions about how impairment type influences involvement. Participants with PSY experienced their university involvement in ways different from most other participants. However, we had more limited information about PSY than about other impairment categories, necessitating further exploration of these students' involvement. The only participants with episodic impairments were those with psychological disabilities; understanding how participants with these types of impairments experience campus involvement is important. We also noticed that LD students had patterns of involvement different from other participants. LD students mentioned that involvement helped them manage their disability; they were also more involved than any other impairment group, a dynamic meriting further investigation.

Future research must consider racial, ethnic, sexual orientation, and other demographic differences when recruiting disabled participants and research team members. Factors that influence disabled students' involvement may differ by social identities, and researchers' interactions with participants are shaped by the similarity or difference of their identities. Researchers of varied backgrounds also may interpret data in ways that enhance the study's credibility.

There were specific barriers and encouragers to involvement that were mentioned only by members of fraternities or sororities. In these settings, group dynamics, GPA requirements, and expectations of leadership roles presented barriers exacerbated by impairments. The role fraternity and sorority life plays for members with disabilities merits additional study.

Students who lived off-campus also seemed to experience different barriers, particularly having to do with weather and transportation. Further study of disabled students' involvement in various higher education settings, such as commuter institutions, community and liberal arts colleges, as well as other geographical settings, would help to validate the findings of this study.

Decades of research on cocurricular involvement in college have demonstrated its linkage to student success. Our data show that disabled students are more likely to be involved if universities create encouraging environments and limit the ableism implicit in many campus practices. Such changes would benefit both disabled students and the larger campus community.

Correspondence concerning this article should be addressed to Nancy J. Evans; nancyjevans1947@gmail.com

REFERENCES

Astin, A. W. (1984). Student involvement: A developmental theory for higher education. *Journal of College Student Development, 25*(4), 297–308.

Bialka, C. S., Morro, D., Brown, K., & Hannah, G. (2017). Breaking barriers and building bridges: Understanding how a student organization attends to the social integration of college students with disabilities. *Journal of Postsecondary Education and Disability, 30*(2), 157–172.

Belfrage, C., & Hauf, F. (2017). The gentle art of retroduction: Critical realism, cultural political economy, and critical grounded theory. *Organization Studies, 38*(2), 251–271. https://doi.org/10.1177/0170840616663239

Bowman, N. A., & Trolian, T. L. (2017). Is more always better? The curvilinear relationships between college student experiences and outcomes. *Innovative Higher Education, 42*(5), 477–489. https://doi.org/10.1007/s10755-017-9403-1

Dolmage, J. T. (2017). *Academic ableism: Disability and higher education.* University of Michigan. http://dx.doi.org/10.3998/mpub.9708722

Dugan, J. P., & Komives, S. R. (2007). *Developing leadership capacity in college students: Findings from a national study.* A Report from the Multi-Institutional Study of Leadership. National Clearinghouse for Leadership Programs.

Dugan, J., & Komives, S. (2010). Influences on college students' capacity for socially responsible leadership. *Journal of College Student Development, 51*(5), 525–549. doi:10.1353/csd.2010.0009

Ellen, R. (1982). *Environment, subsistence, and system: The ecology of small-scale social formations.* Cambridge University.

Elliott, R., & Timulak, L. (2021). *Essentials of descriptive-interpretive qualitative research: A generic approach.* American Psychological Association.

Evans, N. J., Broido, E. M., Brown, K. R., & Wilke, A. K. (2017). *Disability in higher education: A social justice approach.* Jossey-Bass.

Fletcher, A. J. (2017). Applying critical realism in qualitative research: Methodology meets method. International *Journal of Social Research Methodology, 20*(2), 181–194. https//doi.org/10.1080/13645579.2016.1144401

Fox, A., Hedayet, M., Mansour, K., Kommers, S., & Wells, R. (2022). College students with disabilities' experiences with financial, social, and emotional costs on campus in the United States. *International Journal of Disability, Development and Education, 69*(1), 106–120. https://doi.org/10.1080/1034912X.2021.1966758

Harper, S. R., & Quaye, S. J. (2015). Making engagement equitable for students in U.S. higher education. In S. J. Quaye & S. R. Harper (Eds.), *Student engagement in higher education: Theoretical perspectives and practical approaches for diverse populations* (2nd ed., pp. 1–14). Routledge.

Hurtado, S., Milem, J., Clayton-Pederson, A., & Allen, W. (1999). Enacting diverse learning environments: Improving the climate for racial/ethnic diversity in higher education. *ASHE-ERIC Higher Education Report 26*(8). Association for the Study of Higher Education. https://files.eric.ed.gov/fulltext/ED430514.pdf

Katzman, E. R., & Kinsella, E. (2018). 'It's like having another job.' The invisible work of self-managing attendant services.

Disability & Society, 33(9), 1436–1459. https://doi.org/10.1080/09687599.2018.1497949

Kimball, E., Friedensen, R. E., & Silva, E. (2017). Engaging disability: Trajectories of involvement for college students with disabilities. In E. Kim & K. C. Aquino (Eds.), *Disability as diversity in higher education: Policies and practices to enhance student success* (pp. 61–74). Routledge.

Kimball, E. W., & Thoma, H. S. (2019). College experiences for students with disabilities: An ecological synthesis of recent literature. *Journal of College Student Development, 60*(6), 674–693. doi:10.1353/csd.2019.0062

Krueger, R. A. (1994). *Focus groups: A practical guide for applied research* (2nd ed.). Sage.

Linton, S. (1998). *Claiming disability: Knowledge and identity.* New York University Press.

Mamiseishvili, K., & Koch, L. C. (2011). First-to-second year persistence of students with disabilities in postsecondary institutions in the United States. *Rehabilitation Counseling Bulletin, 54*(2), 93–105. https://doi.org/10.1177/0034355210382580

Mayhew, M. J., Rockenbach, A. N., Bowman, N. A., Seifert, T. A., & Wolniak, G. C. (with Pascarella, E. T. & Terenzini, P. T.). (2016). *How college affects students: 21st century evidence that higher education works* (Vol. 3). Jossey Bass.

Mooney, M. A. (2016). Human agency and mental illness. *Journal of Critical Realism, 15*(4), 376–390. DOI: 10.1080/14767430.2016.1193675

Moos, R. H. (1979). *Evaluating educational environments: Procedures, measures, findings, and policy implications.* Jossey-Bass. https://doi.org/10.1016/0149-7189(82)90080-5

Moreno, D. R. & Sanchez, S. M. (2013). The influence of Latina/o Greek sorority and fraternity involvement on Latina/o college student transition and success. *The Journal of Latino–Latin American Studies, 5*(2), 113–125. https://doi.org/10.18085/llas.5.2.y1113g2572x13061

Museus, S. D., Yi, V., & Saelua, N. (2018). How culturally engaging campus environments influence sense of belonging in college: An examination of differences between white students and students of color. *Journal of Diversity in Higher Education, 11*(4), 467–483. https://doi.org/10.1037/dhe0000069

Pendakur, S. L., Quaye, S. J., & Harper, S. R. (2019). The heart of our work: Equitable engagement for students in US higher education. In S. J. Quaye, S. R. Harper, & S. L. Pendakur (Eds.), *Student engagement in higher education: Theoretical perspectives and practical approaches for diverse populations* (pp. 1–16). Routledge.

Porteous, J. P. (1977). *Environment & behavior: Planning and everyday urban life.* Addison-Wesley.

Price, M. (2012). *Mad at school: Rhetorics of mental disability and academic life.* University of Michigan. https://doi.org/10.3998/mpub.1612837

Reed, M. J., & Kennett, D. J. (2017). The importance of university students' perceived ability to balance multiple roles: A comparison of students with and without disabilities. *Canadian Journal of Higher Education, 47*(2), 71–86.

Seidman, I. (1998). *Interviewing as qualitative research: A guide for researchers in education and the social sciences* (2nd ed.). Teachers College Press.

Shakespeare, T. (2014). *Disability rights and wrongs revisited.* Routledge.

Strange, C. C. & Banning, J. (2001). *Education by design: Creating campus learning environments that work.* Jossey Bass.

Strayhorn, T. L. (2019). *College students' sense of belonging: A key to educational success for all students* (2nd ed.). Routledge.

Vaccaro, A., Daly-Cano, M., & Newman, B. M. (2015). A sense of belonging among college students with disabilities: An emergent theoretical model. *Journal of College Student Development, 56*(7), 670–686. https://doi.org/10.1353/csd.2015.0072

Vaccaro, A., & Newman, B. M. (2016). Development of a sense of belonging for privileged and minorized students: An emergent model. *Journal of College Student Development, 57*(8), 925–942. https://doi.org/10.1353/csd.2016.0091.

"We're not the Gods of Accommodations:" Disability Resource Professionals and Accommodation Decision-Making

Morgan M. Strimel   Grace L. Francis   Jodi M. Duke

In institutions of higher education, disability resource professionals (DRPs) have the responsibility of upholding compliance with federal legislation regarding college students with disabilities. Specifically, DRPs are tasked with determining reasonable accommodations to ensure access to all aspects of the campus community while simultaneously maintaining the integrity of academic programs. Despite the complexity of this role, there is limited research and guidance on how to make accommodation decisions. Further, existing guidance provides inconsistent recommendations for practice. As a result, DRPs use multiple, largely unexplored processes to determine accommodations unique to their institutional or professional discretion. The purpose of this study, therefore, was to explore how DRPs approach accommodation decision-making for college students with disabilities. DRP participants discussed factors they considered when making accommodation decisions, processes used to determine accommodations, and exceptions to these processes. The authors conclude with directions for future research and recommendations for higher education disability resources.

Across the United States, 19% of students enrolled in higher education have at least one disability (NCES, 2019). Students with disabilities[1] in college and university settings are protected from discrimination by the Americans with Disabilities Act (ADA, 1990) and Section 504 of the Rehabilitation Act (1973). In accordance with this legislation, institutions of higher education must ensure equal access to programs, services, and spaces for all qualified disabled students by means of reasonable accommodations and equitable design (Yull, 2015). As a result, colleges and universities typically employ disability resource professionals (DRPs), who are responsible for "promoting accessible campus environments for students with disabilities, working with students and others to identify reasonable accommodations that remove barriers to access, and ensuring that accommodations determined to be reasonable are provided and effective" (Association on Higher Education and Disability, n.d.a.).

A DRP's ability to build relationships, collaborate with various stakeholders and find creative solutions to complex situations is critical to their role (Evans et al., 2017). These abilities are particularly essential in the accommodation process, as DRPs engage in a skilled inquiry regarding accommodation requests—the central function of their work (Meeks & Jain, 2015). Specifically, the accommodation process involves (a) evaluating disabled students' accommodation requests on an individualized basis and (b) making determinations that meet the barriers identified by the

---

[1] Because many members of the disability community reclaim the term disabled, we use person-first (i.e., student with a disability) and identity-first (i.e., disabled student) language interchangeably throughout this article.

Morgan Strimel (https://orcid.org/0000-0002-9256-5302) is Research Assistant in Disability Services. Grace Francis (https://orcid.org/000-0002-8707-9430) is Associate Professor of Special Education, and Jodi Duke (https://orcid .org/0000-0003-2313-0935) is Associate Professor of Special Education; all at George Mason University.

student while (c) maintaining the integrity of the institution's academic program standards (Hatzes et al., 2002). According to the ADA (1990), determining accommodations must be an interactive process, with disabled students and DRPs working collaboratively to identify accommodations that are appropriate for the student. Regardless of the specific approach to engaging in the interactive process, accommodations should be (a) defensible, (b) directly related to the functional impact of the student's disability (Ofiesh et al., 2004), and (c) *reasonable* as outlined by federal law (ADA, 1990).

The reasonableness of accommodations is a requirement set forth by the ADA (1990), and although several examples exist of what reasonable accommodations may include (e.g., interpreter services, screen reader software), the law does not provide specific steps that DRPs can follow to determine the reasonableness of a student request (Krebs, 2019). What the law does tell DRPs, however, is that reasonable accommodations must not place an undue hardship upon the institution, pose a threat to others, or result in a fundamental alteration (i.e., compromising an essential component) of a program or service (ADA, 1990; Rehabilitation Act, 1973). Regardless of the components considered, reasonable accommodations are intended to live at the nexus of a student's disability and corresponding barrier and require careful attention to process and detail to achieve (Meeks & Jain, 2015).

REVIEW OF THE LITERATURE

Several researchers have developed models that provide guidance for DRPs to carry out the accommodation process and achieve reasonableness in their decisions, despite the complexities of accommodation decision-making (Gaddy, 2012; Hsiao et al., 2018; Laird-Metke, 2016; Lindstrom, 2007; Meeks & Jain, 2015; Ofiesh et al., 2004). Ofiesh and colleagues

(2004), for example, offered a six-step approach to determine accommodations that includes: (a) identifying a diagnosis from relevant medical documentation, (b) understanding the academic context causing the barrier, (c) comparing the barrier to the impact of the student's disability, (d) evaluating the severity of the disability, (e) synthesizing these factors and (f) developing an appropriate accommodation. Additionally, Hsiao and colleagues (2018) developed a decision-making model that called for gathering the input of faculty members to identify course-specific requirements and student barriers before collaborating with faculty to determine and implement accommodations. Finally, Meeks and Jain (2015) emphasized the importance of conducting an individualized assessment of a student's barriers and learning environments and basing decisions of the reasonableness of accommodations on a student's narrative of the impact of their disability (as opposed to medical documentation). While these models reflect consideration of similar factors, it is evident that they vary in data collection approaches for each factor and the extent to which each is important to accommodation decision-making.

In addition to guidance from the literature, DRPs also have access to guiding documents from the Association of Higher Education and Disability (AHEAD), the leading professional organization on disability in higher education, to assist in the accommodation process. Specifically, AHEAD published *The Professional's Guide to Exploring and Facilitating Access*, which provides a "fluid" seven-step process to guide accommodation meetings (n.d.c., para. 1). Within this document, DRPs are encouraged to listen to a student's self-report (i.e., narrative impact of their disability), consider environmental barriers, use professional judgment, seek medical documentation on an as-needed basis (e.g., if the request is not clear), and consult with faculty/academic departments as necessary.

Complementary to this document is AHEAD's *Supporting Accommodation Requests: Guidance on Documentation Practices*, which emphasizes the use of case-by-case analyses to determine accommodations. In this document, DRPs are encouraged to use the student self-report as a primary form of documentation, followed by their own professional judgment, before examining third-party documentation if the connection between the student's request and their disability is unclear (AHEAD, 2012).

CONCEPTUAL MODEL

In light of the limited guidance available regarding accommodation decision-making, Banerjee and colleagues (2015) found that 53% of DRPs used their professional judgment as the primary source for making accommodation decisions. What *professional judgment* entails, however, is a topic largely unexplored and, as noted by Banerjee and colleagues (2015), is likely subject to DRPs' inherent subjectivity as human beings (e.g., opinion, biases, beliefs). Notably, a potential way to address these concerns among DRPs and their accommodation decision-making practices is to engage in *reflexivity*, a common practice in qualitative research (Merriam & Tisdell, 2016) that involves "an explicit self-consciousness and self-assessment" (Holmes, 2020, p. 2) about one's perceptions, identities, and positions (e.g., social, political) to understand how they might influence actions, choices, and interactions (Holmes, 2020; May & Perry, 2017). In other words, engaging in reflexivity is the continual practice of self-scrutiny and careful attention to the impact of biases and personal beliefs in everyday life.

The concept of reflexivity has expanded beyond practices in educational research to on-the-job practices used within the professional landscape. For example, in the field of social work, D'Cruz and colleagues (2007)

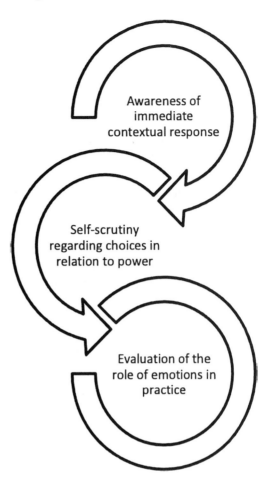

FIGURE 1. Variations of Reflexivity
Note. This figure depicts the path of engaging in reflexivity, starting with an awareness of an immediate contextual response. Through all phases, this reflexive process is intentional and cyclical (see D'Cruz et al., 2007).

explored how practitioners in child and family welfare organizations understood reflexivity, which they described as "a concept that is increasingly gaining currency in professional practice literature, particularly in relation to working with uncertainty . . . and as an important feature of professional discretion and ethical practice" (p. 1). According to the authors, the concept of reflexivity involves three primary variations (see Figure 1). These variations include (a) one's "immediate" response to a particular context and their ability to "process information and create knowledge" that inform choices, (b) self-scrutiny to evaluate created knowledge and subsequent choices in relation to power, and (c) evaluation of the role of emotions in choices made in practice (D'Cruz et al., 2007, p. 2). Each variation of reflexivity, despite presenting dynamic actions for professionals in practice, overlaps with another and interacts to create a holistically reflexive approach to apply to high-stakes decisions.

Although D'Cruz and colleagues' (2007) work focused on social work practitioners' on-the-job decision-making, their approach to conceptualizing reflexivity presents implications for higher education disability resources; disability resources as a field is not unlike social work in that high-stakes decision-making is generally grounded in vague guidelines necessitating professional discretion. There is a paucity of research, however, on the application of reflexivity within the disability resources profession and the extent to which it is used in practice among disability resource professionals.

Purpose

While scholars and professional organizations provide guidance and recommendations on how to make accommodation decisions, there exists minimal research on DRPs' actual decision-making processes (Lindstrom, 2007). As a result, it is essential to deeply understand how DRPs make accommodation decisions for students with disabilities (Banerjee et al., 2015), particularly considering the subjective nature of this practice. The purpose of this study, therefore, was to explore how DRPs approach accommodation decision-making for college students with disabilities. The following question guided this research: What are the practices of disability resource professionals when making accommodation decisions for college students with disabilities?

METHOD

The three-member research team comprised a doctoral student in special education with experience as a DRP, a special education faculty member whose research focused on college students with autism spectrum disorder, and a special education faculty member whose research focused on young adults with significant disabilities and family support. Team members practiced reflexivity by interrogating the impact of their microcultures (e.g., experiences with disabilities, work experiences, monolingual English speakers, first-generation college students) throughout data collection and analysis (e.g., questioning why they reacted strongly to a participant's description of the social model of disability). Team members also shared the epistemological view of critical constructivism, maintaining that knowledge is developed by perceptions of individual experiences (Coghlan & Brydon-Miller, 2014).

Given that team members maintained the view of participants as experts, they used a qualitative interpretive design to collect thick descriptions of participants' experiences (Merriam & Tisdell, 2016). Key tenants of interpretive design involve (a) asking open-ended and exploratory questions; (b) collecting first-person accounts to answer research questions; (c) engaging in a descriptive-interpretative analysis by reflecting meanings of participant data line by line; (d) creating codes, categories, and themes to capture meanings; and (e) critically considering researcher positionalities throughout the research process (Elliott & Timulak, 2005).

Participants

The research team used convenience sampling methods to recruit participants (Merriam & Tisdell, 2016). Specifically, the researchers distributed a flyer with a description of the study and a link to the survey on the member

Table 1
Participant Demographics

Participant	Age	Disability	Years as a DRP
3	31–40	Non-disabled	10+
4	51–60	Disabled	10+
7	41–50	Non-disabled	5–10
8	51–60	Disabled	10+
10	21–30	Non-disabled	5–10
11	41–50	Non-disabled	5–10
12	21–30	Disabled	Less than 3
13	61–70	Non-disabled	10+
15	31–40	Disabled	5–10
16	31–40	Non-disabled	5–10
17	51–60	Disabled	10+
18	41–50	Disabled	3–5
19	41–50	Disabled	10+

listserv for AHEAD, the member listserv for the College Autism Network, and two researchers' Twitter accounts. The anonymous survey included 22 questions covering participant demographic information, processes used for accommodation decision-making, and (c) perceptions of the influence of identities and experiences in relation to these processes. Within the survey, participants were offered the option to leave their names and contact information to participate in a one-hour follow-up interview.

Of the 51 participants who agreed to participate in the survey, a total of 13 DRPs across the United States participated in the interview portion of this study. All 13 participants indicated that English was the primary language spoken in their homes (n = 13). Most participants identified as white (n = 12), and over 75% identified as women (n = 10). More than half of the participants identified as an individual with a disability (n = 7). Four participants worked in the US Southeast, one in the Midwest, two

in the Southwest, four in the West, and two worked in the Northeast. For participant information, see Table 1.

Interviews

The research team conducted all interviews over Zoom. The primary facilitator began the interviews by explaining the purpose of the study and measures that would be taken to maintain participants' confidentiality and by seeking consent for audio recording. Of the 13 participants, 12 consented for their interviews to be recorded. During the interviews, the primary facilitator engaged participants in conversations while a secondary facilitator took rigorous field notes, asked clarifying questions as needed, and conducted member checks at the end of each interview. The researchers used a semi-structured interview protocol to allow for fluidity during conversations with participants (Merriam & Tisdell, 2016). Before the interviews took place, the research team piloted and refined the protocol with two DRPs who did not participate in this study. The interview protocol included open-ended questions regarding participants' backgrounds, processes used for making accommodation decisions, and perceptions of identities and experiences that influence the accommodation process. This paper focuses on the accommodation decision-making processes participants discussed during their interviews.

Data Analysis

The first author transcribed, cleaned, and de-identified data from the 12 recorded interviews and the field notes from the non-recorded interview. Each member of the research team then individually open-coded one transcript line by line, assigning notes and keywords that reflected the meaning of clusters of similar data to identify preliminary codes within the data (Elliott & Timulak, 2005; Merriam & Tisdell, 2016). Following open coding, the team convened to compare codes and developed an initial codebook after discussing similarities and differences found in codes for the first transcript (Elliott & Timulak, 2005). The initial codebook included codes such as *accommodation process* and *standard accommodations*. Next, each researcher used the initial codebook to independently code another transcript, using the same line-by-line process. This process resulted in a third and final codebook that included 12 codes, including *specific accommodation decision-making process* and *complications of determining reasonable accommodations*. Using this finalized codebook, the first author coded all transcripts and field notes with qualitative analysis software (Dedoose, Version 4.12). Finally, the team used coded data to identify key themes representing the meanings of data, including those presented in this manuscript. These included (a) factors influencing the accommodation process, (b) factors considered when making accommodation decisions, and (c) accommodation decision-making processes.

Trustworthiness

The research team engaged in several measures to ensure trustworthiness throughout the entire research process, including (a) developing and maintaining an audit trail of decisions made throughout the research process, (b) pilot testing and refining the interview protocol with DRPs who did not participate in this study, (c) member checking with participants during and directly after interviews to review preliminary themes captured from conversations, (d) cleaning transcripts and field notes, (e) engaging in weekly peer debriefing as a research team, (f) conducting rigorous memoing to explore emergent themes across triangulated data (Merriam & Tisdell, 2016), and (g) research team members critically interrogating their positionality to understand how it may have influenced the research process.

Limitations

First, the sample is not reflective of the diverse identities of DRPs, as participants were primarily middle-aged white women. Second, this study was limited in its recruitment procedures, which included two relevant professional organizations and two researchers' Twitter accounts. This recruitment process limited opportunities to participate to members of these fee-based organizations or those who follow members of the research team on Twitter. Third, the research team was not able to disaggregate accommodation decision-making procedures based on demographic information due to the small sample size and the need to protect participant identities, limiting an understanding of how these factors influenced processes used to determine accommodations. Fourth, despite our efforts to minimize the influence of our biases on the interpretation of data, our positionalities as three white women may have inherently shaped how we engaged with a participant sample of primarily white women and subsequently interpreted the data.

FINDINGS

In the following section, major themes and subthemes from the findings are detailed. The major themes included: (a) factors influencing the accommodation process, (b) factors considered when making accommodation decisions, and (c) accommodation decision-making processes. During the data analysis process, each participant was assigned a number. Participants' numbers are included after each quote to demonstrate the breadth of perspectives represented in this sample. Full participant information is available in Table 1.

Factors Influencing the Accommodation Process

Participants described several factors that influenced their accommodation decision-making processes. This theme included three subthemes: (a) perspectives of the accommodation process, (b) collaboration with coworkers, and (c) collaboration with other professionals.

Perspectives of the Accommodation Process. Before discussing their decision-making processes, many participants broadly described their perspectives on the accommodation process and how those perspectives influenced their approach to decision-making. Some participants, for example, expressed concerns about a "medicalized model of disability thinking" (12) that they observed other DRPs using and, consequently, avoided these medicalized model practices during the accommodation process themselves. According to participants, these practices included framing the accommodation process through "compliance," carrying out "transactional" interactions with disabled

students, "going by exactly what the law requires and nothing more," and "push[ing] [students] through like a factory" (19).

Other participants went a step further and questioned the existence of the accommodation process in general and discussed how it could be troubling to them. For example, some participants questioned why students with disabilities were the only college student population who must "constantly prove that [they] have that [disability] identity" (e.g., "we don't ask students of color to prove . . . they're students of color.") (16). To this point, one participant wondered, "why should students with disabilities experience more barriers . . . to get accommodations?" compared to the experiences of non-disabled students, emphasizing that higher education, as a whole, is "built on ableism" (8). These participants also felt that DRPs should not act as gatekeepers to access as they are "not gods of accommodations" (8). Even further, one participant expressed that to "flatten the power structure" in higher education, DRPs should be "generous with [providing] accommodations" to students with disabilities (7).

Collaboration With Coworkers. Participants described various ways in which they collaboratively approached accommodation decisions with their coworkers. For some, collaboration only occurred in instances where they "struggl[ed] with the decision," (8) emphasizing that getting a second opinion in these instances allowed them to "better serve" (12) disabled students since there is "a lot that goes into" (8) accommodation decisions. Further, participants emphasized that "[having] a debate" with coworkers about accommodations was, at times, "extremely helpful" (12). This was especially true when they were leaning toward denying an accommodation request: "if I'm going to say no, I just check with another professional to make sure" (19).

On the other hand, several participants identified ongoing collaboration with coworkers (e.g., a team approach) as a practice built into the structure of their disability resource centers (DRCs). In these instances, participants described collaborative decision-making processes as a space to "share ideas," "support each other," and "work as a team" to not "make decisions alone, ever" (8, 3). One participant described their DRC's collaborative decision-making structure and, in doing so, effectively summed up the descriptions of others:

> Some days you might have two [students], some days you might have 15 [students] to present [to the DRP team] . . . to determine eligibility for services. You . . . present [the student] and say, "student John Smith, diagnosis of anxiety, asking for a single dorm room, has a letter from the psychiatrist." And if we approve it, great, and then we send a notification to the student when we're done to invite them in . . . [to] explain how to use their accommodations (16).

Collaboration With Other Professionals. Participants discussed collaborating with university faculty to determine accommodations. One participant, for example, emphasized that "the only way [DRPs] can determine reasonable [accommodations]" is if they do so "in conjunction with a professor" (15). This sentiment was echoed by another participant, who described collaborating with faculty by first looking jointly at the "profile of the student" and the course "objectives" to then "pull from [the DRP's] bag of tricks" to determine appropriate accommodations (13). Although participants agreed that collaboration with faculty was important, they also emphasized that the support they received from faculty ranged: "sometimes you're going to get professors that put up a huge fight . . . sometimes you're going to get professors who are like, 'yeah, whatever'" (16).

In addition, participants noted collaborating with other university professionals while making accommodation decisions. For example, participants described collaborating with their general counsel (i.e., the institution's legal team) when they were "on the fence" (15) about complex accommodation decisions. In these cases, participants noted that the general counsel would "be legally defending the university" (15) if a student disagreed with an accommodation decision and therefore valued their opinion. Further, participants described collaborating with professionals outside of the university, including professional learning communities from organizations (e.g., AHEAD). Within these communities, participants worked with other professionals across the country for "niche kinds of questions" (e.g., uncommon accommodation requests; 19). Overall, participants who collaboratively approached accommodation decisions emphasized that "one of the most important things in this field is to not feel like you have to do this alone" (8).

Factors Considered When Making Accommodation Decisions

Participants discussed several factors they considered when making accommodation decisions. This theme included three subthemes: (a) objective factors considered, (b) reasonableness of the accommodation request, and (c) subjective factors considered.

Objective Factors Considered. Participants outlined objective factors (e.g., those not influenced by personal thoughts or feelings) such as documentation, university program standards, and relevant legislation that they considered when making accommodation decisions. Some participants, for example, emphasized a heavy reliance on legal guidance, such as "state and federal requirements" (18), regarding access as well as "current [legal] cases" (e.g., Office for Civil Rights complaints) that were relevant to "guide [their] practices" (3). Specifically, legal factors involved in accommodation decision-making included considering whether the student was "a qualified individual with a disability" per Section 504 of the Rehabilitation Act (1973), whether the student's accommodation request was "reasonable" per the Americans with Disabilities Act (1990), and whether the student was "substantially limited" by their impairment in academic settings (17).

Moreover, several participants identified documentation from a healthcare provider as an essential objective factor considered when making accommodation decisions: "[I] may approve accommodations if there is a clear nexus [between the student's disability and the accommodation request] based on the documentation" (18). Specifically, some participants emphasized relying "heavily" on documentation that was "completed by a licensed clinician or medical provider" so that they could "have evidence" of "what [students were] experiencing" (3). For some, this need for documentation was because some students were "requesting accommodations that [were] not reasonable" (4). Conversely, participants noted documentation as a factor that they considered only on an as-needed basis, such as when "there is no connection between the disability and the accommodation request" (17). For example, one participant stated that they "follow AHEAD guidance on documentation guidelines" and therefore only needed documentation "based on a student's request" if a decision was not clear to them from the student's narrative of the impact of their disability (10).

Reasonableness of the Request. Participants discussed how they considered the standard of reasonableness of accommodations as set forth by the Americans with Disabilities Act (1990) as a factor in their decision-making processes, particularly given the vague definition of the term (i.e., "reasonable is a big gray area that we can swim in"; 19). Because reasonableness is "nebulous" (3), several participants described it in terms of what it is not. Reasonable accommodations, according to participants, cannot

(a) "change the [learning] experience for other students," (b) "give [students with disabilities] an advantage," (c) "help [students]," or (d) create a "reduction of essential course requirements" (4, 16, 18). As one participant described, determining reasonableness is "really trying to find that fine line between making sure the student gets the services they need to equally access the class . . . without crossing that line to give them more help" (12).

Conversely, some participants spoke of reasonable accommodations in terms of what they are as opposed to what they are not. For example, participants noted that reasonable accommodations "fit the impact of the disability" and "mitigate the barriers on campus" (16). One participant outlined the components of reasonableness they used as a guide to determine accommodations:

> When I look at reasonable, the first piece to that is . . . does it make sense in terms of what's the identified barrier, and would this accommodation actually remove that barrier? And is it implementable? And then the next stage to that is, would it result in a fundamental alteration or a lowering of the academic standards? And then lastly . . . [I consider] undue administrative, financial burden [for the university] (17).

Subjective Factors Considered. Participants described subjective factors (those influenced by personal thoughts or feelings), such as student self-report and professional judgment, that they considered during the accommodation process. Relying too heavily on documentation and diagnoses, specifically, was noted by one participant as aligning with the "medicalized model" (7) of disability (e.g., "We shouldn't be counting on a psychologist or doctor who's never actually been in the [college] environment . . . how could they possibly know what the barriers are?"; 8). Instead, participants discussed aligning their work with AHEAD's guidelines on documentation, which emphasizes the use of "professional judgment" as needed, such as when disabled students "don't have paperwork" or who "may not have access to insurance or a doctor" to provide documentation during the accommodation process (7).

In addition, many participants highlighted student self-reports as an essential factor to consider when making accommodation decisions: "start with a student's story and lead with that" (8). Participants emphasized that consideration of the self-report was "best practice" for DRPs and described the importance of hearing it from "a viewpoint of curiosity" (7) to best understand the experiences of students with disabilities. Further, participants emphasized that when soliciting self-reports from students, they were certain to "let [students] know that [they] do see them as an expert" (7) in their disability. Participants indicated that engaging students in conversations about their needs and experiences resulted in students "sharing information with us that is deeply personal . . . [DRPs] have the opportunity to make them feel like they belong" (8).

Accommodation Decision-Making Processes

Participants shared their specific decision-making processes while working to determine accommodations with disabled students. This theme included two subthemes: (a) step-by-step accommodation processes and (b) guiding questions for determining accommodations.

Step-by-Step Accommodation Processes. Participants described a specific beginning, middle, and end to the processes used when determining accommodations for disabled students. To begin accommodation meetings, some participants discussed their use of "ice-breakers" (e.g., "Where are you from?") to "build rapport" with students before asking disability-related questions (15). To lead into disability-related conversations, though, most participants differed in their approach. One participant, for example,

discussed asking "pointed questions" (13) about students' disabilities and potential accommodations, while another expressed the importance of beginning with an open-ended question (e.g., "Why don't you tell me a little bit about your diagnosis?") to subsequently hear the "linear narrative" presented by students (15). In contrast, another participant shared that they first showed students with disabilities a list of the "most common accommodations" available at their institution, as this was a "good place to start a conversation," particularly if students were new to the college setting (7).

During the middle portion of accommodation meetings, participants shifted the focus of meetings to engage in what some called *the interactive process* to determine appropriate accommodations for students with disabilities: "[DRPs] are going to follow the interactive process and ensure that we are working with students individually to determine what accommodations are appropriate" (17). Descriptions of this process were consistent among participants, as summarized by one participant:

> After students submit their registration form and documentation, then they meet individually with myself or our assistant director . . . we've already read their documentation and their registration form, but [we] really hear their story and get to know who they are, as a person and how we can support them. At that point, we determine, based on the documentation and the need, what accommodations would be appropriate (10).

Participants who did not label their method as 'the interactive process,' however, discussed similar approaches that involved talking to disabled students "about which accommodations make the most sense based on [the student's] application, documentation, and narrative," and only approved accommodations if they felt there was a "nexus" between these items and the student's request (18).

Finally, participants ended accommodation meetings with "wrap-up" strategies to "make sure [students] understand all the very specific policies and procedures" regarding their responsibilities as students with disabilities (15). Some participants noted explicitly explaining "the next steps of implementing accommodations" to ensure that "[students] don't have any issues" when accessing them. Finally, participants described their practice of connecting students "to other resources that might be helpful" to them and discussing "interactions with faculty" before concluding accommodation meetings (3).

Guiding Questions for Determining Accommodations. Participants shared guiding questions that they asked themselves as they considered accommodation requests. For some participants, these questions were specifically related to the student. As an example, one participant asked themselves, "Is the student really struggling with [schoolwork] or is there something else?" (e.g., "not know[ing] how" to complete their assignments) because these "are two different problems" (12). Another participant provided a detailed description of guiding questions they asked themselves during the accommodation process:

> What's the impact of engaging in [academic] tasks? Do [students] have particular symptoms that it exacerbates? Do they have limitations for the amount of time that they can be engaged in those types of tasks because it . . . causes fatigue because they've got limited mental energy and effort to ascribe to that? Do they need to take breaks? What does that look like over time and in general? (17).

Other guiding questions were more focused on external factors (e.g., the environment, course design) rather than the students themselves: "Can I think of another way that the student can demonstrate their ability to do [an assignment]? Or can the instructor?" (12).

Participants also asked themselves, "where are these barriers coming from?" and whether or not barriers were "socially constructed" (7). Finally, one participant shared that they consistently asked themselves, "what kind of technology or assistance can I provide?" to disabled students either within or outside of the context of accommodations (19).

Exceptions to Standard Decision-Making Procedures

Participants described exceptional situations that altered their approach to accommodation decision-making. This theme included two subthemes: (a) processes for standard and complex accommodations and (b) processes for clinical or field-based accommodations.

Processes for Standard and Complex Accommodations. Participants discussed differing decision-making processes for accommodations they considered to be "standard" (10; e.g., "this standard set of accommodations that are very much the norm . . . [such as] extra time, computer use") or "known entities" (11). When presented with a standard accommodation request, participants shared that they were "very quick to approve them" without needing to "[make] sure those dots were connected" between the factors they would typically consider (e.g., medical documentation, student self-report, professional judgment; 11). Participants indicated that this streamlined process was due to these requests being "pretty obvious;" therefore, "not much thought" needed to go into them (16). Further, participants emphasized that standard accommodations were easy to approve because such requests "aren't going to compromise anything" (19) and, in general, "support so many students for so many things" (10).

Conversely, participants described alternative approaches to decision-making for requests they considered "complex" (e.g., "a single room," "priority enrollment," 8). Some participants consulted with others (e.g., DRC colleagues, faculty) with whom they did not typically communicate: "most professors I don't need to talk to; it's just those who have those exceptional accommodations" (8). Other participants described "slow[ing]" down to figure out "what's causing the confusion or what's causing the complexity" of the request, reminding themselves that "everything's a case-by-case analysis" (17). Moreover, one participant described their DRC's approach to complex accommodation requests as "MacGyvering" (i.e., creative problem-solving) and provided an example of it in practice:

> We've gotten very good at alternative ways [to accommodate] . . . something as simple as the housing accommodation for someone who has an autoimmune illness . . . we don't need a separate room. We can just have [maintenance] clean the bathroom twice a day or three times a day instead of [changing] housing [assignment]. It's just thinking differently (19).

Processes for Clinical or Field-based Accommodations. Several participants discussed specific variations in processes for determining accommodations within clinical or field-based degree programs (e.g., medical school, social work, teacher education). Participants emphasized that in these programs, "it was most likely that an accommodation might create an issue" because professors were "more concerned" about accommodations "compromising" their coursework (19). These concerns often necessitated "a little sleuthing" to understand the bounds of reasonableness (12). Specifically, participants noted that "not all accommodations can translate to a third-party clinical experience" (4) and, further, the implementation of accommodations depends on "the site in [the student's] practicum" (e.g., elementary school classroom; 12). As a result, participants described needing to understand what the "university's requiring," what "the actual law is requiring," and how these both fit within the program standards to

then determine if "there [is] some wiggle room" for accommodations (4).

Specifically, participants discussed teacher education degree programs, noting that teacher fieldwork requirements were especially complicated (e.g., "I think it's almost harder in . . . the education realm"; 8). One participant highlighted an example of an accommodation that may be reasonable on a college campus but would be unreasonable within the realm of teacher preparation fieldwork: "a student who has a medical marijuana license cannot show up to . . . an education setting . . . impaired at all" (4). As a result of these complexities, one participant described their approach to working through accommodation requests with teacher preparation program faculty, particularly when resistance from professors towards accommodations occurs:

> First of all, have [administration] defined the [education program] standards and really articulated why [an accommodation is] a problem? What is the impact [of an accommodation]? And what would be the impact of accommodating it? . . . cohort programs are inevitably a little ableist. Right? Because we assume everybody can move at the same pace. Start with your program standards . . . why is [a requirement] so important? . . . I think really having to step back and dig deep and look at, is it a fundamental alteration [the requirement]? (8).

Overall, when participants considered accommodations in clinical or field-based settings, they emphasized going back to "the law" (17) as the foundation for decision-making to determine if an accommodation request resulted in a fundamental alteration of an academic standard or requirement. Participants also emphasized the importance of keeping in mind what would be unreasonable based on licensure requirements, university standards, program standards, and the student's disability (e.g., considering "a waiver of a particular aspect of the program that's required for licensure" as an unreasonable request; 17).

DISCUSSION

The purpose of this study was to explore how DRPs approach accommodation decision-making for students with disabilities. This study builds on previous literature that highlighted a variance in decision-making practices within the disability resources field by deeply exploring the multiple, complex layers of DRPs' processes to determine accommodations for disabled students and the extent to which reflexivity is practiced in the field (Banerjee et al., 2015; Lindstrom, 2007). To assess the use of reflexivity, the authors interpreted findings through D'Cruz and colleagues' (2007) variations of reflexivity model (see Figure 1) that describes a cyclical assessment of self-scrutiny with regard to emotional responses and choices in various contexts. The findings of this study answer the call of AHEAD, the leading organization in higher education disability resources, to understand accommodation decision-making processes used within the field, which currently considers such "practices and procedures" as a research priority for the disability resources field (AHEAD, n.d.b., para. 2).

Participants described numerous factors they considered while making accommodation decisions, including those that were both subjective (e.g., professional judgment) and objective (e.g., relevant federal regulations). While each factor participants noted was consistent with guidance from either AHEAD or the literature, their strategies for considering them to determine accommodations varied. This finding is consistent with those of Madaus and colleagues (2010), who emphasized that DRPs generally do not follow rigid procedures when considering accommodation requests. The use of varying factors and processes is also consistent

with previous research that highlighted the ways DRPs adapt to situations when information is limited (e.g., no disability documentation), leaning into their professional judgment to make accommodation decisions (Banerjee et al., 2015). This may suggest, given the various policies and procedures across DRCs, the degree to which certain factors are considered in the accommodation process is relative to the institution in which a DRP is employed and what the institution requires for students to establish accommodations.

Interestingly, participants not only described their overall processes for making accommodation decisions but also provided examples of exceptions to these processes. Clinical or field-based accommodations, for example, were noted as requiring a more in-depth investigation into accommodations sought by students with disabilities, while other requests (e.g., extra time on exams) expedited the decision-making process. These in-depth examples of variations in decision-making processes add to the work of Meeks and Jain (2015), who discussed the ways in which DRPs' approaches to standard versus nonstandard accommodation requests can vary. However, the criteria DRPs use to delineate between standard and nonstandard requests and the extent to which biases and personal beliefs influence that choice remain unclear. As a result, this finding highlights a key instance in which reflexivity is absent from accommodation decision-making processes to understand hidden factors that may influence choices in DRPs' approach to decision-making and subsequent choices in final decisions.

However, before describing their accommodation decision-making processes, some participants discussed their own perspectives on the accommodation process. Notably, these conversations were unprompted and occurred naturally throughout the interviews, shedding light on the importance of these beliefs to participants and the degree to which they influence their work, as well as participants' engagement in an evaluation of their emotions, as outlined by D'Cruz and colleagues (2007; see Figure 1). Further, it is evident that DRPs' interpretations of the ADA's requirement of reasonable accommodations, a key component of the law that ensures access for disabled students, differed among participants. This finding reflects Banerjee and colleagues' (2015) hypothesis that vague descriptions of this requirement in the law may lead DRPs to interpret it in various ways that potentially align with their own preferences and beliefs. As such, it may be the case that the vagueness of the law leaves room for personal beliefs and experiences to influence DRPs' accommodation decision-making processes, opening the door for future exploration into how reflexivity could serve to minimize their impact.

IMPLICATIONS

These findings lead to several implications for higher education disability resources and for individual DRPs. The disability resources field may consider how to address the continued variance in accommodation decision-making processes used by DRPs. Because several participants identified guidance from AHEAD as the foundation of their individual decision-making practices, AHEAD may consider their role in influencing processes used and what guidance they put forth moving forward on what they identify as effective practices. Although the variance in accommodation processes is not inherently negative and a one-size-fits-all approach would be both inappropriate and ineffective (Dolmage, 2017), one must consider the experiences of disabled students throughout this process and how they may benefit from consistency and predictability across the board.

Further, AHEAD or other higher education disability resources organizations may develop free and fully accessible resources (i.e., available in open-access journals, accessible for free online) for DRPs to reference as they refine their accommodation decision-making processes. Specifically, resources should focus on guiding DRPs to work equitably with disabled students to find the nexus between barriers in the academic environment and reasonable accommodations. Examples may include additional guiding documents, extensive professional development opportunities, workshops, webinars, conferences, or mentoring opportunities with seasoned professionals. Free and reasonable access to such resources is imperative, particularly given that more than 60% of DRPs rely on professional development once they are on the job to learn the functions of their role (Banerjee et al., 2015). This reliance on professional development is presumably due to the scarcity of degree or certificate programs available to those pursuing careers in disability resources, highlighting a need for the disability resources field to continue advocacy for higher education programs to ensure consistent training.

Individual DRPs may consider the findings of this study as an opportunity to reflect on their own accommodation decision-making practices and engage in opportunities to enhance their knowledge of reflexivity. Specifically, a reflection on factors considered and processes used to make accommodation decisions may shed light on why particular decisions are made and whether practices differ among different populations of students with whom they are working. Further, because several participants discussed their perspectives of the accommodation process and how these perspectives influence their approach to accommodation decision-making, DRPs should also reflect on their own perspectives of the work they do (e.g., adopting a social model of disability) to critically explore the underlying factors that guide their interactions with students with disabilities. A proposed process of embedding reflexivity into accommodation decision-making is depicted in Figure 2, in which reflection on personal beliefs and experiences is an aspect of a DRP's input while working with disabled students to critically explore and reduce the impact those beliefs have on the final accommodation decisions.

To begin this process, DRPs may find it helpful to identify their varied identities and experiences (e.g., complete a social identity map). From there, they can reflect on how each identity or experience shapes their perceptions, particularly related to disability, and then recognize when they influence accommodation decision-making (e.g., through journaling, memos, or peer debriefs). Becoming intentional in education of this nature is important to reflexive practice because, as noted by D'Cruz and colleagues, "a certain amount of self-confidence is required to engage in critical or reflexive approaches to practice, with confidence associated with practice experience and levels of expertise" (p. 14).

Finally, because of the varied ways in which accommodation decisions for students with disabilities are currently made, it is recommended that DRPs, DRCs, and the field at large consider disabled students' experiences with, and perspectives on, the processes used. Universities and national organizations, for example, could launch a large-scale collection of student feedback on the accommodation process to then inform any future directions with the procurement of guidance for DRPs. DRCs, too, could initiate a smaller-scale survey with students affiliated with them to understand the effectiveness of their current institutional practices. Finally, individual DRPs can also solicit informal feedback from students with disabilities at the conclusion of their accommodation meetings or shortly thereafter on the process used to determine their accommodations.

Input: Perspectives of the accommodation process, objective factors (e.g., documentation), reasonableness of the request, subjective factors (e.g., self-report)

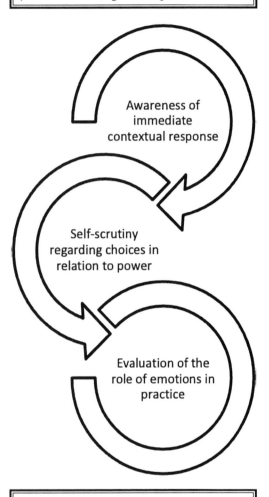

Output: Strategies for discretionary accommodation decision-making (e.g., careful analysis of personal factors, consulting with others, locating the bounds of reasonableness, creative problem-solving)

FIGURE 2. Adapted Reflexivity Model for Accommodation Decision-Making

Future Research

Although the present study highlights several implications for higher education disability services, it also revealed that there is much more work to be done regarding accommodation decision-making practices. First, future researchers may consider purposefully selecting participants with varying demographic characteristics (e.g., number of years in the profession, educational background) to better understand influencing factors that inform practices. Second, a deeper exploration of DRPs' perspectives on the accommodation process is warranted to better understand how this relates to practice and provide information to leading organizations that would inform suggestions for practitioners moving forward; future research of this nature may use the proposed model of reflexivity in Figure 2 as a starting place for such an exploration. Third, as this work relates directly to disabled students, it is critical to better understand the accommodation process from their perspective and use this as the primary tool to inform future practice.

Correspondence concerning this article should be addressed to Morgan M. Strimel at George Mason University; mthomp26@gmu.edu

REFERENCES

Association on Higher Education and Disability. (n.d.a.). *Program and professional standards and ethics.* Retrieved January 9, 2022, from https://www.ahead.org/professional-resources/program-standards-ethics

Association on Higher Education and Disability. (n.d.b.). *Research priorities for the field of postsecondary disability.* Retrieved January 9, 2022, from https://www.ahead.org/research/research-at-ahead/research-priorities

Association on Higher Education and Disability. (n.d.c.). The professional's guide to exploring and facilitating access. Retrieved January 9, 2022, from https://www.ahead.org/professional-resources/accommodations/documentation/professional-resources-accommodations-professional-guide-access

Association on Higher Education and Disability. (2012, October). *Supporting accommodation requests: Guidance on documentation practices.* Retrieved January 9, 2022, from https://www.ahead.org/professional-resources/accommodations/documentation

Americans With Disabilities Act of 1990, 42 U.S.C. § 12101 et seq. (1990).

Banerjee, M., Madaus, J. W., & Gelbar, N. (2015). Applying LD documentation guidelines at the postsecondary level: Decision making with sparse or missing data. *Learning Disability Quarterly, 38*(1), 27–39.

Coghlan, D., & Brydon-Miller, M. (2014). Critical constructivism. In S. Steinberg (Ed.), *The SAGE encyclopedia of action research* (pp. 204–206). SAGE. https://dx.doi.org/10.4135/9781446294406.n90

Dolmage, J. T. (2017). *Academic ableism.* University of Michigan Press. https://doi.org/10.1177/14705931221087710

D'Cruz, H., Gillingham, P., & Melendez, S. (2007). Reflexivity: A concept and its meanings for practitioners working with children and families. *Critical Social Work, 8*(1), 1–18.

Elliott, R., & Timulak, L. (2005). Descriptive and interpretive approaches to qualitative research. In J. Miles & P. Gilbert (Eds.), *A handbook of research methods for clinical and health psychology* (pp. 147–159). Oxford University Press.

Evans, N., Broido, E., Brown, K., & Wilke, A. (2017). *Disability in higher education: A social justice education.* Wiley.

Gaddy, S. (2012). 2–part process can help you determine reasonableness of requested accommodations. *Disability Compliance for Higher Education, 18*(2), 6–6.

Hatzes, N. M., Reiff, H. B., & Bramel, M. H. (2002). The documentation dilemma: Access and accommodations for postsecondary students with learning disabilities. *Assessment for Effective Intervention, 27*(3), 37–52. https://doi.org/10.1177/073724770202700304.

Holmes, D. (2020). Researcher positionality—A consideration of its influence and place in qualitative research—A new researcher guide. *International Journal of Education, 8*(4), 1–10.

Hsiao, F., Zeiser, S., Nuss, D., & Hatschek, K. (2018). Developing effective academic accommodations in higher education: A collaborative decision-making process. *International Journal of Music Education, 36*(2), 244–258.

Krebs, E. (2019). Baccalaureates or burdens? Complicating "reasonable accommodations" for American college students with disabilities. *Disability Studies Quarterly, 39*(3). https://doi.org/10.18061/dsq.v39i3.6557

Laird-Metke, E. (2016). Disability decisions by committee: An increase in risk and decrease in student well-being. *Disability Compliance for Higher Education, 21*(7), 8.

Lindstrom, J. H. (2007). Determining appropriate accommodations for postsecondary students with reading and written expression disorders. *Learning Disabilities Research and Practice, 22*(4), 229–236. https://doi.org/10.1111/j.1540-5826.2007.00251.x

Madaus, J. W., Banerjee, M., & Hamblet, E. C. (2010). Learning disability documentation decision making at the postsecondary level. *Career Development for Exceptional Individuals, 33*(2), 68–79. https://doi.org/10.1177/0885728810368057

May, T. & Perry, B. (2017). *Reflexivity: The essential guide.* SAGE.

Meeks, L. M., & Jain, N. R. (Eds). (2015). *The guide to assisting students with disabilities: Equal access in health science and professional education.* Springer.

Merriam, S. B. & Tisdell, E. J. (2016). *Qualitative research: Guide to design and implementation* (4th ed). Jossey-Bass.

Ofiesh, N. S., Hughes, C., & Scott, S. S. (2004). Extended test time and postsecondary students with learning disabilities: A model for decision making. *Learning Disabilities Research and Practice, 19*(1), 57–70. https://doi.org/10.1111/j.1540 -5826.2004.00090.x

Rehabilitation Act of 1973, 29 U.S.C. § 701 et seq.

Yull, A. (2015). The impact of race and socioeconomic status on access to accommodations in postsecondary education. *Social Policy, 23*(41), 353–392.

Exploring First-Year Students' Demands and Resources in the South African Context

Karina Mostert   Carlien Kahl   Nomfanelo V. Manaka

The growing concern about the mental health and psychological distress of first-year students warrants a greater understanding of their well-being. This study explored the insights of 16 staff and service providers who engage with first-year students at a South African peri-urban campus and built on quantitative studies using the Job Demands-Resources (JD-R) model to understand student well-being. In-depth interviews offered insight into the demands and resources experienced by a largely rural student population. Five themes emerged: (a) transition to university life, (b) the nature of the academic environment, (c) the economic experiences of studying, (d) accommodations and facilities, and (e) the complex lives of first-year students. The study informs the JD-R model from a student context. Implications for practice and future research are discussed.

There is a growing concern about the psychological distress and well-being of students in higher education (Cobo-Rendón et al., 2020; Luescher et al., 2018), with first-year students being at higher risk for stress-related illnesses (Friedlander et al., 2007; Geng & Midford, 2015). Yet, few studies have focused on both negative and positive processes underlying the psychological well-being of students (Lesener et al., 2020). Further, there is a paucity of systematic and empirical research investigating the complexities of first-year students' psychological well-being, specifically in non-Western countries such as South Africa (Makhubela, 2021).

As a developing country, South Africa has significant challenges, such as high dropout, poor success, and slow-moving throughput rates in higher education institutions (van Zyl et al., 2020). Numerous students enrolling in university are first-generation students who come from socioeconomic deprivation and poverty contexts. Accordingly, many university students are worried about basic needs such as food, transport, accommodations, and safety, which hampers their ability to be fully focused and present in their academic studies (van Zyl et al., 2020).

One of the main contributing factors to the scarcity of research on first-year student well-being is the lack of a valid and scientific theoretical model to incorporate the intricate and dynamic processes of student well-being (Kulikowski et al., 2019; Lesener et al., 2020). As a result, researchers have started using the Job Demands-Resources model (JD-R; Bakker & Demerouti, 2017), which offers a dynamic theoretical framework applied in the university

Karina Mostert is Professor of Industrial Psychology with Management Cybernetics, Carlien Kahl is a Doctor of Psychology with an independent practice consulting with Management Cybernetics, and Nomfanelo V. Manaka completed her master's Dissertation with the WorkWell Research Unit; all of the Faculty of Economic and Management Sciences at the North-West University, South Africa. The Deputy Vice-Chancellor's office: Teaching and Learning, North-West University, funded the research.

context (e.g., Lesener et al., 2020; Salanova et al., 2010). The JD-R model explains how working conditions (categorized into demands and resources) uniquely and independently influence employee well-being and organizational outcomes, such as absenteeism and productivity. As Bakker and Demerouti (2017) proposed, demands may initiate the health impairment process (i.e., chronic demands engender burnout and eventually physical health issues). Job resources, on the contrary, may initiate the motivational process (i.e., resources that are motivating and influence work engagement positively), resulting in positive outcomes such as productivity.

Studies using the JD-R model in the university context have been predominantly quantitative, measuring a limited scope of specific demands and resources (Lesener et al., 2020). Two studies explored a somewhat broader range of study demands and resources (Kulikowski, 2019; Salanova et al., 2010), yet their qualitative components offered a narrow exploration of the phenomenon through closed-ended options and quantitative analysis. To our knowledge, only two studies have tested the assumptions of the JD-R model in samples of first-year university students specifically: one with a sample of 225 Dutch students (Pluut et al., 2015) and another with a sample of 936 South African university students (Mokgele & Rothmann, 2014). Although it is encouraging to see that the assumptions of the JD-R model were replicated in a South African sample, the study used a quantitative design. It did not account for or explore the unique contextual factors of South African first-year university settings.

There is a call of great urgency from South African researchers and practitioners to re-evaluate and deepen our understanding

of factors contributing to the psychological well-being of university students (Pretorius & Blaauw, 2020). Still, most approaches and measures originate from Western, educated, industrialized, wealthy, and democratic contexts (Henrich et al., 2010). Such practices are increasingly scrutinized by South African researchers, mainly because we live in a country with Western and non-Western cultures, that is diverse and multi-ethnic,[1] and where a large portion of society adheres to a collectivistic cultural orientation[2] (Blokland, 2016). South African researchers acknowledge the value of approaches and research findings of the Western world and are careful not to substitute one viewpoint and understanding with another. The need remains to critically engage with our culture-specific context and investigate how universal and more culture-specific approaches could inform each other (Morton et al., 2020).

Finally, all studies using the JD-R model in student samples employed quantitative measures of demands and resources as identified by student participants. It is often a limitation in empirical studies when researchers rely solely on self-report. Speckman and Mandew (2014) point out that university student support structures could be a valuable source of information. Staff appointed at various levels or departments in the structure of a university who work with or offer services to first-year students have a strategic and well-positioned role in providing information, which might include more holistic and objective perspectives on student struggles and needed resources than students themselves could provide. Since such structures have an integrated understanding of university students' development, experience, and performance, they could provide additional insights, which can be applied to develop the demands

---

[1] The term *ethnicity* refers to a specific group's cultural characteristics and can include norms, values, attitudes, and typical behaviors (Verkuyten, 2005).

[2] Where people define their identity in terms of tribal and ethnolinguistic affiliations (Blokland, 2016).

and resources components of the JD-R model in the university context.

Based on the above, there is a clear need for rigorous qualitative exploration of the JD-R model, especially for first-year students' experiences of demands and resources in a non-Western country such as South Africa. This study reports on the findings of the first in-depth qualitative study on the demands and resources components of the JD-R model. It explores the insights and perspectives of staff and service providers who engage with first-year students at a South African campus in a peri-urban area (i.e., an urban setting with a surrounding rural area; Merriam-Webster Dictionary, 2022).

THEORETICAL FRAMEWORK: THE JOB DEMANDS-RESOURCES MODEL

The JD-R model (Bakker & Demerouti, 2017) is the most widely applied, empirically tested, and leading approach to well-being research in occupational health psychology. The core assumptions of this model include classifying all types of characteristics in the work environment into two major categories: job demands and job resources. Job demands refer to "those physical, psychological, social, or organizational aspects of the job that require sustained physical and/or psychological effort and are therefore associated with certain physiological and/or psychological costs" (e.g., high pace and amount of work). Job resources refer to "those physical, psychological, social, or organizational aspects of the job that are functional in achieving work goals, reduce job demands and the associated physiological and psychological costs, or stimulate personal growth, learning, and development" (e.g., social support, opportunities to learn and grow) (p. 274).

The JD-R theory incorporates the health impairment and the motivational processes, thus including both negative and positive processes underlying well-being. The health impairment process is where high job demands are consistently present, leading to high levels of strain (e.g., exhaustion, anxiety, psychological health complaints) and predicting adverse organizational outcomes (e.g., intention to leave). The motivational process occurs when the presence of resources buffers the effect of high demands, leading to high levels of motivation (e.g., engagement, commitment) and predicting positive organizational outcomes (e.g., high job performance). And the theory has expanded where personal resources (i.e., self-efficacy, resilience, optimism) are incorporated into the model. Therefore, employees can proactively mobilize job resources through job crafting, which helps them stay engaged in their work.

The JD-R Model in the Student Context

Several studies have used the JD-R model in the university context (Clements & Kamau, 2018; Lesener et al., 2020; Mokgele & Rothmann, 2014; Pluut et al., 2015; Robins et al., 2015; Salanova et al., 2010; Wolff et al., 2014) and demonstrated the transferability of the JD-R model to different educational settings. These studies demonstrated that contextualized study-related factors could be classified into demands (e.g., academic overload, the difficulty of academic tasks, study-leisure conflict) and resources (e.g., social support, growth and developmental opportunities, and decision latitude). Also, environmental characteristics modeled as demands and resources contribute to our understanding of student well-being and performance (Pluut et al., 2015). For example, study-related demands are positively related to student burnout (Lesener et al., 2020; Robins, 2015; Wolff et al., 2014), while study-related resources are positively associated with student engagement, psychological well-being, and life satisfaction (Lesener et al., 2020;

Mokgele & Rothmann, 2014; Robins et al., 2015). Empirical evidence has been found for health impairment and motivational processes (Lesener et al., 2020; Mokgele & Rothmann, 2014; Wolff et al., 2014). Finally, studies incorporating personal resources demonstrated the importance and usefulness of personal resources in protecting against student burnout and fostering engagement (Robins et al., 2015; Wolff et al., 2014).

RESEARCH METHOD

This paper forms part of a larger project called StudyWell: Student Well-being and Success. The project aims to develop a culturally informed, validated, and comprehensive model of first-year student well-being that is flexible to use in South African and other student contexts. It could accommodate the exploration and measurement of (a) a range of contextual variables inside and outside of the university context; (b) individual resources, states, and behavior that contributes to the understanding of student well-being; (c) negative and positive processes of student well-being; and (d) a variety of university settings (e.g., urban, peri-urban, and rural settings) and participants (i.e., first-year students themselves and support structures involved with first-year students). This paper reports on the perspectives of various individuals at the university regularly involved with first-year students at this particular campus.

An interpretive descriptive approach facilitated the researchers' understanding of participants' diverse, subjective experiences and insights on first-year study demands and resources. Interpretive description seeks to understand participants' real life, where they develop subjective meanings of their experiences (Thorne, 2016). Such experiences often have complex meanings. Using a constructivist approach allowed the researchers to access participants' authentic explanations and interpretations. The researchers positioned themselves as co-constructors of participants' understandings. Researchers used video, audio, and written notes to record their reflections. They also engaged in debriefing sessions throughout the research process (particularly during and after site visits). Such reflexivity allowed researchers to monitor their own interpretations and biases to maintain the authenticity of participants' voices and ensure reliability (Patton, 2015; Tracy, 2020). Trustworthiness was ensured by accessing multiple perspectives for high-quality information.

Participants' Community Context and Ethics

We researched a peri-urban university campus in South Africa that serves a large rural area from which students are drawn. Peri-urban universities may be geographically isolated from structural and human resources (Bot et al., 2001; Msila, 2010). The context of this paper (including participants, the university campus, and the environment in which they live) is described by The Gaffney Group (2011).[3] They indicate that close to 93% of the area is considered rural and 7% urban. The majority of community members living in this setting are African (96.6%) and primarily Setswana-speaking (82%; one of the 11 language groups in South Africa). Only 2.2% have English as a home language. The university language policy includes English, Setswana, and Afrikaans, but most learning materials are only available in English.

With high levels of illiteracy, low levels of school completion, and high employment rates, many households suffer extreme poverty and depend on government social grants of

---

[3] The Gaffney Group compiles data from numerous South African government databases using 2011 Countrywide Census Data, which is updated annually by Yes Media.

$26–120 per month for survival. People living in the region have limited access to water, electricity, and infrastructure (including adequate schooling, basic sanitation, and healthcare facilities). The significance of educational background, socioeconomic status, and access to essential resources has implications for first-year students' social, family, and community capital—aspects closely associated with experiential capital influencing academic success (Thomas & Maree, 2021).

Ethics permission to conduct the study was granted (NWU-HS-2014-0165) with gatekeepers who facilitated participants' access. A trusted gatekeeper recommended which participants could best speak to how structures influenced first-year students' study demands and resources. They provided the contact information of possible participants the researchers used to send e-mail forms containing ethics information, recruitment invitations, and referral requests. The researcher obtained voluntary informed consent from the participants following the invitations, where withdrawal carried no negative consequence.

Sampling and Saturation

Purposive, voluntary sampling (Patton, 2015) facilitated the selection of a range of participants from academic and support staff who worked with, supported, or provided services to first-year students. Participants were in contact with first-year students throughout the academic year in various capacities and worked with, supported, or provided services to first-year students regularly. Snowball sampling meant that recruited participants could recommend potential participants to inform on specific study demands and resources. Data were collected concurrently with the analysis until no new information was contributed to the current study, which meant the data were saturated (Gentles et al., 2015) and ensured rigor.

There were 16 sixteen participants, of whom two were Caucasian, Afrikaans, and English-speaking, while the remaining participants were all African. The 14 African participants spoke a range of languages in the home, including Setswana (n = 10), SiSwati (n = 2), English (n = 1), and Oshimwambo (n = 1). Participants included lecturers (n = 3), an administration officer (n = 1), finance officers (n = 2), residence officers (n = 2), a sports manager (n = 1), and a counselor (n = 1), as well as senior students who included a peer mentor and student-instructor (n = 1) and student council members working in orientation services (n = 5). Participants had 1 to 21 years of experience working with first-year students. Their cultural diversity and gender were reflective of the institution's profile (seven males and nine females; DHET, 2018). The campus was considered resourced (i.e., infrastructure and buildings; access to water, electricity, academic and educational materials, and support systems); however, as in the larger community, university structures strained to manage large numbers of students and provide for their needs.

Data Collection Methods

The researchers conducted conversational, in-depth interviews (Chilisa, 2012) through in-person sessions or video-conferencing applications from 2017 to 2019. Bilingual translators (English-Setswana and English-Afrikaans) were present during interviews, allowing participants to converse in their preferred language (Patton, 2015). Interviews lasted between 30 and 90 minutes and were audio-recorded, transcribed, and translated into English where needed. The central question was: "Can you please tell me about your experiences working with first-year students at this university?" The researchers aimed to understand the study demands, challenges, or obstacles students faced from participants' perspectives; the resources participants considered essential to first-year students; and resources they facilitated, gave access to, created, or provided to first-year students.

Data Analysis

Data were analyzed using primary and secondary coding cycles with two independent co-coders, i.e., this paper's second and third authors (Tracy, 2020). The co-coders read the data transcripts, followed by independent open coding (Saldaña, 2016). Next, they met after the first cycle to review their independent analysis, discuss similarities and differences, and host consensus discussions. The co-coders reviewed the open codes, merged similar codes, and decided on a naming structure to organize related codes using prefixes, symbols, and capitalization (Friese, 2019). The co-coders conducted secondary coding to group similar codes conceptually (Miles et al., 2014; Tracy, 2020). They organized code groups into categories and themes using ATLAS.ti version 8 through memos and analysis tools (i.e., generating smart codes using the query tool, code co-occurrence explorer, and the code-document table). The first author of this paper reviewed the themes, and all authors held consensus discussions deciding on the final themes. The ATLAS.ti audit trail, co-coding, and consensus ensured rigor and trustworthiness.

RESULTS

Data analysis revealed five primary themes, each with several sub-themes (see Table 1). The themes are discussed below.

Theme 1. Transitioning to University

Participants reported that first-year students struggled with expected adjustment processes and unmet or unrealistic expectations. Students experienced many academic challenges in the new university environment and dealt with difficulties that their families experienced back home. Participants were aware that "There are so many challenges . . . [moving from] where [first-year students] come from—not only the school system but also their cultures back at home" (P1, 162:138).

What was especially challenging for first-year students was navigating and adapting to a new cultural environment to which many were unaccustomed. The new environment was individualistic, achievement-driven, and did not consider that first-years' arrived from non-Western homes with different ethnic and cultural identities:

> Where [students] come from, not only the school system but also their cultures back at home—it is not so individualistic and achievement-driven . . . Because since they come from more of a "let's help each other, share background," they also help each other and share tests and quizzes and all kinds of other things, which they then get in trouble for because that is seen as plagiarism or cheating in our world here. So, they have many things to get used [to] and adjust to (P1, 162:19).

In addition, conditions that severely exacerbated the transition process and experience at the campus included political unrest, disruptions, and violence during the #FeesMustFall protests[4], harming their healthy adjustment to university and their well-being. The violent unrest that occurred on campus resulted in the destruction of university property and intimidation of staff: "This office was burnt—when was it—last year at the beginning of the year" (P10 & P11, 171:60). The strikes negatively impacted the academic schedule, including changed class schedules and timetables, delayed submission of academic work and access to

---

[4] South Africa's student protests associated with the #FeesMustFall movement demanded free and decolonized education (cf. Ngcobo et al., 2016).

Table 1.
Summary of Themes, Sub-Themes, and Associated Keywords and Phrases

Themes	Sub-themes	Associated supportive keywords and phrases
Theme 1. The complex lives of first-year students	Personal crises place additional demands on students' adjustment to university	Pressure, personal problems, complications, psychological problems
	Students rely on personal resources leading to growth and responsibility	Self-motivation, self-awareness, resilience, social skills, cause and effect, social relationships
	Formal psychological resources and support	Psychologist, psychiatrist, peer counselors
	Informal resources and support	Staff members, friends, older students
Theme 2. The nature of the academic environment	High study-related workload	High volume of work, difficult course content, lack of academic and practical skills (academic writing, referencing, computer skills), lack of lecturer support, changes in class schedules, module clashes
	Language concerns	Difficulty understanding, writing, and expressing ideas using English as second language, poor English education in school, fear of stigmatization when practicing English outside the classroom, first-language-English-speaking students struggling with writing, support from lecturers and senior students to address language-related problems
	Uncertain and unsupportive academic environment complicates navigating academics	Lack of academic support, negative attitudes from lecturers, unmet expectations from the university, need to teach students communication skills to approach lecturers with problems, help and support from other lecturers to assist students with the transition
	Infrastructure and services	Insufficient infrastructure (buildings): Overcrowded lecture halls, disproportioned student-lecturer ratio, difficulty for lecturers to teach effectively, students do not learn the necessary practical skills, imbalance compared to other delivery sites Supportive services: library, computer and reading laboratories, on-campus internet
	Supportive people and resources that assist and facilitate demands and challenges	Lecturers, staff, residence wardens, peer mentors, senior students (academic friends)

Table 1, continued.

Themes	Sub-themes	Associated supportive keywords and phrases
Theme 3. The economic experience of studying	Financial difficulties	Insufficient bursaries, lack of information and communication on funding opportunities, financial stress placing greater burden on students' adjustment, no access to computers or the internet to acquire information or apply for funding, unanticipated costs, uncertainty whether bursaries will pay out
	Support from the university to relieve financial strain	Provide information to students on funding opportunities before enrolling in university and while still in school, funding, meal-a-day program and food packages (stigmatization experienced by students who utilized it)
	External and internal financial resources	External bursaries, external loans, institutional bursaries (orphan, academic merit, leadership bursaries)
Theme 4. Accommodations and facilities	Challenges for on-campus students	High academic requirements, limited on-campus accommodations, lack of space, difficulty adjusting due to different social backgrounds, conflict with roommates, lack of recreational facilities
	Support and resources for on-campus students	Cultural, social, and sports activities, supportive role from university staff, support from residence house committees
	Challenges for off-campus students	Personal safety, being mugged, theft of personal belongings, crime, lack of transport, exclusion from on-campus activities
	Support and resources for off-campus students	Access to university-accredited accommodations, transport provided by the university
Theme 5. Transition to university: Adjustments and expectations	Adjustment to a new environment	University life differs from high school, independent learning, individualistic environment, culture shock, orientation program too generalized, first-generation students
	Course enrolment	Unavailable courses, enrollment in alternative courses, mismatch with course fit and study ideals
	The effect of political unrest on students' adjustment	Destruction of university property; intimidation; negative impact on academic schedules, academics, and access to resources; disrupted orientation program; resilience despite challenges
	Multicultural experiences as a resource through social relationships	University life experienced as multicultural, multilingual, and diverse; different values; the importance of forming friendships; social support

academic resources: "Months of no class, and then trying to catch up and bullets around you and going on with teaching—do you think that would really give you a good idea of the first-year experience?" (P1, 162:86). However, participants reported that students remained resilient despite the negative experiences associated with the strike actions on their campus: "Well, at least we can say that our students are really resilient. Even last year with all the things happening, we completed our programs; it was stress, and it was hectic, but we did it" (P1, 162:87).

Adjustment to university was particularly challenging for first-generation students due to the high expectations and pressure for them to succeed: "Many of my students are first-generation students . . . It is important for them to . . . make it here. The problem is just that sometimes the difficulties are so many" (P1, 162:101). While a structured and informative orientation program was provided to assist new students with the adjustment process, participants reported that first-year students experienced it as too generalized: "But it seems like it [the orientation program] is not enough, so in the beginning, it seems like they do not get enough information as to how this life works on campus and where exactly they can go if they have certain needs" (P1, 162:54).

Participants explained that supportive relationships were a valuable resource and that students found ways to support one another across diverse cultures, languages, and socioeconomic backgrounds. Forming friendships was an essential part of adjusting to a new environment and embracing cultural diversity: "Friendship and unity are very [important]. Understanding one another, understanding one's culture, understanding one's religion, and the most important thing that I teach them is to respect" (P2, 163:72).

Theme 2. The Nature of the Academic Environment

As can be anticipated, students struggled with a high study-related workload. They experienced the content as taxing and very challenging. This was especially difficult because they did not have the academic linguistic skills required at a university level. Many first-years, for whom English was not their home language, experienced difficulty understanding and expressing themselves academically in English: "I think the language is definitely a big problem because it is not only about understanding what I teach in class, which is in English, it is also about understanding the textbook" (P1, 162:107).

Lecturers simplified the module content to assist students in understanding work in English better: "I try to use the textbook where I, of course, it is terminology, but I try to make it simpler. So, I read the original [text], and then I repeat it in simpler language" (P1, 162:5). Participants explained how first-year students start learning each other's home language to improve communication and connect socially: "I understand Setswana . . . I've been working with [first-years who] come from maybe Western Cape. Now, they speak Xhosa, they speak Swati, or Zulu . . . [The] language barrier [is a problem], but as the months go on, you understand [somewhat]." (P12.5, 172:29). However, language proficiency in English remained necessary for academic performance: "[Students] should be able to write a good essay assignment. And what they learn in these two modules is to be able to write a good academic essay—not only in English but in all the modules" (P8, 169:10).

Students also struggled with practical skills lecturers assumed they had to complete their academic coursework. However, they had not necessarily mastered these skills: "they are expected . . . to type their assignments, while many of them have not seen a computer. That's very demanding and confusing. By the end of a semester, they are still trying to get hold of what is happening" (P4, 165:44). In general, participants experienced the academic environment as uncertain and unsupportive, complicating their ability to navigate academic life at university. Even though resources were available, it did not automatically imply access or use of these resources: "[Students rarely] go to the library" (P6, 167:59).

In addition to language barriers, participants understood that students faced cultural differences in their home and university life. Such discrepancies were noted in how the university is structured to teach module content without consideration for students' cultural practices in the teaching design. The system operates within an individualistic orientation, while most students are culturally embedded in a collectivist orientation. This presents a barrier to learning effectively and does not accommodate first-year students' needs:

> especially with students from the rural areas . . . especially the Setswana community. At home, students are not supposed to talk [back] to the parents, and as a result, they don't ask questions, and that's a very serious problem. Even at the end of the lecture, you say: Any questions? They don't ask questions. [You later] realize that they don't understand after giving them a test, and you'll see that not all of them performed. (P8, 169:4)

Theme 3. The Economic Experiences of Studying

Participants highlighted extreme financial difficulties as a significant stressor for first-year students that permeated all other aspects of their lives and well-being. Participants reported a severe lack of sufficient bursaries and funding opportunities, especially first-years who: "are [mostly] from disadvantaged homes" (P8, 169:32). Applying for financial assistance was complicated as students lacked access to computers and the internet to apply for bursaries. However, participants working in the financial department tried to assist by providing computer stations so students could "be assisted in applying online. [They] bring their documents, they are scanned in this office, then they apply online . . . We put five computers in the hallway here, so we can assist those students coming to apply" (P10 & P11, 171:9). Participants further explained that students were uncertain whether they would receive the bursaries for which they applied. Notice of funding applications was often delayed for weeks or even months, while students had to cope until they were finally notified of their bursaries. These delays had a destructive effect on their successful engagement with their academic program and increased the risk of dropout.

It was also clear that students were unaware of, did not plan for, or did not understand the total costs involved in studying at university when they initially registered:

> [Students say to us] I only raised money to pay for my accommodations and registration . . . it was a problem because I have to buy books. I have to eat every day, and I have to study. Lectures will ask us to do certain things, projects, which costs me money . . . I don't have money for such; it was a problem . . . mentally, you have to survive. (P11, 171:71)

One initiative from the university to relieve financial strain included sports scholarships. These scholarships covered all financial needs for students who were athletes, but unfortunately not for non-athletes: "Your accommodations and meals and all that will be ready for those first-years coming in, but then in a [typical] student coming from a poor background who is not part of an [sport] institute, they will not" (P9, 170:17). Another initiative of the university to relieve the financial strain of students was a nutrition support program called "meal-a-day." This initiative provided food packages to students from disadvantaged backgrounds. However, the challenge with this program was that students felt stigmatized and categorized as "struggling" when they made use of this program. As a result, participants reported that first-years decided not to collect the food packages: "What I hear from the students is that, if you are known to take [the food packages], you are in the needy category . . . This is sad because the opportunity is there" (P1, 162:42). Female students had additional basic needs, and often, participants would assist with these needs:

> [there are] so many things [women] need money, for example, maybe to buy sanitary pads and this and that. So, I have to step in as a mother and see what is it that I can do. Sometimes I go as far as giving them money to go buy those things. (P3, 164:6)

Theme 4. Accommodations and Facilities

Participants differentiated between on-campus students who resided in campus-based residences and those students who lived off campus in private or university-approved accommodations. Accommodations and study facilities were experienced differently by on- and off-campus first-year students. There were challenges for on-campus students. Besides the academic requirements to be accepted and maintain your place for on-campus accommodations (i.e., having and maintaining a high academic average performance), the campus had limited placements available: "First-years get residence here according to their [university admission] scores" (P2, 163:126). Also:

> So, it's a struggle here; it's a struggle for our students . . . the yearly cries that we hear from them getting accommodation here, stuff like that . . . The place is full . . . It's really painful for some. I mean, even that

guy who got that 100% in mathematics [but it was full]. (P2, 163:34)

Students who lived on campus had access to essential resources, such as clean water and electricity, even when the surrounding areas in town had limited and interrupted services. Participants reported that on-campus students lived in a supportive, safe environment, making their dealing with study demands more manageable. Senior on-campus students also interacted with and motivated first-years; they "take them through the journey of their first year and, actually tell them that they will make it. Give them that courage" (P3, 164:15). Living off campus had numerous challenges that made life difficult for students. The personal safety of off-campus students was particularly concerning: "We hear about cases whereby [students] complained that [other people at off-campus accommodations] stole their laptops and [their mobile phones]" (P12.2, 172:39), and "[criminals] are always on the road waiting for people. You [students] can get mugged . . . You don't have data you have to stay here or sleep at the library or computer lab for [for Internet]" (P2, 163:73). Fearing for their safety had an immensely adverse effect on their academic studies:

> [Students say . . .] I can't focus on work right now because I don't know where I will live tonight . . . even now, there's been quite a few cases of girls being attacked and raped on their way home . . . you can't just focus on your studies because you have to also worry about finances and about being safe and about where you live, and whether there will be water or electricity. (P1, 162:37)

Off-campus students often experienced difficulty attending campus activities due to a lack of transport, which excluded them from cultural, social, and sports activities. However, some students who lived off campus had access to support, such as university-accredited accommodations, a safer alternative: "Three outside accommodations that are accredited by the university . . . so, especially on NSFAS and other bursaries, we [the university] pay for that accommodation" (P10, 171:21). The university also assisted off-campus students with transport to and from their accredited residences. However, it only ran at specific times throughout the day.

Theme 5. The Complex Lives of First-year Students

In addition to the challenges experienced at university and their academic studies, many first-year students came from impoverished families. Participants explained they had challenging personal circumstances, placing additional demands on their adjustment and experience at university: "[Students] are leaving [their] families at home with no food and no [additional] family and things like that, so they come already stressed" (P7, 168:1). Participants also noted how first-year students found it challenging to cope with the pressure and extent of personal crises.

Students relied on formal (provided by the university) and informal sources of support, both on- and off-campus. Formal support for students included on-campus psychologists, intern psychologists, registered counselors, guidance from lay counselors, and career counseling. Peer counselors and senior students also volunteered to counsel students: "In the office, we train them [senior students] with basic counseling skills [and] they have first aid. I would like to think of them as mental health first aiders on the campus" (P7, 168:10). A residence officer explained that first-year students preferred to come to them rather than formal psychological support:

> I had two of them [first-year students] who tried to commit suicide because I was forcing them to go to a psychologist . . . But with the help of the psychologist, I told them that I have this situation, my

problem is that they don't want to come there. They said: No, it's fine to monitor the situation. If you need advice, you will tell us, and then we will tell you what to do. (P3, 164:8)

Other students relied on friends and fellow students that formed part of their informal support structure, including socializing with friends and playing Indigenous games. Participants explained that first-years also relied on personal resources to deal with their individual crises. In their view, this led to individual growth and responsibility linked with self-motivation, self-awareness, resilience, social skills, and recognizing the cause and effect of their choices:

> I'm looking at . . . the internal motivation of the students . . . [what] you need to have is that level of determination motivation . . . How can I [get there from] where am I so far . . . Then you start tapping into their resources! So that the internal person can recognize their competencies and then be able to tap into the resources available for them. (P7, 168:48)

DISCUSSION

Students' Demands in the Context of a Peri-Urban Campus

The results clearly showed that first-year students do not only experience academic demands and pressure (Demetriou et al., 2017; Pather et al., 2017) but also those related to complex interactions between academic, political, social, and cultural realities. Transitioning to university entailed the culture shock first-year students experience (Azmitia et al., 2013). However, this study showed an apparent discrepancy between the university's individualistic-orientated structure and students' collectivist orientation and values. The need for more culturally cohesive support was emphasized (Adams et al., 2012). Students also had to deal with often violent and disruptive political strikes that had harmful effects because of the destruction of university property, intimidation, and lack of access to study resources (e.g., Naidoo & McKay, 2018).

As reported in other studies, students experienced the academic environment as very challenging, with high academic pressure that could influence their academic success (Sommer & Dumont, 2011) and potentially lead to their dropping out of university (Fourie, 2020; Scott, 2019). Participants reported that students struggled to perform well at university when English was their second, third, fourth, or even fifth language. Academic achievement is linked to language proficiency, especially at institutions where English is predominantly used as the language of instruction and differs from students' home languages (Thomas & Maree, 2021). Sader and Gabela (2017) affirm that English, as a second or third language, is a barrier to academic class engagement.

The economic experiences of studying highlighted that financial matters were considered a severe stressor among students from disadvantaged backgrounds (Nyar, 2019; Pillay & Ngcobo, 2010). There was also unique contextual knowledge about the total costs involved in attending university. Students often were not informed beforehand of the total study costs involved with studying at university. In general, access to higher education in South Africa was barred by the high costs of fees and lack of bursaries (Pillay & Thwala, 2012). This problem was exacerbated by the lack of information and advanced communication tools (e.g., the Internet; Naidoo & McKay, 2018). The current study emphasized complications associated with limited Internet access and connectivity related to rural areas, even when the campus is in a peri-urban town (Leibowitz, 2017).

There was a clear difference in the demands that on-campus and off-campus students experienced regarding accommodations and facilities. A limited number of on-campus accommodations were available (Nel et al., 2016), and students experienced high pressure to perform academically to access and maintain a place in an on-campus residence. Yet, living in on-campus residences also presented challenges in terms of dealing with diverse cultural values and norms. Off-campus students experienced demands related to personal safety, difficulties with transport, and exclusion from on-campus resources and activities. Off-campus students especially had to deal with theft and violent crime. Such findings align with reports related to crime and violence and difficult living circumstances that hinder students' focus on their studies (Pather et al., 2017; van Breda, 2017).

Clark (2005) emphasized that multiple factors inside and outside the university may influence students in their first year. This was very clear in the current study, where students had complex personal lives that included pressure from home, personal problems, and associated psychological well-being issues. Participants related how first-years often experienced high levels of psychosocial vulnerability that impeded their academic success (van Breda, 2018) and was exacerbated by the additional demands within the university environment, especially in scarce resource settings.

Students Resources in the Context of a Peri-Urban Campus

Regarding the transition to university, adjustments, and expectations, participants emphasized the nature of multicultural experiences as a resource embedded within social relationships (Wilcox et al., 2005). Such support helped increase the number of resources students viewed as accessible to them to replace insufficient (or lack of) resources. The present study displayed culturally meaningful activities and relations amid the diversity of relational interactions at the peri-urban campus, providing a unique take on conditions.

The nature of the academic environment referred to resources such as academic support, supportive lecturers, residence officers, peer mentors, and senior students (academic friends). Empowering rural first-years may help these students develop the critical academic skills they require to participate successfully in the university environment (Steyn et al., 2014). The unique language integration in the current study illustrated how language commonalities facilitated cultural cohesion and friendships. In this study, the role of lecturers' supportive strategies to bridge language gaps made a difference in students' mastery of English and academic content.

First-year students relied on support from the university to relieve financial strain. People and services within the university can facilitate access to and knowledge of funding applications. The current study illustrated the extent of support for first-year students through access to knowledge and access to pragmatic care. Such structures facilitated access through inter-relational support, often beyond the call of duty (extending the work of Scott, 2019).

Accommodations and facilities resources differed for on- and off-campus first-years. Resources included cultural, social, and sports activities; the supportive role of university staff and residence officers for on-campus students (Wilcox et al., 2005); and access to university-accredited accommodations and university transport provided for off-campus students (similar to Mbara & Celliers, 2013). The present study showed that social support positively contributed to first-year students' overall well-being, which helped student life adjustment (Wilcox et al., 2005). Current findings also provide culturally embedded examples of practices and interactions with Indigenous games and meaningful connections with staff as parent figures to build strong relationships.

The current study provides a distinct comparison of the on- and off-campus experiences. For example, how accessible essential infrastructure (e.g., water, electricity, safety) and academic resources (e.g., computer labs, Internet, library) were for on-campus compared to off-campus students influenced overall well-being in the first year at university. Also, it is clear how the lack of access to resources made first-year transitions even more complicated when enabling resources were absent, emphasizing the importance of sufficient resources in the face of severe demands.

In dealing with first-year students' complex lives, participants focused on first-year students' reliance on and development of personal resources (self-motivation, self-awareness, resilience), social skills, and understanding of the impact (i.e., the cause and effect of choices made) concerning growth processes within transitions. Some examples of students' coping with study demands aligned with extant findings (Mason, 2018, 2019; van Zyl & Dhurup, 2016). Intrinsic motivation, perceived stress, and attitudes toward seeking help were associated with student adjustment to university (Sommer & Dumont, 2011). The current study showed a preference for relying on informal resources (especially peer mentors) that first-years' felt more comfortable approaching. Such approaches are congruent with first-year students' cultural backgrounds, where elders (family, lecturers, and staff) are held in high esteem in rural upbringing, which influences relational interactions (Ganss, 2016).

LIMITATIONS

The current study explored the perspectives of support structures and services from a specific peri-urban university. The findings may resonate with other higher education environments with similar university and student demographics and experiences. Such experiences may overlap but may also present different demands and resources. Multi-voiced findings that include both support structures and students simultaneously could unfold greater understandings than in-depth discussions with structures alone.

IMPLICATIONS FOR FUTURE RESEARCH AND PRACTITIONERS

Practitioners need to understand first-year students' demands and resources in the context of the multiple study demands and resources that first-year students encounter, especially considering positive and negative dual processes within a sound theoretical framework (Bakker & Demerouti, 2017). Accessing structural perspectives provide insight from multiple vantage points for people and services dedicated to first-year students. Such insights could help first-year students discern the challenges they face and approach appropriate resources to help them adjust to university, promoting well-being on various levels (academically, psychologically, pragmatically, and socially). The university expects first-year students to develop their personal resources by dealing with their study demands. In the context of additional demands (e.g., disruptions, protests, complex personal problems or conditions), academic challenges significantly affected first-year students' transitions. While resources are essential to mobilize, they may change, and the absence of resources may place additional demands on first-years. Universities could utilize their resource structures to orient first-year students and emphasize holistically meeting students' actual and complex needs. The current study challenges conventional responses to encourage in-depth, empirically informed decisions. Practitioners' responses should understand and promote multi-level, complex interactions of study demands and resources that foster first-year students' well-being amid diverse, culturally embedded contexts. Practitioners can mobilize institutional resource provision and access and promote and strengthen first-year students' personal resources.

CONCLUSION

The current study contributed to developing an informed theoretical model (i.e., the JD-R model) in exploring the unique demands and resources that first-year students experience that can be linked to their well-being. The findings were informed by university staff and services perspectives on first-year students' experiences of study demands and resources. The findings highlighted the interactive, complex nature of academic demands that include competencies and use of first-year students' personal resources (mastery, resilience, social capital) to navigate academic demands with limited access to resilience-enabling resources (e.g., prior education, English-language skills, fewer supportive opportunities to meet individual study needs). Study resources provide insight into the nature and availability of supporting resources available to first-year students. The existence or provision of resources alone did not meet students' complex needs. However, nurturing and facilitating appropriate resources in meaningful ways were crucial for supporting first-year transitions to university. Our study enhances qualitative understanding of academic study demands in the context of multi-level, interrelated study demands (Nyar, 2019; Scott, 2019), adding to limited examples of non-Western interpretations of cultural identity and well-being interactions in the JD-R model.

Correspondence concerning this article should be directed to Karina Mostert, Faculty of Economic and Management Sciences, North-West University; Karina.Mostert@nwu .ac.za

REFERENCES

Adams, B. G., Van de Vijver, F. J. R., & De Bruin, G. P. (2012). Identity in South Africa: Examining self-descriptions across ethnic groups. *International Journal of Intercultural Relations, 36*(3), 377–388. https://doi.org/10.1016/j.ijintrel.2011.11.008

Azmitia, M., Syed, M., & Radmacher, K. (2013). Finding your niche: Identity and emotional support in emerging adults' adjustment to the transition to college. *Journal of Research on Adolescence, 23*(4), 744–761. https://doi.org/10.1111/jora.12037

Bakker, A. B., & Demerouti, E. (2017). "Job demands-resources theory: Taking stock and looking forward." *Journal of Occupational Health Psychology, 22,* 273–285.

Blokland, L. M. E. (2016). Non-Western (African) views of psychological constructs: Current context of psychological assessment in South Africa. In R. Ferreira (Ed.), *Psychological assessment: Thinking innovatively in the contexts of diversity* (pp. 37–51). Juta Publishers.

Bot, M., Wilson, D., & Dove, S. (2001). *The education atlas of South Africa 2000.* Education Foundation.

Chilisa, B. (2012). *Indigenous research methodologies.* SAGE.

Clark, M.R. (2005). "Negotiating the freshman year: Challenges and strategies among first-year college students." *Journal of College Student Development, 46*(3), 296–316. http://doi.org/10.1353/csd.2005.0022

Clements, A. J., & Kamau, C. (2018). Understanding students' motivation towards proactive career behaviours through goal-setting theory and the job demands-resources model. *Studies in Higher Education, 43*(12), 2279–2293.

Cobo-Rendón, R., López-Angulo, Y., Pérez-Villalobos, M. V., & Díaz-Mujica, A. (2020). Perceived social support and its effects on changes in the affective and eudaimonic well-being of Chilean university students. *Frontiers in Psychology, 11,* Article 590513. https://doi.org/10.3389/fpsyg.2020.590513

Demetriou, C., Meece, J., Eaker-Rich, D., & Powell, C. (2017). The activities, roles, and relationships of successful first-generation college students. *Journal of College Student Development, 58*(1), 19–36. https://doi.org/10.1353/csd.2017.0001

Department of Higher Education & Training (DHET). (2018). *Statistics on post-school education and training in South Africa: 2016* (p. 156). DHET. https://www.dhet.gov.za/DHET Statistics Publication/Statistics on Post-School Education and Training in South Africa 2016.pdf

Fourie, C. M. (2020). Risk factors associated with first-year students' intention to drop out from a university in South Africa. *Journal of Further and Higher Education, 44*(2), 201–215. https://doi.org/10.1080/0309877X.2018.1527023

Friedlander, L. J., Reid, G. J., Shupak, N. & Cribbie, R. (2007). Social support, self-esteem, and stress as predictors of adjustment to university among first-year undergraduates. *Journal of College Student Development, 48,* 259–274.

Friese, S. (2019). *Qualitative data analysis with ATLAS.ti* (3rd ed.). SAGE.

Ganss, K. M. (2016). The college transition for first-year students from rural Oregon communities. *Journal of Student Affairs Research and Practice, 53*(3), 269–280. https://doi.org/10.1080/19496591.2016.1157487

Geng, G., & Midford, R. (2015). Investigating first year education students' stress level. *Australian Journal of Teacher Education, 40*(6), 1–12. https://doi.org/10.14221/ajte.2015v40n6.1

Gentles, S. J., Charles, C., Ploeg, J., & McKibbon, K. A. (2015). Sampling in qualitative research: Insights from an overview of the methods literature. *The Qualitative Report, 20*(11), 20. http://nsuworks.nova.edu/tqr/vol20/iss11/5

Henrich, J., Heine, S. J., & Norenzayan, A. (2010). The weirdest people in the world? *Behavioural and Brain Sciences, 33*(2), 1–75.

Kulikowski, K., Potoczek, A., Antipow, E., & Król, S. (2019). How to survive in academia: Demands, resources and study satisfaction among Polish PhD students. *Educational Sciences: Theory and Practice, 19*(4), 65–79.

Leibowitz, B. (2017). Rurality and education (SARiHE Working Paper No.1). South African Rurality in Higher Education. http://sarihe.org.za/publications

Lesener, T., Pleiss, L. S., Gusy, B., & Wolter, C. (2020). The study demands-resources framework: An empirical introduction. *International Journal of Environmental Research and Public Health, 17*(14). https://doi.org/10.3390/ijerph17145183

Luescher, T. M., Schreiber, B., & Moja, T. (2018). Towards student well-being and quality services in student affairs in Africa. *Journal of Student Affairs in Africa, 6*(2). https://doi.org/10.24085/jsaa.v6i2.3317

Makhubela, M. (2021). Comorbid anxiety and depression psychopathology in university students: A network approach. *South African Journal of Psychology, 51*(1), 35–53. https://doi.org/10.1177/0081246320973839

Mason, H. D. (2018). Learning and study strategies among first-year students at a South African university: A mixed methods study. *Africa Education Review, 15*(4), 118–134.

Mason, H. D. (2019). Factors that enhance academic learning and study behaviours: A qualitative study. *Journal of Psychology in Africa, 29*(1), 67–72. https://doi.org/10.1080/14330237.2019.1568087

Mbara, T. C., & Celliers, C. (2013). Travel patterns and challenges experienced by University of Johannesburg off-campus students. *Journal of Transport & Supply Chain Management, 7*(1), 1–8. http://dx.doi. org/10.4102/jtscm.v7i1.114.

Merriam-Webster Dictionary. (2022). Peri-urban. Retrieved October 26, 2022, from https://www.merriam-webster.com/dictionary/peri-urban

Miles, M. B., Huberman, A. M., & Saldaña, J. (2014). *Qualitative data analysis: A methods sourcebook.* SAGE.

Mokgele, K. R. F., & Rothmann, S. (2014). A structural model of student well-being. *South African Journal of Psychology, 4,* 514. https://doi.org/10.1177/0081246314541589

Morton, N., Hill, C., Meiring, D., & van de Vijver, F. J. (2020). Investigating measurement invariance in the South African Personality Inventory: English version. *South African Journal of Psychology, 50*(2), 274–289. https://doi.org/10.1177/0081246319877537

Msila, V. (2010). Rural school principals' quest for effectiveness: Lessons from the field. *Journal of Education, 48,* 170–185.

Naidoo, A., & McKay, T. J. M. (2018). Student funding and student success: A case study of a South African university.

South African Journal of Higher Education, 32(5). https://doi.org/10.20853/32-5-2565

Nel, K., Govender, S., & Tom, R. (2016). The social and academic adjustment experiences of first-year students at a historically disadvantaged peri-urban university in South Africa. *Journal of Psychology in Africa, 26*(4), 384–389. https://doi.org/10.1080/14330237.2016.1208960

Ngcobo, Z., Manyathela, C., & Bateman, C. (2016, October 10). #FeesMustFall protests turn violent, bus set alight in Jhb CBD. *Eyewitness News*. http://ewn.co.za/2016/10/10/Bus-set-alight-during-Wits-protests.

Nyar, A. (2019). *The first-year experience (FYE) in South Africa: A national perspective* (SANRC FYE Thought Series 2, p. 1–38). South African National Resource Centre for the First-Year Experience and Students in Transition. https://www.sanrc.co.za/index.php/resources/sanrc-fye-thought-series

Pather, S., Norodien-Fataar, N., Cupido, X., & Mkonto, N. (2017). First year students' experience of access and engagement at a University of Technology. *Journal of Education (University of KwaZulu-Natal), 69*, 161.

Patton, M. Q. (2015). *Qualitative research & evaluation methods: Integrating theory and practice*. SAGE.

Pillay, A. L., & Ngcobo, H. S. B. (2010). Sources of stress and support among rural-based first-year university students: An exploratory study. *South African Journal of Psychology 40*(3), 234–240. http://doi.org/10.1177/008124631004000302

Pillay, A. L., & Thwala, J. D. (2012). Are rural students from previously disadvantaged communities prepared for psychology studies at university? *Journal of Psychology in Africa, 22*(3), 419–424.

Pluut, H., Curşeu, P. L., & Ilies, R. (2015). Social and study related stressors and resources among university entrants: Effects on well-being and academic performance. *Learning & Individual Differences, 37*, 262–268.

Pretorius, M. & Blaauw, D. 2020. Financial challenges and the subjective well-being of first-year students at a comprehensive South African university. *Journal of Student Affairs in Africa, 8*(1), 47–63. 10.24085/jsaa.v8i1.3824

Robins, T. G., Roberts, R. M., & Sarris, A. (2015). Burnout and engagement in health profession students: The relationships between study demands, study resources and personal resources. *The Australasian Journal of Organisational Psychology, 8*, E1. https://doi.org/10.1017/orp.2014.7

Sader, S. B., & Gabela, N. P. (2017). Spatialities of widening participation: Narrative of first year students receiving financial aid. *South African Journal of Higher Education, 31*(1). https://doi.org/10.20853/31-1-1056

Salanova, M., Schaufeli, W., Martínez, I., & Bresó, E. (2010). How obstacles and facilitators predict academic performance: The mediating role of study burnout and engagement. *Anxiety, Stress & Coping, 23*(1), 53–70.

Saldaña, J. (2016). *The coding manual for qualitative researchers* (3rd ed.). SAGE.

Scott, I. (2019). *Designing the South African higher education system for student success.* (SANRC - FYE Thought Series 3,

pp. 1–40). South African National Resource Centre for the First-Year Experience and Students in Transition. https://www.sanrc.co.za/content/2019/04/I-Scott-Report.pdf

Sommer, M., & Dumont, K. (2011). Psychosocial factors predicting academic performance of students at a historically disadvantaged university. *South African Journal of Psychology 41*(3), 386–395. http://doi.org/10.1177/008124631104100312

Speckman, M., & Mandew, M. (Eds). (2014). *Perspectives of student affairs in South Africa.* African Minds.

Steyn, M. G., Harris, T., & Hartell C. G. (2014). Institutional factors that affect Black South African students' perceptions of early childhood teacher education. *South African Journal of Education, 34*(3), 1–6.

The Gaffney Group. (2011). North West municipalities. In J. Leon (Ed.), *GAFFNEY's local government in South Africa: Official yearbook 2011–2013* (pp. M941–M1022).

Thomas, T. A., & Maree, D. (2021). Student factors affecting academic success among undergraduate students at two South African higher education institutions. *South African Journal of Psychology*. https://doi.org/10.1177/0081246320986287

Thorne, S. (2016). *Interpretive description*. Routledge. https://doi-org/10.4324/9781315426259

Tracy, S. J. (2020). *Qualitative research methods: Collecting evidence, crafting analysis, communicating impact* (2nd ed.). Wiley-Blackwell.

van Breda, A. D. (2017). Students are human too: Psychosocial vulnerability of first-year students at the University of Johannesburg. *South African Journal of Higher Education, 31*(5), 246–262.

van Breda, A. D. (2018). Resilience of vulnerable students transitioning into a South African university. *Higher Education, 75*(6), 1109–1124. https://doi.org/10.1007/s10734-017-0188-z

van Zyl, A., Dampier, G. & Ngwenya, N. 2020. Effective institutional intervention where it makes the biggest difference to student success: The University of Johannesburg (UJ) integrated student success initiative (ISSI). *Journal of Student Affairs in Africa, 8*(2), 59–71. 10.24085/ jsaa.v8i2.4448

van Zyl, Y., & Dhurup, M. (2016). When things get tough, the tough get going: University students' perceived stress and coping mechanisms. *International Journal of Social Sciences & Humanity Studies, 8*(1), 218–232. https://dergipark.org.tr/en/download/article-file/257160

Verkuyten, M. (2005). *The social psychology of ethnic identity*. Psychology Press.

Wilcox, P., Winn, S., & Fyvie-Gauld, M. (2005). "It was nothing to do with the university, it was just the people": The role of social support in the first-year experience of higher education. *Studies in Higher Education, 30*(6), 77–722.

Wolff, W., Brand, R., Baumgarten, F., Lösel, J., & Ziegler, M. (2014). Modeling students' instrumental (mis-)use of substances to enhance cognitive performance: Neuroenhancement in the light of job-demands-resources theory. *BioPsychoSocial Medicine, 8*(1), 2–22.

Self-Authorship Development of Chinese College Students: Relationships Among Epistemological, Interpersonal, and Intrapersonal Dimensions

Yifei Li   Ellen M. Broido

We describe relationships among epistemological, interpersonal, and intrapersonal development in Chinese college students from the perspective of self-authorship theory. The themes that emerged from interviews with 13 junior or senior students offer insights into unique aspects of self-authorship development in the Chinese higher education context as well as similarities to development in the US context. We used students' narratives about their college experiences to illustrate their journey toward self-authorship. Findings suggest that a style based on hierarchy and interpersonal connection in Chinese culture plays an important role in student development.

In 2019, the number of college students in China was 40.02 million (Ministry of Education, 2020), more than 10 times that in 1998 (3.61 million; Ministry of Education, 1999). With the dramatic expansion of higher education over the last 20 years, policymakers and the public have raised their expectations of higher education, calling for higher quality, including the enhancement of students' innovation and creativity (The State Council, 2018). Additionally, dramatically increasing exposure to ideas, options, and information brought by the internet has added complexity to adult

life in contemporary China, requiring college graduates to critically examine information and decide what to believe based on multiple data sources and their values. Chinese adults also are expected to take initiative and responsibility for self-evaluation and their own development at work. In addition, they should be able to establish norms and roles in relationships, create healthy boundaries inside and outside the family for privacy and personal respect, and undertake other responsibilities relating to partnering and parenting in their private lives (Zhu, 2010).

Self-authorship, an integrative concept in student development theory, is closely related to innovation and creativity, as well as other desired learning outcomes of Chinese higher education. Kegan (1982) originated this term to refer to the fourth order in his five-order human consciousness development theory. Then, Baxter Magolda (1992) defined it fully in the context of college student development. Baxter Magolda (1999) found that self-authorship has three dimensions: epistemological, interpersonal, and intrapersonal, with the ultimate goal of self-authorship being the development of "an internal voice" to author one's life (p. xi). Thus, it is valuable to explore Chinese college

Yifei Li (ORCID: https://orcid.org/0000-0002-5721-6799) is Research Analyst of Institutional Research & Integrated Planning at University of the Fraser Valley. She gratefully acknowledges the support of the Hunan Educational Studies Office (XJK21BJC001). Ellen M. Broido (ORCID: https://orcid.org/0000-0001-7574-4096) is Professor of Higher Education and Student Affairs at Bowling Green State University.

students' development from the perspective of self-authorship theory to better inform the educational practices and research in Chinese higher education. This paper is derived from a doctoral dissertation that explored Chinese college students' self-authorship development and focused on the relationships among development in epistemological, interpersonal, and intrapersonal domains.

REVIEW OF LITERATURE

Baxter Magolda (1998) defined self-authorship as "the ability to collect, interpret, and analyze information and reflect on one's own beliefs in order to form judgment" (p. 143). Later, Baxter Magolda (1999) expanded that definition, writing that self-authorship is "an ability to construct knowledge in a contextual world, . . . to construct an internal identity separate from external influences, and . . . to engage in relationships without losing one's internal identity" (p. 12). This second definition explained the three domains of the construct clearly as the epistemological, interpersonal, and intrapersonal domains. In Baxter Magolda and King's (2012) self-authorship model, there are 10 positions grouped into three major phases: (a) External Meaning Making, (b) Crossroads (a mixture of external and internal), and (c) Internal Meaning Making.

Relationships Among the Three Dimensions of Self-Authorship Development

Some scholars have attempted to understand the relationship among the three dimensions of the self-authorship construct (Baxter Magolda, 2010; Pizzolato & Olson, 2016). Baxter Magolda (2010) believed that each person has a "default, or a 'home'" dimension (p. 41). Individuals use this default dimension as an initial way of analyzing their situation. Some people may use the epistemological dimension; others

may choose the intrapersonal dimension; still others utilize the interpersonal dimension.

Although the home dimension varies from person to person, Baxter Magolda (2010) presented a pattern of development among the three dimensions. The construction of epistemological beliefs typically happens before the integration of identity at the intrapersonal level. "[I]n other words, convictions were in their heads before they could live them in their hearts" (Baxter Magolda, 2010, p. 42). Even when crises emerged from the intrapersonal or interpersonal domains, Baxter Magolda's participants often first approached them epistemologically: "Making decisions about what to change was usually a precursor to doing the intrapersonal and interpersonal work to implement the change. This implies the epistemological dimension is necessary to process beliefs about self and relationships" (p. 42). The interpersonal dimension seemed to be the most challenging area for individuals to develop. However, Baxter Magolda (2010) noted that "[i]t was not until all three dimensions became integrated that participants were able to act on their internal foundations consistently across contexts" (p. 42).

Pizzolato and Olson (2016) also studied the relationship among the three dimensions of self-authorship. They spent a year studying the development of community college students in a welfare-to-work program. Their results validated Baxter Magolda's (2010) findings that development along the three dimensions of self-authorship is not synchronous. However, Pizzolato and Olson (2016) found that "there is no home dimension by type of person, but rather the leading dimension appears to change as a function of the environment, instead of the individual choosing or preferring a lead dimension" (p. 421). Their findings also contradicted Baxter Magolda's (2010) conclusion about the leading role of the epistemological dimension. They found the intrapersonal dimension was the leading dimension for their participants.

However, participants had the most development in the cognitive dimension during the year under study.

King (2010) explored the importance of the cognitive dimension in self-authorship development. However, she admitted that "the term 'cognitive' conveys a broad set of mental activities (e.g., inductive and deductive reasoning, self-monitoring, knowledge retention)" (p. 168), while self-authorship development, for the most part, involves developing epistemology—one facet of cognition. Furthermore, she noted, "A broader definition of the cognitive dimension provides a basis for the dimension to have a stronger impact; it simply casts a broader net that encompasses more elements, and thus has a higher likelihood of playing a stronger role" (p. 169). The difference is worth noting because King (2010) has argued for the cognitive dimension as the foundation of all three dimensions, suggesting cognitive complexity strengthens development in the intrapersonal and interpersonal dimensions. "[W]ithout cognitive complexity, one does not have a cognitive frame of reference that would accommodate integrating several aspects of self or seeing multiple possibilities and choices about the kinds of friendships one constructs" (King, 2010, p. 179). King also provided a possible resolution, which is "to locate cognitive complexity as a foundation that underlies all dimensions; in this foundational role, cognitive complexity is necessary but not sufficient for self-authored meaning-making" (p. 182). She has proposed a new terminology, *connective complexity*, to "better capture this element that underlies development across dimension" (p. 182).

How the dimensions work together has implications for assessment and practice and clarifies the theoretical construct of self-authorship. The varying findings in research on this topic may arise from different populations of the studies. More work needs to be done to systematically examine patterns or relationships across the self-authorship dimensions with different populations and contexts.

Self-Authorship Development of College Students in China

Researchers have pointed out that development in epistemology, identity, and interpersonal relationships is intricately connected to cultural differences (Heine & Lehman, 1997; Heine et al., 1999; Hofer, 2010; Weinstock, 2010). Weinstock (2010) suggested researchers should consider how cultural values and practices "do or do not serve to support the development of a contextual, evaluativist epistemology and self-authorship" (p. 130). Hofer (2010) also concluded that epistemological development varies across cultures. In addition, Heine et al. (1999) noticed the great distinction between the self in Asian cultures and European or American cultures. Heine and Lehman (1997) found East Asian students, when confronting dissonance, strove to maintain the good of the relationship instead of the good of the individual self, unlike European or American students. Since development in epistemology, identity, and interpersonal relationships are domains of self-authorship, it is meaningful and necessary to explore self-authorship development in countries with different cultures, including China, with its unique sociocultural contexts.

Cen (2012) found that Chinese senior college students, in general, were at the crossroads in self-authorship development. Yu et al. (2020) noted 6 out of 8 students in a Doctor of Medicine program who quit pursuing medical careers were following external formulas when making their medical career decisions in the first place. The participants were mostly influenced by their parents when initially choosing to be doctors. Seven of them did not consider other career options until they entered the 6th year in the program when they started working in hospitals, indicating they had just started to use internal voices in self-authorship development.

Participants in the Yu et al. study entered the crossroads a little later than those in Cen's study, perhaps because the "real world" part of their programs occurred later.

Kegan (1994) proposed that people with a connected style preference might face more obstacles to development if important people in their lives did not support their moves toward personal authority. China has a unique socio-cultural context, characterized by a strong hierarchy and collectivism (Bush & Haiyan, 2000). This suggests that Chinese college students may have more difficulty developing self-authorship. Deutsch (2004) confirmed Kegan's assertion. She noticed senior college students in southeastern China considered their parents' expectations when making career decisions. Many of them gave up their initial career plans when facing disapproval from their parents. Bohon (2015) also found that the development of Chinese students in the intrapersonal and interpersonal domains was more mutually dependent than is true for students in the Western cultural context due to the influence of collective cultures.

The researchers discussed above started the important work of examining how culture plays a role in students developing self-authorship. In this paper, we aim to contribute to the research on student development by providing insight into the nuances of Chinese undergraduates' self-authorship development.

METHODOLOGY

We adopted a social constructivist, grounded theory approach in this study. One researcher is Chinese and grew up and lived in China for most of her life. She also received most of her education in China and worked as a college professor there for more than 10 years. Therefore, she has an insider perspective on the college student experience in China, with rich knowledge of Chinese social and higher education cultures. The second author is a White higher education faculty member at a US university who was raised primarily in the US and completed all her formal education there. As such, she thinks from a US perspective. However, she was a visiting faculty member at a university in China and has studied student services work in China. She also has taught about the structure of student services in multiple national contexts, including China, the UK, and South Africa. The first author of the study designed and conducted the research with guidance and writing assistance from the second author.

Sampling

The 13 junior or senior student participants attended one of three higher education institutions, all in one province chosen for convenience. To maximize the diversity of institution types in the study, we used purposive sampling and chose three institutions with different levels of selectivity. We asked teachers and administrators at the three institutions to send out the preliminary survey link with interview invitations to potential participants. The preliminary survey was used to collect demographic information from students who were interested in taking part in the study. We used purposive sampling, maximizing demographic variation, to select the first six participants. We used theoretical sampling to choose subsequent participants after completing the analysis of the first six interviews, identifying remaining participants to explore patterns observed and questions arising from the first interviews. We include some of the participants' demographic information and the order of their interviews in Table 1.

All participants were traditional-aged students. The column, Geographic Origin, indicates where participants were raised and is based on the administrative divisions of China. County towns are the seats of county administration, and most residents are employed in non-agricultural work ("County town," n.d.).

Table 1.
Participant Demographics

Order of Interview	Pseudonym	Geographic Origin	Year in school	Graduation year	Gender identity	Ethnicity	Major	SES
1	Tracy	Countryside	Junior	2019	Woman	Han	English	L
2	Dawkin	Countryside	Junior	2019	Man	Dong	Physical Education	L
3	Tingting	County Town	Junior	2019	Woman	Han	Law	H
4	Qiqi	Secondary City	Junior	2019	Woman	Han	Visual Communication	H
5	Miss P	Secondary City	Junior	2019	Woman	Han	English	H
6	Yang	County Town	Rising Senior	2019	Woman	Han	Finance	H
7	Leon	Secondary City	Rising Junior	2020	Man	Han	Marketing	H
8	Tendo	Secondary City	Graduate	2018	Man	Han	Accounting	H
9	Yan	Countryside	Graduate	2018	Woman	Han	Physics	H
10	Monian	Countryside	Rising Senior	2019	Man	Han	Electronic Science and Technology	L
11	Wangjie	County Town	Senior	2019	Man	Han	Physical Education	L
12	Duanlinxi	Countryside	Junior	2020	Woman	Miao	Business English	L
13	Liubing	Countryside	Junior	2020	Woman	Han	Accounting	L

Larger than county towns, secondary cities have populations of more than 250,000 who engage in non-agricultural work ("Prefecture-level city," 2019). Countryside refers to areas where most people conduct agricultural work ("Countryside," n.d.).

Participants' socioeconomic status (SES) is based on our judgment, given where participants were raised and information from the interviews, particularly their parents' jobs. We put SES into two categories, lower and higher. Overall, people living in the countryside have fewer economic resources and lower-quality schools. The two categories are relative to the other participants in the study. Four participants were from Institution A (highly selective admissions), six were from Institution B (moderately selective admissions), and three were from Institution C (less selective admissions). Six were only children; the other seven were not.

Data Generation

We used synchronous video conferencing to conduct interviews due to our location in the US and the participants' location in China. The first researcher, who shared Chinese as a first language with participants, conducted the interviews in Chinese. Conducting the interviews in the participants' primary language facilitated generating rich data. In addition, the researcher's fluency in Chinese facilitated the interpretation of what participants shared and the ability to fully capture meanings of expressions embedded in the Chinese cultural context, procedures suggested by Nurjannah et al. (2014).

The semi-structured interviews lasted from 85 to 150 minutes and had four phases. First, participants were invited to introduce themselves. Next, participants were encouraged to share five phrases to describe each college year as a way of brainstorming and then to provide detailed explanations of why they chose the phrases and to describe experiences related to

each of those phrases. Finally, the first author briefly summarized the interview and asked participants to synthesize the collective experience. This is a modified version of the format used in the Wabash National Study (WNS) interview protocol. To adapt it to the Chinese context and establish reciprocity with participants, we used multiple strategies to distribute power more equally between the researchers and participants. For example, we asked the participants to decide the time and location for interviews. People with more seniority or status usually have more say in deciding meeting times and locations in China. By having participants set the meeting time and location, we reduced the status differential, making the interviewer more approachable. In addition, we showed each participant the interviewer's physical surroundings with the camera at the beginning during the greetings so that they got to know the interviewer more and felt at ease before the conversation.

Data Analysis

The first author analyzed the Mandarin text using English codes. The second author reviewed English translations of all significant coded text and the initial analysis and provided comments and revisions. We analyzed the data using English codes to facilitate collaborative work. The use of both languages supports the authenticity of the findings as the study is published in English—procedures recommended by Nurjannah et al. (2014). We used constant comparative analysis, with a combination of inductive and abductive thought, in the analytical processes. Attentive to the potential of our prior knowledge influencing our interpretation of the data, we kept our focus on patterns we saw in the data. Additionally, frequent discussion during data analysis ensured the theory arose from the data rather than from our prior thinking. We also used a Chinese higher education practitioner as a peer debriefer. As a native

Chinese speaker also proficient in English and holding a doctorate in higher education administration, she reviewed the Mandarin transcripts and English translations and codes, as well as provided feedback on our analysis.

The first step of data analysis was line-by-line coding. The first author closely read each transcript and field note, noting text relevant to participants' self-authorship and its development; she created codes to capture the essence of the relevant text. Second, related codes were combined into categories; this made patterns of development visible and led to a tentative hypothesis about self-authorship development. Finally, the authors created the theory presented here by consulting the interviews added to approach theoretical saturation, reviewing all memos, and using story-lining and theoretical coding.

Member Checking and Memoing

Congruent with guidelines for constructivist grounded theory (Charmaz, 2012), we conducted member checks with participants by sharing the analysis we had constructed of each individual's development. The analyses were originally written in English, then translated into Chinese, and participants received both versions. Translating English back to Chinese and checking with participants helped verify the adequacy of translations, as Nurjannah et al. (2014) recommended. We chose not to share the overall theory as it is a very abstract version of the collective experience and likely would have been perplexing to participants. Ten of the 13 participants responded, all affirming that the analyses accurately reflected their experiences.

The first author used memoing during research planning, sampling, data generation, and data analysis to map research activities; record planned activities, unforeseen circumstances and changes, the rationale for decisions, and responses to various contingencies; to

reflect on the research process, including factors that influenced quality in the study, decision making and discussions with the second author; and to document the development of codes, categories, and the overall theory. She also included illustrations and diagrams to map her thinking about the data and strengthen data conceptualization.

FINDINGS

In Table 2, we present participants' development in the three domains from where they were at the start of college (as they recollected) and at the time of the interview. For each domain, there are two groups of subcategories indicating different levels of meaning-making complexity. For instance, there are subcategories of Authorities are right, No appreciation of different views, and so on, indicating less complex epistemological meaning-making structures. For each time point, we indicate the number of subcategories demonstrated in each participant's interview. We also provide the total number of subcategories in each cell for easy comparison. Taking Tracy's epistemological development as an example, describing herself at the start of college, she showed thinking or behaviors fitting into three subcategories of simpler meaning-making structures and none of the more complicated structures. At the time of the interview, she still described thinking or behaviors aligned with three subcategories of less complicated meaning-making structures. However, she also described thinking/behaviors demonstrating three subcategories of more complicated meaning-making structures. In the table, we first list all juniors and then the seniors, as the seniors may have more opportunities to develop self-authorship. In examining participants' overall development, as shown in Table 2, we identified three patterns in the relationships between domains of participants' self-authorship development.

Table 2.
Participants' Development in the Three Domains

Year	Name	Domain	Start of college		Time of Interview	
			Less complicated meaning-making	More complicated meaning-making	Less complicated meaning-making	More complicated meaning-making
Juniors	Tracy	Epistemological	3/7	0/6	3/7	2/6
		Interpersonal	1/8	0/6	4/8	0/6
		Intrapersonal	3/10	0/8	6/10	3/8
	Dawkin	Epistemological	2/7	0/6	1/7	3/6
		Interpersonal	2/8	0/6	3/8	1/6
		Intrapersonal	3/10	0/8	0/10	6/8
	Tingting	Epistemological	1/7	0/6	0/7	4/6
		Interpersonal	3/8	0/6	0/8	4/6
		Intrapersonal	4/10	0/8	1/10	5/8
	Qiqi	Epistemological	2/7	0/6	3/7	3/6
		Interpersonal	2/8	0/6	0/8	1/6
		Intrapersonal	NA	NA	2/10	1/8
	Miss P.	Epistemological	NA	NA	1/7	2/6
		Interpersonal	NA	NA	1/8	2/6
		Intrapersonal	2/10	0/8	0/10	4/8
	Leon	Epistemological	1/7	0/6	0/7	3/6
		Interpersonal	1/8	0/6	2/8	2/6
		Intrapersonal	2/10	0/8	0/10	6/8
	Duanlinxi	Epistemological	NA	NA	3/7	2/6
		Interpersonal	1/8	0/6	1/8	5/6
		Intrapersonal	3/10	0/8	0/10	6/8
	Liubing	Epistemological	1/7	0/6	2/7	2/6
		Interpersonal	2/8	0/6	2/8	2/6
		Intrapersonal	4/10	0/8	2/10	3/8

Table 2, continued.

Year	Name	Domain	Start of college		Time of Interview	
			Less complicated meaning-making	More complicated meaning-making	Less complicated meaning-making	More complicated meaning-making
Seniors	Yang	Epistemological	1/7	0/6	2/7	2/6
		Interpersonal	2/8	0/6	2/8	2/6
		Intrapersonal	1/10	0/8	1/10	3/8
	Tendo	Epistemological	1/7	0/6	0/7	5/6
		Interpersonal	2/8	0/6	0/8	3/6
		Intrapersonal	1/10	0/8	0/10	6/8
	Yan	Epistemological	1/7	0/6	1/7	1/6
		Interpersonal	3/8	0/6	2/8	2/6
		Intrapersonal	3/10	0/8	1/10	3/8
	Monian	Epistemological	1/7	0/6	2/7	1/6
		Interpersonal	3/8	0/6	2/8	2/6
		Intrapersonal	5/10	0/8	1/10	5/8
	Wangjie	Epistemological	1/7	0/6	0/7	5/6
		Interpersonal	4/8	0/6	0/8	2/6
		Intrapersonal	5/10	0/8	4/10	3/8

NA indicates the topic did not arise in the interview

Asynchronous Development in the Three Domains

Development in the three domains proceeded at different rates for most participants. For example, Dawkin described balanced development in three domains (all early stage) when he began college but showed greater gains in the intrapersonal domain than in the epistemological and interpersonal domains at the time of the interview. When asked to synthesize his experience at the end of the interview, Dawkin commented,[1]

> In teaching, for example, some people's ideas, like their teaching style and philosophy, are more advanced and at a higher level. I can go to communicate with them about their experience. Then I could obtain something valuable, which I could use when I experience the same thing.

> 就说从教学这一方面吧，可能是有一些人的思想，就是说他的上课模式，还有他的教学理念，就是说更前卫一点，可能相比高度更强一点，我可以能好好跟他沟通交流一下，对于你来说的话可能在经历，还有在一些你所经历过的事情，然后我再走你的路的话，可能就是说有更好的那个东西。

He believed there were different levels of ideas, some superior to others, and he believed his ideas were less valid than some others. This suggests that he had yet to own his personal views, looking for external formulas to follow epistemologically and interpersonally. However, he showed a clear understanding of his own abilities and needs. He reflected, "I have a clearer vision on what I am going to do in the future." Obviously, by the time of the interview, Dawkin was more advanced in the intrapersonal domain than in the epistemological and interpersonal domains.

Tingting and Wangjie started college with balanced development in three domains and showed more epistemological and interpersonal gains than intrapersonal gains. At the time of the interview, Tingting's decision-making about her post-graduation plans showed how she was able to articulate her reasoning despite disagreement from her mother and the general trend in her peers majoring in law. Tingting debated taking both the Graduate Entrance Exam for possible graduate study in law as well as the Judicial Exam, which would allow her to seek employment immediately after graduation, or taking only the Graduate Entrance Exam. She shared,

> I hope to study for two more years instead of hunting for a job because I haven't learned much during four years of college and have no confidence to go to work. Furthermore, with a master's degree, I can find a job with a better salary. I really do not know whether I have brought my ability into full play at [university name], and I want to find out where my ceiling is and how far I can go. Actually, I could not understand why preparing for the two exams at the same time became mainstream. . . . Many students in higher grades tried two [exams], but most of them only passed the Judicial Exam and then had to hunt for jobs. I believe I could try to pass the Judicial Exam [while] in my graduate program. . . . Upon hearing my plan, [my mom] responded intensely, "No matter what, you have to pass Judicial Exam, get the certificate, so that you can find a job, and earn your living." She said, "You decided not to take the Judicial Exam, but if you fail your Graduate Entrance Exam, you will have nothing." She was worried about me, that I could not cope with my failure, about my lagging behind others. I could understand her, so I explained to her that many other students did the same thing as me, preparing for Graduate Entrance Exam and giving up Judicial Exam. Later, she told me she could

---

[1] All quotes are translated from Mandarin, which follows.

understand, and she did not think it over thoroughly previously

我个人的想法就是，相对于说直接拿证出去工作，我还是想多读两年，因为本科这四年并没有学到什么，就这样出去工作很没有底气，而且研究生出去找工作，工资什么的也会好好很多，我真的不知道我自己在XX大学是不是已经到达了我的能力的天花板，我还是想去碰一下自己的天花板到底在哪里，看看自己能走到哪里。其实我不是很明白，为什么法考考研一起准备会成为主流，是因为大家都很迫切，想在短时间内把所有需要完成的都完成了的心态吗？我很多学姐两样一起准备，大多只过了法考，没有考上研，她们现在都在四处找工作，我觉得没有必要，考上研之后，把法考过了就好。很多人抱着的想法就是，两样一起准备，即使考不上研，大不了出去工作，我觉得正是因为以这种心态去考，所以才考不上。……我妈应该是比较急躁性的想法吧，当时跟她说了我的打算之后，她就有点反应激烈说，"不管怎么样你一定要拿那个证出来，拿那个证才能出去工作，才能养活自己。"她会担心说，"你今年不考法考，万一今年考研失败了，就什么都没有了。"她会担心我这种状况，担心我自己心态受不了，比别人慢了一步，我能理解她这种担心，我和她解释了一下，其实也有很多人是和我一样坚定先考研，把法考暂时放下的情况，到后来，她也表示了理解，说她可能想的没有很周到。

Tingting made her decision based on two factors: First, she was not confident she could find a good job. Second, she was not sure if she had reached her full potential in college. This self-reflection demonstrated that she was constructing her own belief about what would be best for her. She recognized her mother's point of view and rationale and showed an understanding of it. She also recognized the perspectives of her peers and students in higher grades. However, her tone was confident when she described what

she wanted to do, risking failing the Graduate Entrance Exam. This shows her more advanced position epistemologically and interpersonally.

But intrapersonally, Tingting admitted that she needed more time to explore her future direction. At the end of the interview, she reflected,

> Who am I on earth? Where to go in the future? What is my direction? What to do in the future? I told myself that I must figure out in five years what in the world I like and what will be my future life. During these five years, I'll experience a lot, and after such full experiences, I'll finally get to know what I really love and want to pursue. The best result, then, would be I will become who I want to be.

> 我到底是谁，然后我以后要怎么走，我的方向在哪里，我以后会怎么办。我跟自己说的是，五年，这五年时间，我一定要想清楚，到底什么是我喜欢的，什么才是我的生活方式，然后在这五年时间，我知道我会经历很多，先把这几年充分的体会了之后，我觉得可能到最后，我就会知道我自己真的热爱的东西是什么，真正向往的生活是什么，然后到那个时候最好的结果，就是成为了我想成为的人。

Instead of looking for external guidance to figure out her direction, Tingting looked to herself to be the one to author her life. But she needed more time and experience to determine who she was, indicating she was still in the process of exploring her identity.

Tracy and Leon started with balanced development in three domains and had slightly more gains in the epistemological and intrapersonal domains than in the interpersonal domain. At the time of the interview, Leon was able to construct his own beliefs. When asked whether he had improved in his "shortcoming" of caring about what others said, Leon responded,

> A little better, I feel. . . . I feel like I am not that focused on how others look at

me or others' opinions. Taking majors, for example, many people still believe business administration and marketing are not good majors. But for me, I am able to know these majors better, with my own understanding, or I am able to find how the major fits me.

会有一点吧，感觉，但是会更好一点。......就是感觉自己没有那么去计较其他人怎么看我，或者其他人的一些看法。就拿专业来说，比如说还是很多人都觉得工商管理和市场营销这两个是不好的专业，但是我自己的话，能够去认清楚这些专业，有自己的一些理解在里边，或者说能够发现它跟我的结合合适的地方。

Leon started to see the connection between his major and himself as an individual unique from others and was able to differentiate others' viewpoints from his own. That he was not focused on how others perceived him indicates his internal voice was strengthening. In addition, using his understanding to make meaning of his major shows that, in the epistemological domain, he was listening to his internal voice regarding how he viewed the major.

Qiqi provided no data indicating her intrapersonal position at her entry to college, so it is hard to tell in which domain she gained the most. But she ended university more advanced in the interpersonal domain than in the epistemological and intrapersonal domains. Duanlinxi also did not indicate her epistemological position at college entry. But she ended up in a more advanced intrapersonal position than in the other two domains. Miss P. did not indicate her epistemological and interpersonal positions at the start of college, but she ended up more advanced in the intrapersonal domain than in the other two domains. Yang, Tendo, Yan, Monian, and Liubing all started college with balanced development in three domains, and it was difficult to determine which domain(s), if any, were leading at the time of the interview.

In other words, their development in the three domains seems almost synchronous.

No single domain had the most developmental progression in college. When we consider the 10 participants for whom we have data about their developmental position at both the start of college and the time of the interview, five showed equal developmental gains across the three domains. The other five participants varied in which domain(s) showed meaningful development. Four showed greater development in two domains. One showed gains in one domain. There is no obvious pattern as to which domain had the most growth during college.

Although it is challenging to determine which domain showed the most development in college, there was a pattern in terms of the sole leading domain. Among these eight who were at different levels of development in the three domains at the time they were interviewed, three participants' intrapersonal domains were leading; one participant's interpersonal domain was leading; two participants' epistemological and interpersonal domains were leading; and two participants' epistemological and intrapersonal domains were leading. The intrapersonal domain was the most common sole leading domain, and the epistemological domain was never the sole leading domain.

Interconnection Among Domains

Participants' development in each domain influenced development in the other two domains, sometimes hindering and sometimes supporting their development in both other domains. In some cases, the lagging domain(s) hindered participants' development in other domain(s). For example, Yang believed authorities had more valid knowledge than she did, an epistemological belief that limited her making more self-authored decisions when dealing with conflicts with her supervisors (interpersonal domain). Liubing's reliance on her parents (interpersonal) hindered her epistemological development. She recognized her parents' shortcomings but still trusted them to make decisions for her since she believed they kept her best interest in mind.

In other cases, the leading domain(s) served to support participants' development in other domain(s). For example, Tendo's development in the epistemological and intrapersonal domains helped with his interpersonal development. Specifically, his understanding that his parents' viewpoints were not necessarily wrong but were a product of a certain context, combined with an awareness of his love of the field of art, helped him advocate for support from his parents to pursue art while maintaining a mutual relationship with them. Thus, his more advanced epistemological and intrapersonal development facilitated his interpersonal development.

Inconsistent Developmental Status Across Contexts

In different contexts, participants often showed varying developmental statuses. In Yang's case, in the interpersonal domain, she demonstrated solid internal criteria in considering peers' needs when making plans with friends. However, she showed deference to her supervisors' opinions and ideas when confronting her supervisors. Monian believed what professors and senior students said was correct. However, she realized knowledge was subjective and varying viewpoints were equal when she and her dorm mates held different opinions regarding appropriate behaviors in the dormitory.

Participants were most influenced by parents and professors. When confronting parents and professors, as compared to confronting peers, participants showed more external meaning-making structures by deferring to parents' and professors' ideas and opinions. However, when dealing with peer relationships, participants tended to show more advanced self-authorship. With that being said, participants who made meaning externally tended to perceive some peer students as having

more valid knowledge claims than other peers, especially students in higher grades or who were perceived as excellent. For example, Tracy realized from attending departmental meetings that there were a lot of excellent students to learn from and that she was "ordinary" and "nothing" compared with those students.

Participants' development in the interpersonal domain was linked with their epistemological belief about who was the more valid knowledge source. This generated a hierarchy with parents and professors at the top, students in higher grades and excellent students in the middle, and peers at the bottom. When participants who made meaning externally confronted peers perceived as equal knowledge claimants, participants saw knowledge claims as subjective and believed there was no way to determine which claims were more valid. In these contexts, participants often looked inward for their own voice in making meaning.

DISCUSSION AND IMPLICATIONS

We found that development across the three domains of self-authorship was interconnected, linked, and mutually influential. In addition, development in the three domains was asynchronous in most cases. These findings are consistent with previous studies (Baxter Magolda, 2001; Baxter Magolda & King, 2012; Bohon, 2015; King, 2010; Pizzolato & Olson, 2016). In addition, researchers agree that context plays a role in student development; the findings of this study indicate the interplay of sociocultural context and power or hierarchical relationships with students' self-authorship development, particularly influencing the synchronicity of development across domains.

Self-Authorship Development in Chinese Culture

We found that the epistemological domain was never the sole leading domain and that the intrapersonal domain was the most common sole leading domain for participants who developed asynchronously across the three domains. A possible explanation for our findings related to epistemological development is that most participants' epistemological beliefs were about who is a more valid knowledge source—a belief rooted in the hierarchical nature of Chinese culture (Yang et al., 2006). Participants' epistemological beliefs about who is a more valid knowledge source generated a hierarchical order with parents and professors at the top, students in higher grades and excellent students in the middle, and peers at the bottom. When participants interacted with people whom they perceived to be in higher/senior positions, they tended to believe what these authorities said or believed. Another possible explanation is relatively limited sources of information available to college students caused by censorship of the internet, textbooks, and other sources, even though no participants mentioned this point, probably due to their unawareness. These findings are consistent with Baxter Magolda and King's (2012) assertion that participants showed different developmental positions across contexts when they were at the Crossroads stage. Many participants in Baxter Magolda and King's and our study demonstrated lateral growth (horizontal decalage; Perry, 1999) as they showed an internal voice in some, but not all, contexts.

Furthermore, interpersonal development appears to be influenced by hierarchical Chinese culture, which also influences epistemological development. Interpersonal development may have lagged because participants deferred to authorities and found it difficult to be aware of or stick to their own ideas. In other words, in Chinese culture, which values connection among people and interpersonal hierarchy, people in lower-status positions are expected to show obedience to those who are in higher/senior positions to maintain interpersonal

connections. In addition, in the Chinese sociopolitical context, it is generally believed that there are consequences for dissent or critique of authorities. Students are encouraged to accept the words of faculty members, more senior classmates, and other authorities. Our findings suggest that when the epistemological and interpersonal domains are constrained by a culture of hierarchy and connection, the intrapersonal domain becomes the leading domain.

Pizzolato and Olson's (2016) findings were similar to ours. They found that most participants had the intrapersonal domain as the leading domain, while the fewest had the epistemological domain as the sole leading domain. The similarity in our findings may be because participants in Pizzolato and Olson's study lived in a culture similar to the ones in this article, even though they were in two different countries. First, participants in Pizzolato and Olson's study were welfare-to-work students in a community college in the US who "repeatedly experienced relationships as places for power plays and enforcement of rules without consideration of perspectives" (p. 421). Second, 24 of 25 of their participants were female [sic], and females tend to prefer connected voice rather than separate voice, according to Kegan (1994). The participants in their and our studies were in hierarchical and connected cultures.

Kegan's (1982, 1994) observations about the orders of consciousness in human development may provide some explanation for the epistemological and interpersonal development patterns discussed above. While acknowledging people in all stages of the development of consciousness may show connected or separate voice preferences, or have an orientation of independence or inclusion, Kegan (1994) noted, "If one's important connections are unwilling to support our moves toward personal authority, then being faithful to the forward motion of our own lives may indeed involve the extraordinary cost of having to take our leave from these connections" (p. 220).

Kegan's statement suggests that Chinese college students, in general, may face more obstacles in their self-authorship journey for two reasons. First, although they do not necessarily personally prefer a connected voice or inclusion orientation, collectively they are living in a culture valuing connection among people. Thus, they are more likely to choose the connected voice or inclusion orientation. Second, collectively Chinese college students are living in a cultural environment that promotes filial piety and a hierarchical social order. Therefore, their family and other connections may not support their moves toward personal authority but rather expect or demand obedience. This may limit students' ability to recognize different perspectives and value their internal voice and encourage them to obey authorities to stay connected.

With that being said, Kegan (1982, 1994) did not mean people with connected voice preference or orientation of inclusion are at a disadvantage in lifespan development. Kegan believed people with a separated voice preference or an orientation of independence might find it easier to develop from the third order to the fourth but then harder to develop from the fourth order of consciousness to the fifth. For people with the orientation of inclusion, it may be harder to develop from the third order to the fourth but then easier to develop from the fourth order of consciousness to the fifth. Self-authorship development, the focus of this paper, refers to the development process from the third order of consciousness to the fourth order but is not the final step in the human development of consciousness.

Our findings and those of Pizzolato and Olson (2016) differ from Baxter Magolda's (2010) assertion that the "epistemological dimension [was] necessary to process beliefs about self and relationships" (p. 42). King (2010) also considered whether the cognitive dimension played a comparable or a stronger role than the intrapersonal and interpersonal dimensions. She did not argue for a specific conclusion but wanted to start a conversation in the field. From the perspective of equally important roles, she listed one example from Baxter Magolda (2001) to illustrate "the intrapersonal dimension seems to represent the leading edge of development" (p. 172). Due to a lack of clarity about relationships among the three domains, more empirical data and discussions are needed before any conclusions can be made, especially taking into consideration different contexts.

Implications for Practice and Future Research

Our findings suggest that student affairs practitioners and instructors working with Chinese students should promote student development by giving students frequent opportunities to question the reliability of information sources and to consider multiple points of view rather than declaring authorities to be the best source of knowledge. They need to weaken their positions as the sole owners of knowledge, a perspective deeply based in the ideas and practices of Chinese culture. This would encourage students to consider knowledge from multiple sources, including their experiences and internal voice.

In addition, the organizational charts of student organizations need to be less hierarchical, and administrators and student leaders should encourage multiple perspectives and input from students regardless of their experience. This would promote students' epistemological and interpersonal development, especially if it were promoted in multiple venues, such as campus activities, on-campus housing, orientation, career services, and other settings. Institutional missions should be updated to include the promotion of students' holistic development, leading to changes in multiple aspects of the university. In addition, workshops and professional development opportunities, especially regarding how to facilitate students' coping and growth in college, could be arranged for practitioners and professionals, including instructors, supervisors of student organizations, student affairs staff, administrators, and other stakeholders.

We found participants' meaning-making structures shifted in varying contexts. Future researchers could examine how college students' meaning-making structures differ and develop in different contexts, such as jobs, cocurricular activities, and the classroom. Additionally, our findings suggest that hierarchical or connected cultural contexts may influence self-authorship development, so it is valuable to explore if the dynamic exists in similar contexts, such as athletic teams and military groups in the US or other countries. Finally, studies on different cohorts and longitudinal studies on a single cohort are good options for further investigation of how college students' self-authorship development progress in the three domains.

Correspondence concerning this article should be addressed to Yifei Li, University of the Fraser Valley; yifei.li@ufv.ca

REFERENCES

Baxter Magolda, M. B. (1992). *Knowing and reasoning in college: Gender-related patterns in students' intellectual development.* Jossey-Bass.

Baxter Magolda, M. B. (1998). Developing self-authorship in young adult life. *Journal of College Student Development, 39*(2), 143–156.

Baxter Magolda, M. B. (1999). *Creating contexts for learning and self-authorship: Constructive-developmental pedagogy.* Vanderbilt University.

Baxter Magolda, M. B. (2001). *Making their own way: Narratives for transforming higher education to promote self-development.* Stylus.

Baxter Magolda, M. B. (2010). The interweaving of epistemological, intrapersonal, and interpersonal development in the evolution of self-authorship. In M. B. Baxter Magolda, E. G. Creamer, & P. S. Meszaros (Eds.), *Development and assessment of self-authorship: Exploring the concept across cultures* (pp. 25–44). Stylus.

Baxter Magolda, M. B., & King, P. M. (2012). *Nudging minds to life: Self-authorship as a foundation for learning* (ASHE Higher Education Report). Wiley Online Library. DOI: 10.1002/aehe.20003

Bohon, L. L. (2015). *Self-authorship development of Chinese undergraduate students attending a U.S. university* (UMI No. 3663008) [Doctoral dissertation, the College of William and Mary in Virginia]. ProQuest Dissertations and Theses database.

Bush, T., & Haiyan, Q. (2000). Leadership and culture in Chinese education. *Asia Pacific Journal of Education, 20*(2), 58–67.

Cen, Y. (2012). *Growth as product and as process: Student learning outcomes attained through college experiences in China* (UMI No. 3509899) [Doctoral dissertation, Indiana University]. ProQuest Dissertations and Theses database.

Charmaz, K. (2014). *Constructing grounded theory* (2nd ed.). Sage.

Countryside. (n.d.) Retrieved from https://baike.baidu.com/item/农村

County town. (n.d.) Retrieved from https://baike.baidu.com/item/县城/33483

Deutsch, F. M. (2004). How parents influence the life plans of graduating Chinese university students. *Journal of Comparative Family Studies, 35*(3), 393–421. https://doi.org/10.3138/jcfs.35.3.393

Heine, S. J., & Lehman, D. R. (1997). Culture, dissonance, and self-affirmation. *Personality and Social Psychology Bulletin, 23*(4), 389–400. https://doi.org/10.1177/0146167297234005

Heine, S. J., Lehman, D. R., Markus, H. R., & Kitayama, S. (1999). Is there a universal need for positive self-regard? *Psychological Review, 106*(4), 766–794. https://doi.org/10.1037/0033–295X.106.4.766

Hofer, B. K. (2010). Personal epistemology, learning, and cultural context: Japan and the U.S. In M. B. Baxter Magolda, E. G. Creamer, & P. S. Meszaros (Eds.), *Development and assessment of self-authorship: exploring the concept across cultures* (pp. 133–148). Stylus.

Kegan, R. (1982). *The evolving self: Problem and process in human development.* Harvard University Press. https://doi.org/10.4159/9780674039414

Kegan, R. (1994). *In over our heads: The mental demands of modern life.* Harvard University Press. https://doi.org/10.2307/j.ctv1pncpfb

King, P. M. (2010). The role of the cognitive dimension of self-authorship: An equal partner or a strong partner. In M. B. Baxter Magolda, E. G. Creamer, & P. S. Meszaros (Eds.), *Development and assessment of self-authorship: Exploring the concept across cultures* (pp. 167–186). Stylus.

Ministry of Education. (1999). *The statistic communique of the 1998 national education development.* Ministry of Education of the People's Republic of China. Retrieved from http://www.moe.gov.cn/s78/A03/ghs_left/s182/moe_633/tnull_842.html

Ministry of Education. (2020). *The statistic communique of the 2019 national education development.* Ministry of Education of the People's Republic of China. Retrieved from http://www

.moe.gov.cn/jyb_sjzl/sjzl_fztjgb/202005/t20200520_456751.html

Nurjannah, I., Mills, J., Park, T., & Usher, K. (2014). Conducting a grounded theory study in a language other than English: Procedures for ensuring the integrity of translation. *Sage Open, 4*(1), 1–10. https://doi.org/10.1177/2158244014528920

Perry, W. (1999). *Forms of intellectual and ethical development in the college years: A scheme.* Jossey-Bass.

Pizzolato, J. E., & Olson, A. B. (2016). Exploring the relationship between the three dimensions of self-authorship. *Journal of College Student Development, 57*(4), 411–427. https://doi.org/10.1353/csd.2016.0052

Prefecture-level city. (2019). Retrieved from https://baike.baidu.com/item/地级市/2089621?fromtitle=地级城市&fromid=5388642&fr=aladdin

The State Council of the People's Republic of China. (2018). *The State Council's opinions on developing innovation and entrepreneurship with high quality and upgrading the version of*

innovation and entrepreneurship. Retrieved from http://www.gov.cn/zhengce/content/2018-09/26/content_5325472.htm

Weinstock, M. (2010). Epistemological development of Bedouins and Jews in Israel: Implications for self-authorship. In M. B. Baxter Magolda, E. G. Creamer, & P. S. Meszaros (Eds.), *Development and assessment of self-authorship: Exploring the concept across cultures* (pp. 117–132). Stylus.

Yang, B., Zheng, W., & Li, M. (2006). *Chinese view of learning and implications for developing human resources.* https://files.eric.ed.gov/fulltext/ED492822.pdf

Yu, C., Wu, H., & Wu, M. (2020). The choice of "abandoning doctor career" by eight-year medical doctors: Study based on "self-authorship theory." *Chinese Higher Education Studies, 36*(1), 83–89. doi:10.16298/j.cnki.1004-3667.2020.01.13

Zhu, H. (2010). Gao xiao ren cai pei yang zhi liang ping gu xin fan shi [New paradigm of higher education quality assessment]. *Journal of National Academy of Education Administration,* (9), 50–54.

Did You Help? Intervening During Incidents of Sexual Assault Among College Student Bystanders

Lucia F. O'Sullivan   Charlene F. Belu   Rice B. Fuller   Morgan E. Richard

Sexual assault continues to plague college campuses despite years of targeted intervention. Recent prevention efforts have focused on the role of bystanders in reducing rates. However, limited work has explored actual intervention behaviors as opposed to intentions to intervene or reasons why individuals might choose not to help. College students (N = 1219; aged 19–62; 66% women) completed an online survey assessing experiences as a bystander witnessing a sexual assault, willingness to intervene, helping behavior, and associated beliefs and attitudes (rape myth attitudes, perceived peer norms, perceived self-efficacy). Fifteen percent witnessed a recent situation that they believed involved sexual assault, and most students (69%) intervened. Lower rape myth endorsement, greater self-efficacy regarding intervening, and greater perceived norms that peers would intervene on behalf of a peer predicted willingness to intervene. A personal history of sexual assault and knowing of another's assault increased the odds of perceiving an assault was underway. Knowing the victim increased the odds of intervening for all groups except men. Reports were compared among students who identified as men, women, heterosexuals, and sexual minorities. This research advances our understanding of how common it is to witness sexual assault, who is willing to intervene, and cognitive–affective barriers to intervention among college students. Specific recommendations for practitioners and educators are provided.

Rates of sexual assault among young people have remained stubbornly consistent despite decades of education, programming, and intervention (Orchowski et al., 2020). The range of adverse consequences experienced by victims of sexual assault makes it one of the most pernicious public health issues. Sexual assault affects approximately one in five to one in four college women (Cantor et al., 2020; Moreau, 2019), with lower numbers among men (1 in 8 to 1 in 37 college men; Fedina et al., 2018; Ford & Soto-Marquez, 2016; Mellins et al., 2017). Higher rates are found in non-college samples (RAINN, n.d.; Thomson & Tapp, 2022), but college students have been a renewed focus of research because of their high rates of sexual assaults, emphasis on peer culture (Telzer et al., 2018), and increasing rates of college attendance in Western countries (Statista, 2019). What is needed are ways to radically shift these rates downward by examining further how assaults might be prevented.

A promising development in prevention efforts has been the focus on bystanders in mitigating the harm of a potential assault (Banyard et al., 2009; Barone et al., 2007; CDC, 2022; The White House, 2014). Bystanders are witnesses to crimes, emergencies, or high-risk situations; they are not directly involved as perpetrators or victims. Many sexual assaults take place in social contexts, such as parties or other public spaces, where friends of the perpetrator or victim are present (Burn, 2009; Mellins et al.,

Lucia F. O'Sullivan is Professor of Psychology, Charlene F. Belu is a Doctoral Candidate in Clinical Psychology, and Rice B. Fuller are Licensed Clinical Psychologists and Morgan E. Richard is a Doctoral Candidate in Experimental Psychology; all at the University of New Brunswick. The authors greatly appreciate the help of Mary Byers with data collection.

2017). These bystanders have opportunities to intervene before, during, or after an assault to help offset some of the extreme, adverse consequences experienced by victims. Official crime statistics indicate that one third of situations involving sexual assault occur in the presence of bystanders (Planty, 2002); a recent survey found 40% of students have witnessed a sexual assault (Hoxmeier et al., 2017b).

OPPORTUNITIES TO INTERVENE TO PREVENT SEXUAL ASSAULT

Contemporary research has focused on young people's intentions to intervene—that is, self-reported likelihood or willingness to intervene (Banyard et al., 2014; Bennett et al., 2017). Researchers have questioned the value of assessing indirect metrics, such as generalized, hypothetical, or anticipated responses, given the heightened social sensitivity to the topic of sexual assault (Austin et al., 2016; Brown et al., 2014; Hoxmeier et al., 2017b; Linder, 2018; McMahon, 2010) and that the situations in which bystander intervention is warranted are typically stressful and anxiety-provoking for the bystanders themselves (Yule & Grych, 2020). Further, there is a long research history of demonstrating that a focus on intentions and beliefs is misguided, given that they are typically poor predictors of actual behavior (Sutton, 2006).

The few studies that have assessed actual intervention behavior among college students tend to assess whether they have ever intervened (lifetime) after witnessing a potential assault or else they are asked to speculate whether they would intervene in hypothetical scenarios that the researchers construct (e.g., Banyard et al., 2014; Bennett et al., 2017). Recall for more distal (versus recent) events in memory is often poor, and demand characteristics of such scenarios undermine the validity of responses.

Of particular importance is that we know little about whether young people have opportunities to intervene but choose not to intervene for some reason (i.e., missed opportunities). There are a few notable exceptions to research on students and intervention opportunities with scenarios where a potential assault was underway. The first is a study by Hoxmeier et al. (2017a) that found 19% of the student sample had witnessed a male friend taking an intoxicated woman back to his room; 25% did not intervene in that situation. The researchers did not explore reasons for students' decisions, recent experiences, or missed opportunities across other sexual assault scenarios. However, this study is valuable as it helps broaden the focus to other decision outcomes in situations requiring intervention. Follow-up research assessed the consistency of students' responsive bystander intervention to six scenarios warranting intervention and showed that students took action only half of the time (Hoxmeier et al., 2019). However, this study also did not assess reasons for not intervening.

Another study of first-year college students assessed whether students had encountered any of 10 scenarios, such as hearing someone make an offensive joke, seeing a drunk and vulnerable person at a party, or witnessing someone acting in a harassing or sexually aggressive manner toward another person (Yule & Grych, 2020). Students reported whether they had witnessed any of the scenarios in the prior three months and whether they had intervened. If they had intervened, they indicated which behaviors they had engaged in, and if they had not, they checked reasons for not intervening from a list of four barriers. Most (93%) reported recently being in at least one of the 10 scenarios; half reported intervening. Almost three-quarters (73%) also reported that they did not take action in at least one of the scenarios. They typically reported not feeling responsible (58%) or lacking skills (45%) versus fearing harm (29%) or feeling inhibited (13%).

Although valuable for helping to clarify students' decisions for not intervening, a more comprehensive picture of the factors that facilitate or hinder intervention in a sexual assault scenario is needed. These studies acknowledged the value of examining both occasions where students intervened and those where they did not but provided only researcher-derived scenarios and barriers to intervening (Hoxmeier et al., 2017a, 2019; Yule & Grych, 2020). The conclusions drawn from these findings might be most relevant to the researchers' beliefs about typical scenarios and not ones that were necessarily salient or meaningful to the students themselves. Some of the scenarios might not have been perceived as indicative of assault, such as seeing someone with unexplained bruises or hearing an offensive joke. The primary goal of the current study was to advance this work further by addressing some of these gaps. The overall aim is to understand better potential facilitators and barriers of responsive bystander behavior in college students by exploring situations that students observed and believed were or could have led to sexual assault. To that end, we asked college students to report a recent incident that they perceived to be an actual or potential assault scenario.

CONCEPTUAL FRAMEWORK FOR UNDERSTANDING BYSTANDER INTERVENTION

Latané and Darley's (1970) theory of the determinants of responsive bystander behavior proposed that intervening as a bystander was dependent on being aware that a potential crime was underway, interpreting the situation as requiring intervention, assuming responsibility to intervene, knowing how to intervene, and then actually intervening in some way, such as calling the police or physically removing a person from the interaction. Identification of factors associated with bystander response

decision-making in sexual assault situations is imperative because such in-the-moment interventions could constitute primary prevention efforts by reducing the incidence of assault. The current study incorporates these various decision points and related cognitive–affective components. The bystander approach is believed to effect change primarily by shifting sociocultural attitudes and behaviors related to sexual assault and promoting a communal approach to health promotion more broadly (McMahon et al., 2015). Identifying these factors might reduce the harm of assault by supporting victims and preventing secondary harms in cases where they can identify known perpetrators.

Since that initial work, the cognitive–affective components of the bystander intervention process have been assessed in various studies and have shown moderate effects for endorsement of rape myths (i.e., false beliefs about sexual assault that shift blame to the survivor; Amar et al., 2014; Katz et al., 2013), self-reported likelihood or willingness to intervene (Banyard et al., 2014; Nicksa, 2014), self-efficacy regarding intervening on behalf of an individual targeted by another for sexual assault (Banyard, 2008; Exner & Cummings, 2011), and small effects on actual behavior (Katz & Moore, 2013; Kleinsasser et al., 2015). These factors predict lifetime reports of having intervened (Amar et al., 2014; Bennett et al., 2014) and thus are a useful starting point for understanding who offers help to another when a potential assault is underway.

Another conceptual framework used to understand bystander behavior is social norms theory (Berkowitz, 2003), which is valuable because it taps some of the personal and social factors known to predict whether an individual will engage in responsive bystander behavior (Labhardt et al., 2017). Norms are social beliefs that capture perceptions of the "rules and standards that are understood by members of a group, and that guide or constrain social behaviors without the force of law" (Cialdini & Trost, 1998, p. 152). Individuals tend to adjust their own attitudes and behavior to reflect their perception of a corresponding peer norm. One study found that perceived peer norms regarding bystander intervention was the only predictor of willingness to intervene, even after considering personal attitudes toward sexual assault (Brown & Messman-Moore, 2010). Thus, perceived norms seem key to decisions to intervene, and we incorporated it as a factor for study here.

In addition, research has shown that bystanders are more likely to provide help if they are women, have a greater awareness of sexual assault as a social problem or from close experience, endorse fewer rape myths, and have high self-efficacy regarding their ability to intervene (Bennett et al., 2014, 2017; Brown et al., 2014; Linder, 2018). Others have identified characteristics of the context itself associated with bystander response, in particular, the relationship between the bystander and the victim or perpetrator. Bystanders are more willing to intervene as familiarity or closeness to the victim increases and less likely as familiarity or closeness to the perpetrator increases (Bennett et al., 2017).

In line with this conceptual framework, a second goal of the study was to replicate some of the findings from the previous literature by selecting variables that researchers have shown are important for understanding sexual assault of young people and bystander response. However, we advanced this past research by exploring these factors comprehensively, as well as incidents that students experienced and perceived to be assaultive or as having the potential for assault. We examined characteristics of individuals who were likely to perceive an incident as possibly leading to assault, and another novel component was examining students' responses, with a particular emphasis on reasons for not intervening (barriers) after witnessing any

incident with the potential for assault. We explored most recent experiences rather than lifetime occasions and actual experiences rather than hypothetical ones. We also controlled for socially desirable responses throughout—features not incorporated into most past research.

THE CURRENT STUDY

The overall objective of this research was to provide information about bystander responsiveness in terms of actual behavioral outcomes among college students who had recently witnessed a sexual assault or potential assault. Our first goal was to assess college students' reports of observing a sexual assault or potential sexual assault in the prior year. Of those who reported that they had observed such an incident, this study explored whether witnessing the incident led to efforts to intervene during an incident of sexual assault, a decision not to intervene (i.e., missed opportunities) after some consideration, or a decision that they had misinterpreted the incident as one involving sexual assault (i.e., re-evaluated). Our second goal was to replicate and expand upon previous work in this area by examining a comprehensive range of individual and contextual factors associated with willingness to intervene, recognizing a scenario as involving sexual assault, and actually intervening as a bystander. Where possible, we have included illustrative quotes when students chose to elaborate on their responses. We explored all reports on the basis of gender and sexual identity. The research questions and hypotheses were as follows:

> RQ1: What proportion of students witnessed a sexual assault (or potential sexual assault)?
>
> RQ2: What proportion of students who witnessed an assault (or potential assault) intervened as a bystander, decided not to intervene (i.e., missed opportunities), or ultimately decided that they

had misconstrued the interaction (i.e., re-evaluated)?

RQ3: What reasons did students give for their decisions not to intervene?

RQ4: Which individual and contextual factors were associated with reports of witnessing a sexual assault, willingness to intervene, and intervening as a bystander?

H1: Lower rape myth endorsement, perceiving peers as supportive of bystander intervention as a norm, higher self-efficacy regarding preventing sexual assault, stronger perception of assault as a student problem, personal history of assault, and knowledge of another student's sexual assault will predict having perceived a sexual assault was underway and having a greater willingness to intervene.

H2: Knowing the victim of a sexual assault will be associated with greater odds, while knowing the perpetrator of a sexual assault will be associated with lower odds of having intervened as a bystander to help prevent a sexual assault.

METHOD

Participants

A study of attitudes and experiences of sexual assault included a sample of 1,219 college students (801 women, 401 men, 3 transgender men, 4 transgender women, and 10 not specified). In addition, 81.6% identified as heterosexual, 8.3% as bisexual, 2.9% as gay or lesbian, 0.8% as asexual, and 7.0% as other (i.e., unknown, unlabeled, or questioning). Eligibility requirements included being currently enrolled as a student and being at least 19 years old. Ages ranged from 19 to 62 years (M = 23.14, SD = 6.06). Most (80.3%) were undergraduate (vs. graduate) students. Overall, 85.7% identified as White/Caucasian, 6.6% as Asian, 1.3% as African origin/Black, 2.0% as Aboriginal, 2.3% as biracial/multiracial, and

1.9% indicated mixed or other racial/ethnic backgrounds. This race/ethnicity breakdown is characteristic of the larger college population. The college itself is the oldest public university in North America and is situated in a region of Canada that is predominantly European Canadian. The proportion of women who participated in the current study was higher than the proportion representative of the institution (49.7% women). No information regarding the prevalence of sexual violence at this institution was available. Bystander intervention programming was not offered at the institution before this study.

Measures

Demographic questionnaire. An experimenter-derived questionnaire was used to obtain demographic information, including age, sex (male, female), gender (man, woman, transgender man, transgender woman, other), race/ethnicity, and sexual identity (heterosexual, lesbian, gay, bisexual, asexual, questioning, don't know, no labels preferred, other). Information was gathered on participants' educational level (undergraduate, graduate/professional degree), place of residence (on or off campus), and with whom they lived (alone, roommate, friend, partner, family, other).

Bystander experiences. Items assessing whether a participant has witnessed a sexual assault were adapted from the Defense Equal Opportunity Climate Survey (White House Task Force, 2014). Participants were asked if they observed a situation that they believed was or could have led to a sexual assault while on campus or at a college-sponsored event or program. Those who had observed such a situation reported the degree of familiarity with the victim and perpetrator (e.g., stranger, student I recognized, acquaintance, friend, someone of authority, other) and reported how they responded (e.g., I stepped in and separated the people involved, I asked the person who appeared to be at risk if they needed help, I confronted the person who appeared to be causing the situation, I created a distraction, I asked others to step in as a group and diffuse the situation, I told someone in a position of authority about the situation, I considered intervening but could not safely take any action, I decided not to intervene). Those who took no action provided their reasons from a list (e.g., I didn't know how, it wasn't my business, I wasn't comfortable) with an option for "other" and a prompt to elaborate.

Rape myth attitudes. The Illinois Rape Myth Acceptance Scale Short-Form (Payne et al., 1999) is a 20-item widely adopted scale used to assess endorsement of sexual assault myths. Respondents indicate agreement from (1) *strongly disagree* to (5) *strongly agree*. Items assess attitudes that ignore the legitimacy of rape, suggest that women enjoy being raped, and suggest that women lie about or exaggerate rape. Higher scores indicate a stronger endorsement of rape myths. Given the extreme sensitivity of the items, we also collapsed rape myth acceptance into no endorsement of rape myth acceptance if they answered "strongly disagree" for each item versus some endorsement. The Cronbach alpha was .94 in the current study.

Perceived peer norms. Perceptions of peer norms were assessed by six items adapted from the Bystander Confidence Measure (White House Task Force, 2014). Items were rated from 1 (*not at all likely*) to 4 (*very likely*), with higher scores indicating stronger perceived norms for intervening when witnessing a sexual assault. An example of the items included, "Based on behavior you have observed on campus (or at events sponsored by the college), how likely are students to report other students who continue to engage in sexual harassment or unwanted sexual behaviors after having been previously confronted?" The Cronbach alpha was .78.

Perceived self-efficacy to intervene. Students' self-efficacy was measured by three items

adapted from a Readiness to Help scale (Banyard et al., 2014). An example included, "I do not think that there is much I can do about sexual violence on this campus." Responses ranged from 1 (*strongly disagree/not at all true*) to 5 (*strongly agree/entirely true*). Higher scores indicated greater self-efficacy. The Cronbach alpha was .89 for the current study.

Sexual assault awareness. Students' awareness was assessed by the item "I think that sexual violence is a problem at this college," with responses ranging from 1 (*strongly disagree/not at all true*) to 5 (*strongly agree/entirely true*). Knowledge of student sexual assault was assessed by asking participants to indicate if, during the prior year, a friend or acquaintance told them (*no/yes*) about being a victim of a sexual assault.

History of sexual assault. Using the Sexual Experiences Survey–SF Victimization (Koss et al., 2007), participants indicated any experience of five types of unwanted sexual contact (i.e., touching of a sexual nature, oral sex, vaginal sex, anal sex, and anal and vaginal penetration) since starting college (*never* to *11+ times*). As per recommended adaptations (Abbey et al., 2005), participants were asked about these forms of unwanted sexual contact under three assault conditions (taken advantage of you when you were too drunk or out of it to stop what was happening, threatened to physically harm you or someone close to you, used physical force). Unless reporting "never," participants were classified as having some history of sexual assault.

Social desirability. Social desirability was assessed by the Socially Desirable Response Set Five-Item Survey (Hays et al., 1989). Items were assessed from 1 (*definitely false*) to 5 (*definitely true*) (e.g., "No matter who I am talking to, I'm always a good listener"). Higher scores indicated greater socially desirable responses. The Cronbach alpha was .64 in the current study.

Bystander willingness. The Bystander Attitudes Scale-Revised (McMahon et al., 2014) assessed willingness to intervene in situations associated with sexual assault (e.g., check in with a friend who looks drunk when they go into a room with someone at a party). Eleven items were measured from (1) *not at all likely* to (5) *extremely likely* (Cronbach alpha = .87).

Procedure

All undergraduate and graduate students at a mid-sized comprehensive Canadian college were invited via email to participate in a confidential online survey; a second invitation was sent one week later. The study was advertised via student news, university blogs, and Facebook pages. Participants represented 12.0% of the student body. All provided consent before starting. Upon completion, participants could link to a separate page to provide their contact information and enter a lottery for a $10 gift card. All procedures were approved by the research ethics board.

Data Analyses

We first predicted reports of witnessing a sexual assault as a bystander (witnessed) using logistic regression analyses. Predictors were rape myth attitudes, perceived peer norms, self-efficacy, degree sexual assault is perceived to be a problem for students, own sexual assault history, and knowledge of another's sexual assault by gender (men, women) and by sexual identity (heterosexual, sexual minority). We used the same variables to predict willingness to intervene using separate hierarchical linear regression analyses. Next, we used logistic regression analyses to predict reports of having intervened [the behavioral outcome] for the small subset who reported having witnessed a scenario involving sexual assault and who described their response (*n* = 174). In these analyses, we used familiarity with the perpetrator and victim as predictors (separate analyses for men and women and for heterosexual and sexual minority students). We controlled for age in all analyses as it is

negatively correlated with reports of willingness to intervene (Banyard & Moynihan, 2011; Diamond-Welch et al., 2016) and for socially desirable responses. We did not control for race/ethnicity as results are mixed regarding the need to do so (Hoxmeier et al., 2017) and because of limited diversity at this college. On the other hand, researchers have consistently found that men are less willing than women to intervene on behalf of another in a sexual assault scenario (Burn, 2009). A study examining perceptions of same-gender versus mixed-gender sexual assault revealed differences in the likelihood of labeling the event as assault (Ballman et al., 2016). Thus, we examined gender and sexual identity as moderators.

RESULTS

Bystander Experiences

With regard to RQ1, a notable minority of participants (*n* = 184; 15.1%) indicated that they had witnessed a sexual assault or potential assault since the start of the academic year. Of those participants, 174 reported on these experiences, and 130 (74.7%) reported that they intervened as a bystander. One third (36.8%; 64/174) reported that the person they saw being sexually assaulted was a stranger, whereas the remaining 110 students (63.2%) reported that the victim was someone they knew. Most (62.1%; 108/174) indicated that they did not know the perpetrator (vs. to some extent). With regard to RQ2, 44 of these 174 asked the person at risk if they needed help, 37 separated the people involved, 9 confronted the person causing the situation, 16 created a distraction, 7 asked peers to step in, 10 told an authority, and 7 reported "other." However, 31 decided not to intervene, and another 12 reported that they considered intervening but decided not to take any action—all missed opportunities. Among the 43 students who chose not to intervene, equal numbers indicated that they did not know how to respond or did not feel it was their business (n = 16; 37.2%). Slightly fewer students reported not feeling comfortable doing so (n = 14; 32.6%). Additionally, nine students (20.9%) re-evaluated the situation and decided it did not warrant their intervention.

Men, Women, Heterosexual and Sexual Minority-Identified Participants

The four continuous scores (rape myths, peer norm, efficacy, and awareness) varied significantly by gender, $F(4, 1178) = 28.12, p < .000$, $\eta p^2 = .087$, and by sexual identity, $F(4, 1178) = 9.50, p < .000, \eta p^2 = .031$. Women had lower rape myth endorsement (Ms = 1.29 and 1.74; $F[1, 1186] = 85.99, p < .000; \eta p^2 = .07$) and perceived norms for intervening than did men (Ms = 2.82 and 3.02; F[1, 1186] = 13.33, $p <$ .000; $\eta p^2 = .01$), but higher self-efficacy around preventing sexual assault (Ms = 3.61 and 3.20; $F[1, 1186] = 39.06, p < .000; \eta p^2 = .03$), and greater awareness of assault on campus ([Ms = 3.52 and 2.98; $F[1, 1186] = 34.24, p < .000$; $\eta p^2 = .03$). More men (87.5%) endorsed rape myths compared to women (66.1%), $\chi^2(1) = 62.56, p < .001, \eta = .23$; more women (24.0%) than men (14.9%) had been assaulted since the start of college, $\chi^2(1) = 30.91 p < .001, \eta = .16$, and were told of a sexual assault, $\chi^2(1) = 13.39$, $p < .001, \eta = .11$.

Students who identified as a sexual minority (versus heterosexual) had lower rape myth endorsement (Ms = 1.31 and 1.47; $F[1, 1186] = 21.82, p < .000; \eta p^2 = .02$) and lower perceptions of peer norms to intervene (Ms = 2.74 and 2.92; $F[1, 1186] = 11.46, p < .001$; $\eta p_2 = .01$), higher self-efficacy around preventing sexual assault generally (Ms = 3.66 and 3.42; $F[1, 1186] = 12.31, p < .000; \eta p^2 = .01$), and greater awareness of sexual assault on campus (Ms = 3.62 and 3.27; $F[1, 1186] = 18.33, p < .000; \eta p_2 = .02$). A higher proportion of heterosexual than sexual minority-identified students

(75.4% and 63.2%) reported some endorsement of rape myths, $\chi^2(1) = 13.75, p < .000, \eta = .11$. No differences were found in history of sexual assault since the start of college, $\chi^2(1) = 1.96, p = .159, \eta = .04$, but a higher proportion of sexual minority students were recently told of a friend's assault (34.2% and 18.1%), $\chi^2(1) = 28.48, p < .000, \eta = .15$.

Predicting Reports of Having Witnessed a Sexual Assault as a Bystander

For men, perceiving peers as willing to intervene was linked to lower odds of witnessing an assault (OR = 0.50) (RQ4; Table 1). One's history of assault (vs. no history) was associated with almost four times the odds of witnessing an assault (OR = 3.97) as was being told of another's assault (OR = 4.62). For women, each increase in mean self-efficacy increased the odds of witnessing an assault by 50%. History of assault doubled the odds of witnessing an assault (OR = 2.27), as did being told of a sexual assault by another (OR = 2.20). For heterosexual students, a history of assault and being told by another person of their sexual assault increased the odds of witnessing a sexual assault 2–3 times (OR = 2.36 and 2.79). For sexual minority students, perceptions that peers would intervene decreased the odds (OR = 0.52), whereas increases in self-efficacy tripled the odds (OR = 2.97), and one's history of assault quadrupled the odds (OR = 4.10) of witnessing an assault.

Predicting Bystander Willingness to Intervene

For men, rape myth attitudes, perceived peer norms, self-efficacy to intervene, and awareness of assault were each associated with bystander willingness to intervene, $F(8, 382) = 24.84$, $p = .000$ (Table 2). Lower endorsement of rape myths, stronger beliefs that peers would intervene, greater self-efficacy to intervene,

Table 1.
Logistic Regression Analyses Predicting Reports of Witnessing a Sexual Assault by Gender and Sexual Identity

Variables	Male (n = 380)			Female (n = 738)			Heterosexual (n = 926)			Sexual Minority (n = 201)		
	OR	95% CI	p	OR	95% CI	p	OR	95% CI	p	OR	95% Ci	p
Block 1	Nagelkerke R^2 = .02, p = .217			Nagelkerke R^2 = .04, p = .000			Nagelkerke R^2 = .04, p = .000			Nagelkerke R^2 = .04, p = .081		
Age	0.94	.87–1.02	.141	0.90	0.84–0.96	.001	0.90	0.84–0.95	.001	0.92	0.83–1.01	.081
Social desirability	1.12	.65–1.93	.696	1.09	0.75–1.60	.647	1.06	0.75–1.50	.751	1.28	0.68–2.40	.443
Block 2	Nagelkerke R^2 = .28, p = .000			Nagelkerke R^2 = .18, p = .000			Nagelkerke R^2 = .17, p = .000			Nagelkerke R^2 = .38, p = .000		
Rape myth attitudes	1.64	0.90–2.99	.110	0.88	0.48–1.65	.689	1.08	0.72–1.61	.721	2.25	0.72–6.99	.163
Peer norms	0.50	0.26–0.96	.037	0.79	0.58–1.07	.128	0.80	0.58–1.12	.195	0.52	0.29–0.92	.024
Self-efficacy	1.46	0.86–2.50	.164	1.54	1.12–2.12	.008	1.35	1.00–1.82	.050	2.97	1.47–6.00	.002
Awareness	1.15	0.73–1.82	.538	1.05	0.82–1.36	.685	1.07	0.84–1.37	.572	1.41	0.82–2.42	.217
Sexual assault history	3.97	1.61–9.76	.003	2.27	1.46–3.54	.000	2.36	1.49–3.72	.000	4.10	1.75–9.61	.001
Told of sexual assault	4.62	1.93–11.10	.001	2.20	1.41–3.44	.000	2.79	1.75–4.44	.000	1.90	0.82–4.39	.133

and greater awareness of assault as a problem predicted greater willingness among men to intervene. For women, lower rape myth endorsement, stronger beliefs that peers would intervene, greater self-efficacy, and being told of a sexual assault predicted willingness to intervene, $F(8, 740) = 37.25$, $p = .000$. The pattern of results for heterosexual students was similar to that of men: Lower endorsement of rape myths, beliefs that peers would intervene, greater self-efficacy, and greater awareness of sexual assault predicted willingness to intervene, $F(8, 930) = 64.48$, $p = .000$. The pattern for sexual minority participants was different, however. Only lower rape myth endorsement and higher self-efficacy predicted willingness to intervene, $F(8, 201) = 16.10$, $p = .000$.

Predicting Reports of Bystander Intervention Behavior

For men, intervening on behalf of a victim was not predicted by the extent to which the respondent knew the victim (Table 3). For women and heterosexual students, each increase in the degree of familiarity with the victim almost doubled the odds of intervening (OR = 1.89 and 1.90). Among sexual minority students, knowing the victim increased the odds of intervening seven times (OR = 7.05). Knowing the perpetrator was not associated with helping a victim for any group.

DISCUSSION

This study was designed to assess students' bystander experiences of witnessing the sexual assault (or potential assault) of a peer, their willingness to intervene, and actual efforts to that end. Our study indicates that sexual violence continues to be a serious problem for young people, as others consistently have found (CDC, 2022; Muehlenhard et al., 2017). One in five students had been assaulted since starting college, and a similar proportion reported

learning of another's assault. Most perceived sexual violence to be a problem for students, but even so, 72% endorsed rape myths to some degree, typically beliefs that women enjoy or are responsible for rape.

Witnessing Sexual Assault or Potential Sexual Assault

A minority of students (15%) reported that they had witnessed a recent situation that involved sexual assault. This rate is lower than previous work that found 40% of students had witnessed a sexual assault (Hoxmeier et al., 2017b). Our participants were asked to recall events since the start of the academic year. This rate might be comparable to previous research if they were asked to report at the end of the academic year—after eight months—instead of throughout the academic year.

Of those who reported on the events that they witnessed, almost two thirds stated that the sexual assault involved a victim who was a friend or acquaintance, yet only one third indicated that they knew the perpetrator. Students may be more vigilant to potential assaults when socializing in groups that include strangers, even though most assaults involve known assailants (Koss et al., 1987). They might be less aware of or able to discern the assault actions or intentions among those individuals who they know. Practitioners should take this finding to heart and help educate students about the most common characteristics of sexual assault scenarios, especially emphasizing the heightened risk associated with alcohol use in social situations (Abbey et al., 2014).

Who was most likely to have witnessed sexual assault? A clear pattern emerged: a peer's or one's own history of assault doubled to quadruple the odds of witnessing an assault. We cannot, of course, be sure that they accurately perceived a situation to involve a sexual assault, but this may indicate that students who had supported a peer or been assaulted themselves

Table 2.
Hierarchical Linear Regression Analyses Predicting Bystander Willingness

Variables	Men (n = 380)				Women (n = 738)				Heterosexual (n = 926)				Sexual Minority (n = 201)			
	r	β	sr	ΔR²	r	β	sr	ΔR²	r	β	sr	ΔR²	r	β	sr	ΔR²
Controls				.08***				.03***				.05***				.09***
Age	.03	.05	—		.00	.01	—		.01	.02			-.13*	-.07		
Social desirability	.27	.27***	—		.18***	.18***	—		.23***	.23***			.29***	.27***		
Variables				.27***				.28**				.30***				.31***
Rape myth	-.36***	-.20***	-.17		-.34***	-.24***	-.22		-.44***	-.30***	-.28		-.33***	-.18*	-.16	
Peer norms	.05	.11*	.11		.03	.08*	.08		.00	.09**	.08		-.01	.02	.02	
Self-efficacy	.48	.35***	.31		.46***	.37***	.32		.49***	.34***	.29		.55***	.45***	.40	
Awareness	.33***	.18**	.15		.23***	.01	.00		.32***	.09**	.07		.30***	.06	.04	
Assault history	-.04	-.06	-.06		.07*	-.01	-.01		.11**	.01	.01		.02	-.07	-.07	
Told of assault	.17	.03	.03		.15***	.09*	.08		.16***	.05	.05		.16*	.05	.04	

*p < .05. **p < .01. ***p < .001.

Table 3.

Logistic Regression Analyses Predicting Reports of Bystander Intervention Behavior in Sexual Assault Situations

Variables	Men (n = 33)			Women (n = 118)			Heterosexual (n = 110)			Sexual Minority (n = 43)		
	OR	95% CI	p	OR	95% CI	p	OR	95% CI	p	OR	95% CI	p
Block 1		Nagelkerke R^2 = .13, p = .236			Nagelkerke R^2 = .01, p = .590			Nagelkerke R^2 = .04, p = .241			Nagelkerke R^2 = .16, p = .082	
Age	0.99	0.83–1.17	.864	.99	0.86–1.14	.910	.940	0.84–1.05	.266	1.33	0.94–1.89	.106
Social desirability	2.57	0.83–7.96	.101	1.56	0.66–3.72	.314	1.68	0.77–3.68	.196	2.01	0.59–6.85	.264
Block 2		Nagelkerke R^2 = .48, p = .008			Nagelkerke R^2 = .19, p = .000			Nagelkerke R^2 =.26, p = .001			Nagelkerke R^2 = .44, p = .006	
Knew victim	5.33	0.82–34.60	.080	1.89	1.30–2.76	.001	1.90	1.27–2.83	.002	7.05	1.10–45.06	.039
Knew perpetrator	0.55	0.09–3.06	.482	1.07	0.61–1.85	.821	1.42	0.72–2.82	.312	0.32	0.07–1.46	.141

Note. All students reported having witnessed a sexual assault (or potential assault) situation.

were better able to make this determination and were more vigilant or sensitized to warning signs compared to those with no experience. For practitioners, though, questions remain as to how we can shift the burden away from those with histories so that all share a responsibility to intervene. Effective communication of the characteristics of assaults among the students of a given college (or else collectively across regional colleges), including prevalence, victim–perpetrator relationship, and the social contexts of assaults, would help educate and sensitize students to scenarios with the potential for assault. Emphasizing peer norms, in line with our theoretical framework, and providing information about how others believe it is important to intervene in situations where people may be distracted and overlook an assault incident that is underway will be important. Addressing common violence-related cognitions (e.g., rape myths, hostile attitudes, victim blaming), especially among all-male peer groups, and emphasizing peer disapproval of forced sex will help offset initial hesitation to intervene.

That would not be enough, of course. Correctly interpreting a situation as requiring intervention and believing oneself able to intervene are central features of the bystander model. Senn et al. (2015) developed an efficacious prevention program that teaches college women to trust their instincts about unsafe situations. Higher perceived self-efficacy to intervene was related to greater odds of having witnessed a sexual assault for women but almost three times greater odds for those who identified as a sexual minority individual. Those who feel they could effectively intervene may be better able to recognize when an assault is underway and be better positioned to intervene. Identifying campus contexts or policies that increase the risk for violence, including perceptions of administration disinterest, while improving campus inclusivity and distributing assault policies and procedures in poster campaigns or social media will provide the scaffolding necessary to prompt individual action (Bonar et al., 2020).

Contrary to our expectations, both awareness of sexual assault as a problem on campus and endorsing rape myths were unrelated to having witnessed an assault for all groups. Perhaps recognizing that an assault is underway is unrelated to attributions of responsibility or feelings that helping a victim is warranted. Believing one's peers would intervene lowered the odds of reporting an assault (as we anticipated) by half for men and sexual minority-identified students. Others have found that men's perception of peers' willingness to intervene was predictive of their own willingness to intervene (Austin et al., 2016; Brown & Messman-Moore, 2010) in line with social norms theory (Berkowitz, 2003). This finding may reflect a diffusion of responsibility effect: believing one's peers would intervene to stop an assault may lead to attenuated attention to potential assaults. It would be important to break this down further in research to help ensure we do not reinforce beliefs about willingness rather than actual efforts.

Decisions to Intervene on Behalf of a Victim

Addressing our second and third research questions, we found that 69% of those who had witnessed a sexual assault indicated that they intervened on behalf of the victim. Students reported that they were most likely to use direct forms of intervention, such as asking the victim if they were okay, stepping in, or removing the person from the situation. They reported few indirect efforts, such as distracting the perpetrator, asking others to help, or telling an authority. Indirect forms of intervention like these should be taught as they can be highly effective and are often a reasonable choice if harm to the bystander is a possibility.

However, approximately 30% of students elected not to intervene (usually because they did not know how, thought it was inappropriate, or felt uncomfortable) or else considered intervening or re-evaluated the scenario as not warranting intervention after all. Re-evaluating the scenario calls into question the decision-making factors individuals use to judge whether a sexual assault is underway, as well as whether individuals are more prone to dismissing evidence of a potential assault relative to other crimes, topics that need to be addressed in future research. We focused on the degree of familiarity with the individuals involved. Knowing the victim or perpetrator did not predict whether men tried to help. In fact, knowing the perpetrator did not predict intervention for any of the four groups. However, knowing the victim doubled the odds ..at women and heterosexual-identified students helped, and of particular note, increased odds over seven times among those who identified as sexual minorities. Individuals likely experience stronger empathic responses when someone close to them is in danger. We know bystanders are more likely to intervene when they perceive a victim to belong to their own group (Levine et al., 2002). Women and sexual minority students might help those in their network because they are, in fact, at heightened risk for assault in general. These findings underscore the value of knowing about peers' experiences as a prompt to help.

Perceiving Oneself as Willing to Intervene to Prevent Sexual Assault

Research on prosocial behaviors has made clear that a necessary precursor to helping behavior is the willingness to intervene—a factor most closely linked to perceived intentions to intervene on behalf of another (Brown & Messman-Moore, 2010). In line with our conceptual framework and research on intentions (Banyard et al., 2014; Brown & Messman-Moore, 2010; Salazar et al., 2014), lower rape myth endorsement and higher perceived self-efficacy to prevent sexual assault were key predictors of

willingness to intervene for each of our four groups: men, women, heterosexual, and sexual minority-identified students.

For all groups (except those who identified as a sexual minority), perceptions that one's peers would intervene predicted greater willingness to intervene (despite a lower actual likelihood of recognizing an assault was underway). Bystanders' willingness to intervene does not ensure actual helping because they also must recognize an assault is underway and take responsibility while not assuming that someone else will intervene. Perceiving peer support for bystander intervention can reinforce one's belief that one would intervene. Given the sensitivity of sexual assault and the high risks associated with stopping a potential encounter in terms of perpetrator retaliation, anger, and intimidation, alignment in own and peer behavior seems a necessary precursor to actually helping. Research is needed to explore ways to promote convergence here.

Believing that sexual assault is a common and serious problem among students proved a meaningful predictor of willingness to intervene for men and heterosexual students. Denying the reality of sexual assault may promote the endorsement of harmful rape myths, increase victim blaming, and delegitimization of known assaults. Those told of an assault directly may feel heightened vulnerability relative to hearing about an assault through secondary sources, such as gossip. Researchers should assess how learning of an assault directly or indirectly influences willingness to intervene. Interviews of victim–supporter pairs found supporters' own perceptions of risk and threat were heightened by these experiences (O'Callaghan et al., 2019).

Study Limitations and Future Directions

The sample size was not sufficiently large to explore links between all factors and actual intervention behaviors. Greater diversity, especially racial and ethnic diversity, is needed in future research. We used a convenience sample, which was likely subject to volunteer biases, and relied on self-reports that could have been biased despite controlling for socially desirable responses. Even though this study investigated recent as compared to distal experiences or hypothetical scenarios, it was still retrospective and thus limited by recall. A prospective study of best intervention strategies (e.g., causing a distraction) would be valuable.

Teaching students how to recognize and be alert to the range of potential assault scenarios would help them to correctly interpret problematic scenarios. Our findings indicate that a social norms approach—one that reinforces perceptions that sexual assault is common among one's peers and that it is normative (and morally imperative) to help could improve willingness to intervene—an approach Linder (2018) recommends. However, such programming also needs to reinforce students' perceived self-efficacy to intervene. Training in the range of direct and indirect intervention strategies (e.g., Right to Be, n.d.), using in-person and computer-enhanced role-play simulations, as well as reviewing testimonials of students who incorporated effective strategies, could improve actual readiness to intervene. Testimonials allow educators to explicitly name the power dynamics that reify rape myths while making clear that sexual assault surrounds student life (Linder, 2018). Online training in groups would reinforce cooperative aspects of peer intervention. Rather than mandatory training, such as those offered during college orientation, student affairs practitioners could offer creative incentives (e.g., tuition credit, lotteries) to encourage participation in workshops throughout the academic year, integrating messages into online social media used to communicate with students to ensure broad and consistent exposure.

In conclusion, substantial numbers of college students experience incidents of sexual violence either firsthand or as witnesses. Students who perceived a sexual assault was underway appeared likely to intervene in some way. This study is one of the first to compare reports of bystander decisions to intervene or not to intervene across groups. These insights may help mitigate the considerable harm of sexual assault in efforts to generate a viable means of reducing the consistently high rates that plague the lives of young people.

Correspondence concerning this article should be addressed to Lucia F. O'Sullivan, University of New Brunswick; osulliv@unb.ca

REFERENCES

Abbey, A., Parkhill, M. R., & Koss, M. P. (2005). The effects of frame of reference on responses to questions about sexual assault victimization and perpetration. *Psychology of Women Quarterly, 29*(4), 364–373. https://doi.org/10.1111/j.1471-6402.2005.00236.x

Abbey, A., Wegner, R., Woerner, J., Pegram, S. E., Pierce, J. (2014). Review of survey and experimental research that examines the relationship between alcohol consumption and men's sexual aggression perpetration. *Trauma, Violence, & Abuse, 15*(4), 265–282. https://dx.doi.org/10.1177/1524838014521031

Amar, A. F., Sutherland, M., & Laughon, K. (2014). Gender differences in attitudes and beliefs associated with bystander behavior and sexual assault. *Journal of Forensic Nursing, 10*(2), 84–91. https://doi.org/10.1097/JFN.0000000000000024

Austin, M. J. M., Dardis, C. M., Wilson, M. S., Gidycz, C. A., & Berkowitz, A. D. (2016). Predictors of sexual assault–specific prosocial bystander behavior and intentions: A prospective analysis. *Violence Against Women, 22*(1), 90–111. https://doi.org/10.1177/1077801215597790

Ballman, A. D., Leheney, E. K., Miller, K. E., Simmons, B. L., & Wilson, L. C. (2016). Bystander perceptions of same-gender versus mixed-gender rape: A pilot study. *Journal of Aggression, Maltreatment & Trauma, 25*(10), 1079–1096. https://doi.org/10.1080/10926771.2016.1228019

Banyard, V. L. (2008). Measurement and correlates of prosocial bystander behavior: The case of interpersonal violence. *Violence and Victims, 23*(1), 85–99. https://doi.org/10.1891/0886-6708.23.1.83

Banyard, V. L., & Moynihan, M. M. (2011). Variation in bystander behavior related to sexual and intimate partner violence prevention: Correlates in a sample of college students. *Psychology of Violence, 1*(4), 287–301. doi: http://dx.doi.org/10.1037/a0023544

Banyard, V. L., Moynihan, M. M., Cares, A. C., & Warner, R. (2014). How do we know it works? Measuring outcomes in bystander-focused abuse prevention on campus. *Psychology of Violence, 4*(1), 101–115. https://doi.org/10.1037/a0033470

Banyard, V. L., Moynihan, M. M., & Grossman, M. T. (2009). Reducing sexual violence on campus: The role of student leaders as empowered bystanders. *Journal of College Student Development, 50*(4), 446–457. https://doi.org/10.1353/csd.0.0083

Barone, R. P., Wolgemuth, J. R., & Linder, C. (2007). Preventing sexual assault through engaging college men. *Journal of College Student Development, 48*(5), 585–594. https://doi.org/10.1353/csd.2007.0045

Bennett, S., Banyard, V. L., & Edwards, K. M. (2017). The impact of the bystander's relationship with the victim and the perpetrator on intent to help in situations involving sexual violence. *Journal of Interpersonal Violence, 32*(5), 682–702. https://doi.org/10.1177/0886260515586373

Bennett, S., Banyard, V. L., & Garnhart, L. (2014). To act or not to act, that is the question? Barriers and facilitators of bystander intervention. *Journal of Interpersonal Violence, 29*(3), 476–496. https://doi.org/10.1177/0886260513505210

Berkowitz, A. D. (2003). Applications of social norms theory to other health and social justice issues. In H. W. Perkins (Ed.), *The social norms approach to preventing school and college age substance abuse: A handbook for educators, counselors, and clinicians* (pp. 259–279). Jossey-Bass.

Bonar, E. E., DeGue, S., Abbey, A., Coker, A. L., Lindquist, C. H., McCauley, H. L., Miller, E., Senn, C. Y., Thompson, M. P., Ngo, Q. M., Cunningham, R. M., & Walton, M. A. (2020). Prevention of sexual violence among college students: Current challenges and future directions. *Journal of American College Health.* Advance online publication. https://doi.org/10.1080/07448481.2020.1757681

Brown, A. L., & Messman-Moore, T. L. (2010). Personal and perceived peer attitudes supporting sexual aggression as predictors of male college students' willingness to intervene against sexual aggression. *Journal of Interpersonal Violence, 25*(3), 503–517. https://doi.org/10.1177/0886260509334400

Brown, A. L., Banyard, V. L., & Moynihan, M. M. (2014). College students as helpful bystanders against sexual violence: Gender, race, and year in college moderate the impact of perceived peer norms. *Psychology of Women Quarterly, 38*(3), 350–362. https://doi.org/10.1177/0361684314526855

Burn, S. M. (2009). A situational model of sexual assault prevention through bystander intervention. *Sex Roles, 60*(11–12), 779–792. https://doi.org/10.1007/s11199-008-9581-5

Cantor, D., Fisher, B., Chibnall, S., Harps, S., Townsend, R., Thomas, G., Lee, H., Kranz, V., Herbison, R., & Madden, K. (2020, January 17). *Report on the AAU Campus Climate Survey on Sexual Assault and Misconduct.* Association of American Universities, Westat. https://www.aau.edu/sites/default/files/AAU-Files/Key-Issues/Campus-Safety/Revised%20Aggregate%20report%20%20and%20appendices%201-7_(01-16-2020_FINAL).pdf

Centers for Disease Control and Prevention (2022). *Fast facts: Preventing sexual violence.* https://www.cdc.gov/violenceprevention/sexualviolence/fastfact.htmlCenters for Disease Control and Prevention (2015). *Sexual assault: Prevention strategies.* www.cdc.gov/ViolencePrevention/sexualviolence/prevention.html

Cialdini, R. B., & Trost, M. R. (1998). Social influence, social norms, conformity and compliance. In D. T. Gilbert, S. T. Fiske, & G. Lindzey (Eds.), *The Handbook of Social Psychology* (pp. 151–192). McGraw-Hill.

Diamond-Welch, B., Hetzel-Riggin, M. D., & Hemingway, J. A. (2016). The willingness of college students to intervene in sexual assault situations: Attitudes and behavior differences by gender, race, age, and community of origin. *Violence and Gender, 3*(1), doi: 10.1089/vio.2015.0023

Exner, D., & Cummings, N. (2011). Implications for sexual assault prevention: College students as prosocial bystanders. *Journal of American College Health, 59*(7), 655–657. https://doi.org/10.1080/07448481.2010.515633

Fedina, L., Holmes, J. L., & Backes, B. L. (2018). Campus sexual assault: A systematic review of prevalence research from 2000 to 2015. *Trauma, Violence, & Abuse, 19*(1), 76–93. https://doi.org/10.1177/1524838016631129

Ford, J., & Soto-Marquez, J. G. (2016). Sexual assault victimization among straight, gay/lesbian, and bisexual college students. *Violence and Gender, 3*(2), 107–115. https://doi.org/10.1089/vio.2015.0030

Hays, R. D., Hayashi, T., & Stewart, A. L. (1989). A five-item measure of socially desirable response set. *Educational and Psychological Measurement, 49*(3), 629–636. https://doi.org/10.1177/001316448904900315

Hoxmeier, J. C., Acock, A. C., & Flay, B. R. (2017a). Students as prosocial bystanders to sexual assault: Demographic correlates of intervention norms, intentions, and missed opportunities. *Journal of Interpersonal Violence, 35*(3–4), 731–754. https://doi.org/10.1177/0886260517689888

Hoxmeier, J. C., McMahon, S., & O'Connor, J. (2017b). Beyond yes or no: Understanding undergraduate students' responses as bystanders to sexual assault risk situations. *Journal of Interpersonal Violence, 35*(23–24), 5772–5796. https://doi.org/10.1177/0886260517723143

Hoxmeier, J. C., O'Connor, J., & McMahon, S. (2019). 'She wasn't resisting': Students' barriers to prosocial intervention as bystanders to sexual assault risk situations. *Violence Against Women, 25*(4), 485–505. http://dx.doi.org/10.1177/1077801218790697

Katz, J., & Moore, J. (2013). Bystander education training for campus sexual assault prevention: An initial meta-analysis. *Violence and Victims, 28*(6), 1054–1067. https://doi.org/10.1891/0886-6708.VV-D-12-00113

Katz, J., Olin, R., Herman, C., & DuBois, M. (2013). Spotting the signs: First-year college students' responses to bystander-themed rape prevention posters. *Journal of Community Psychology, 41*(4), 523–529. https://doi.org/10.1002/jcop.21552

Kleinsasser, A., Jouriles, E. N., McDonald, R., Rosenfield, D. (2015). An online bystander intervention program for the prevention of sexual violence. *Psychology of Violence, 5*(3), 227–235. doi: http://dx.doi.org/10.1037/a0037393

Koss, M. P., Abbey, A., Campbell, R., Cook, S., Norris, J., Testa, M., Ullman, S., West, C., & White, J. (2007). Revising the SES: A collaborative process to improve assessment of sexual aggression and victimization. *Psychology of Women Quarterly, 31*(4), 357–370. https://doi.org/10.1111/j.1471-6402.2007.00385.x

Koss, M. P., Gidycz, C., & Wisniewski, N. (1987). The scope of rape: Incidence and prevalence of sexual aggression and victimization in a national sample of higher education students. *Journal of Consulting and Clinical Psychology, 55*(2), 162–170. https://doi.org/10.1037/0022-006X.55.2.162

Labhardt, D., Holdsworth, E., Brown, S., & Howat, D. (2017). You see but you do not observe: A review of bystander intervention and sexual assault on university campuses. *Aggression and Violent Behavior, 35*, 13–25. https://doi.org/10.1016/j.avb.2017.05.005

Latané, B., & Darley, J. M. (1970). *The unresponsive bystander: Why doesn't he help?* Appleton-Century-Crofts.

Levine, M., Cassidy, C., Brazier, G., & Reischer, S. (2002). Self-categorization and bystander non-intervention: Two experimental studies. *Journal of Applied Social Psychology, 32*(7), 1452–1463. https://doi.org/10.1111/j.1559-1816.2002.tb01446.x

Linder, C. (2018). *Sexual violence on campus: Power-conscious approaches to awareness, prevention, and response.* Emerald Publishing.

McMahon, S. (2010). Rape myth beliefs and bystander attitudes among incoming college students. *Journal of American College Health, 59*(1), 3–11. doi: http://dx.doi.org/10.1080/07448481.2010.483715

McMahon, S., Allen, C. T., Postmus, J. L., McMahon, S. M., Peterson, N. A., & Lowe Hoffman, M. (2014). Measuring bystander attitudes and behavior to prevent sexual violence. *Journal of American College Health, 62*(1), 58–66. https://doi.org/10.1080/07448481.2013.849258

McMahon, S., Banyard, V. L., & McMahon, S. M. (2015). Incoming college students' bystander behaviors to prevent sexual violence. *Journal of College Student Development, 56*(5), 488–493. https://doi.org/10.1353/csd.2015.0050

Mellins, C. A., Walsh, K., Sarvet, A. L., Wall, M., Gilbert, L., Santelli, J. S., Thompson, M., Wilson, P. A., Khan, S., Benson, S., Bah, K., Kaufman, K. A., Reardon, L., & Hirsch, J. S. (2017). Sexual assault incidents among college undergraduates: Prevalence and factors associated with risk. *PLoS One, 12*(11). https://doi.org/10.1371/journal.pone.0186471

Moreau, G. (2019, July 22). Police-reported crime statistics in Canada, 2018 (Catalogue no. 85-002-X). Statistics Canada. https://www150.statcan.gc.ca/n1/pub/85-002-x/2019001/article/00013-eng.htm

Muehlenhard, C. L., Peterson, Z. D., Humphreys, T. P., & Jozkowski, K. N. (2017). Evaluating the one-in-five statistic: Women's risk of sexual assault while in college. *Journal of Sex Research, 54*(4–5), 549–576. https://doi.org/10.1080/00224499.2017.1295014

Nicksa, S. C. (2014). Bystander's willingness to report theft, physical assault, and sexual assault: The impact of gender, anonymity, and relationship with the offender. *Journal of Interpersonal Violence, 29*(2), 217–236. https://doi.org/10.1177/0886260513505146

O'Callaghan, E., Shepp, V., Ullman, S. E., & Kirkner, A. (2019). Navigating sex and sexuality after sexual assault: A qualitative study of survivors and informal support providers. *Journal of Sex Research, 56*(8), 1045–1057. https://doi.org/10.1080/00224499.2018.1506731

Orchowski, L. M., Edwards, K. M., Hollander, J. A., Banyard, V. L., Senn, C. Y., & Gidycz, C. A. (2020). Integrating sexual assault resistance, bystander, and men's social norms strategies to prevent sexual violence on college campuses: A call to action. *Trauma, Violence, & Abuse, 21*(4), 811–827. https://doi.org/10.1177/1524838018789153

Payne, D. L., Lonsway, K. A., & Fitzgerald, L. F. (1999). Rape myth acceptance: Exploration of its structure and its measurement using the Illinois rape myth acceptance scale. *Journal of Research in Personality, 33*(1), 27–68. https://doi.org/10.1006/jrpe.1998.2238

Planty, M. (2002). *Third-party involvement in violent crime, 1993–1999.* (Bureau of Justice Statistics Special Report). U.S. Department of Justice.

RAINN. (n.d.). *Campus sexual violence: Statistics.* Retrieved February 25, 2023, from https://www.rainn.org/statistics/campus-sexual-violence

Right to Be. (n.d.). Bystander intervention. Retrieved February 12, 2023, https://righttobe.org/bystander-intervention-training/

Salazar, L. F., Vivolo-Kantor, A., Hardin, J., & Berkowitz, A. (2014). A web-based sexual violence bystander intervention for male college students: Randomized controlled trial. *Journal of Medical Internet Research, 16*(9), e203. https://doi.org/10.2196/jmir.3426

Senn, C. Y., Eliasziw, M., Barata, P. C., Thurston, W. E., Newby-Clark, I. R., Radtke, H. L., & Hobden, K. L. (2015). Efficacy of a sexual assault resistance program for university women. *New England Journal of Medicine, 372*, 2326–2335. https://doi.org/10.1056/NEJMsa1411131

Sutton, S. (2006). Predicting and explaining intentions and behavior: How well are we doing? *Journal of Applied Social Psychology, 28*(5), 1317–1338. doi: 10.111/j.1559-1816.1998.tb01679.x

Statista. (2019). *College & university – statistics and facts.* https://www.statista.com/topics/829/college-and-university

Telzer, E. H., Van Hoorn, J., Rogers, C. R., & Do, K. T. (2018). Social influence on positive youth development: A developmental neuroscience perspective. *Advances in Child Development and Behavior, 54*, 215–258. https://doi.org/10.1016/bs.acdb.2017.10.003

Thompson, A., & Tapp, S. N. (2022, September). *Criminal victimization, 2021.* Bureau of Justice Statistics, U.S. Department of Justice. https://bjs.ojp.gov/content/pub/pdf/cv21.pdf

University of Victoria (2021). Bystander intervention. https://www.uvic.ca/services/studentlife/initiatives/bystander-intervention/index.php

The White House. (2014, April 29). *Not alone—Protecting students from sexual assault.* https://obamawhitehouse.archives.gov/the-press-office/2014/04/29/fact-sheet-not-alone-protecting-students-sexual-assault

White House Task Force to Protect Students from Sexual Assault. (2014). *Climate surveys: Useful tools to help colleges and universities in their efforts to reduce and prevent sexual assault.* https://www.justice.gov/archives/ovw/page/file/910426/download

Yule, K., & Grych, J. (2020). College students' perceptions of barriers to bystander intervention. *Journal of Interpersonal Violence, 35*(15–16), 2971–2992. https://doi.org/10.1177/0886260517706764

Research in Brief   Jason C. Garvey, EXECUTIVE ASSOCIATE EDITOR

Estimating Differences in the Effects of Living–Learning Community Participation on Black Students' Sense of Belonging at Predominantly White and Historically Black Colleges and Universities

Terrell L. Strayhorn

Strong social connections and supportive relationships with others on campus have been consistently linked with college students' sense of belonging, a major correlate of educational success (Strayhorn, 2019). Sense of belonging refers to the "psychological sense that one is a valued member of the college community" (Hausmann et al., 2007, p. 804). It is, indeed, "a feeling that members matter to one another . . . and a shared faith that members' needs will be met through their commitment to be together" (Strayhorn, 2019, p. 11). Although a basic human need, belonging takes on heightened importance in some college settings, especially for ethnoracial minorities in majority institutions such as Black students at predominantly White institutions (PWIs), professional schools (Strayhorn, 2020a), and historically Black colleges and universities (HBCUs) (Strayhorn, 2021). The weight of empirical evidence consistently shows that Black students' sense of belonging, like their non-Black peers, is positively associated with critical learning and development

outcomes, including grades, identity, and persistence (Jessup-Anger et al., 2012; Maestas et al., 2007; Rhee, 2008; Strayhorn, 2020b).

Prior scholarship has established that myriad factors shape college students' sense of belonging, including aspects of one's campus environment, namely students' living arrangements and learning conditions (Johnson et al., 2007). To this end, many colleges and universities established cultural centers, first-year seminars within year-long experiences, and living–learning communities (LLCs)[1] as high-impact practices (i.e., time-intensive academic experiences that provide structured opportunities potent for catalyzing growth; Kuh & O'Donnell, 2013; Kuh et al., 2017) that connect academic and social aspects of college life, emphasize certain learning foci, and provide supportive social networks for students to engage in challenging educational opportunities (Inkelas & Weisman, 2003). Such initiatives are also increasingly present at HBCUs (Strayhorn, 2021). Existing research has demonstrated the

---

[1] LLCs are typically defined as "a group of students who live together in the same on-campus building and share similar academic or special interests" (Inkelas et al., 2018, p. 1).

Terrell L. Strayhorn is Professor of Higher Education & Women's, Gender & Sexuality Studies at Illinois State University and Director of Center for the Study of HBCUs and Visiting Scholar at Virginia Union University.

many academic, cognitive, and socioemotional gains that accrue to students in LLCs compared to their non-LLC peers (Johnson et al., 2007; Inkelas & Weisman, 2003).

Whereas the weight of empirical evidence suggests learning communities are effective (Museus & Chang, 2021), innovative tools for reinvigorating undergraduate education and promoting student success, causal studies indicate that the on-campus, residential component of LLCs is key (Caviglia-Harris, 2021; Inkelas et al., 2006). Existing research on LLCs has burgeoned since their emergence in the 1980s. Today, LLCs vary considerably in terms of structure and organization (Inkelas & Soldner, 2011). LLCs are increasingly utilized to deepen and enrich students' collegiate experiences (Matthews et al., 2012). For example, Jessup-Anger et al. (2019) analyzed qualitative interview data from 8 sophomore students (5 women, 3 men) at a private Catholic PWI. They found that students attributed growth in their understanding of social justice issues and increased capacity for civic engagement to their LLC participation. Students also credited their LLC experiences with helping them to develop stronger community values and skills in making social connections.

With notable exceptions, very few investigations have focused on the link between LLC participation and students' sense of belonging, especially at minority-serving institutions (MSIs) like HBCUs. Hoffman et al. (2002) analyzed data from an East Coast PWI and found that LLC students scored higher than non-LLC peers on sense of belonging. Similar results were found for LLC students at public, research-intensive institutions (Inkelas et al., 2007). To our knowledge and following an extensive search of education databases

(Strayhorn et al., in press), no studies exist comparing the influences of LLC participation on Black students' sense of belonging at HBCUs and PWIs, despite decades of research showing that Black students' experiences vary by campus racial composition (Patton et al., 2011). This is the gap addressed by the present study.

The purpose of this study was to estimate differences in the relationship between LLC participation and sense of belonging in college for Black students at HBCUs and PWIs. Because prior studies have shown differences across gender[2] (Garvey et al., 2020), we controlled for this variable in the multivariate analyses. A single research question guided the study: Does Black students' sense of belonging vary by LLC participation and campus racial composition, controlling for gender?

METHODS

This study is based on an analysis of large-scale data from a recent administration of the National Survey of Student Engagement (NSSE), sponsored by the Center for Postsecondary Research at Indiana University (for more, see NSSE, 2021). The larger study surveyed 44,000 students enrolled at 650 US universities, but this analysis is based only on Black respondents living on-campus at HBCUs and PWIs. Constraining the investigation in this way eliminated several mediating factors—namely, residential status and campus dominant racial composition (Patton et al., 2011)—that threaten internal validity. A total of 17,326 Black students were included in the sample, of which 71% were women and 29% were men, reflecting their representation nationally (U.S. Department of Education, 2020). Additional sample characteristics are summarized in Table 1.

---

[2] In this analysis, gender is defined as "gender identity" on the survey, assessed as "man," "woman," and "another gender identity," which includes nonbinary, gender fluid, agender, transgender, genderqueer, among others, in keeping with prior research on gender-variant students (BrckaLorenz et al., 2017).

Table 1.
Description of the Analytic Sample

Characteristic	HBCU		PWI	
	N	%	*N*	%
Gender	2153	76	10049	70
Women	692	24	4285	30
Men	3	< 1	50	< 1
Gender-Variant				
Age	1317	46	5124	36
19 or younger	969	34	3919	27
20–23 years	547	19	5225	37
24 and older				
FG	827	29	4707	33
Yes	2013	70	9641	67
No				
Sense of Belonging	*M*	*(SD)*	*M*	*(SD)*
LLC	42.16	(12.33)	44.35	(11.57)
Non-LLC	37.28	(12.45)	41.56	(12.43)

Note. FG = first-generation status defined as neither parent attended college. Numbers may not equal 100 due to rounding.

Sense of belonging was assessed using five items. Individual responses to each item were averaged to create a composite scale (*alpha* = 0.82). LLC participation was assessed from student responses to an item about participating "in a learning community or some other formal program where groups of students take two or more classes together." Response options were sorted into two categories: LLC participants (*Done*) and non-LLC participants (*Do not plan to do* or *Have not decided*), using "1" and "0," respectively. For more information about the survey, items, and psychometric properties, see NSSE (2021). The appendix (available upon request) provides supplemental methodological information and analyses. Data were analyzed using two-way analyses of covariance (ANCOVAs) that evaluate whether population means on a dependent variable "are the same across levels of a factor, adjusting for differences on the covariate" (Green & Salkind, 2003, p. 191).

RESULTS

An ANCOVA was conducted to compare Black students' sense of belonging at HBCUs and PWIs by LLC participation, controlling for gender. A preliminary analysis evaluating the homogeneity-of-slopes assumption indicated that the relationship between the covariate and the dependent variable did not differ significantly as a function of the independent variables. Results indicated there was a statistically significant interaction between campus racial composition and LLC participation on Black students' sense of belonging, controlling for gender, $F(1, 14275) = 11.72$, $p < 0.001$, partial $\eta^2 = 0.001$, adjusted $R^2 = 0.026$. In short, Black LLC participants reported higher sense of belonging (e.g., $M_{PWI} = 44.35$ [$SD = 11.57$]) than Black non-LLC peers (e.g., $M_{PWI} = 41.56$ [$SD = 12.43$]) at both campus types. Table 1 presents a summary.

DISCUSSION

The purpose of this study was to test for differences in Black students' sense of belonging at HBCUs and PWIs by LLC participation. Results yielded several important conclusions. First, Black LLC participants reported greater sense of belonging ratings than their same-race non-LLC peers, regardless of gender. In other words, LLCs seem to work in boosting Black students' sense of belonging, and these findings hold for Black students regardless of gender identity. LLCs could serve as effective within-college sources of support for Black students, just as they do for White students (Jessup-Anger et al., 2019). It is likely that LLCs structure opportunities for Black students to connect meaningfully with others (e.g., peers, faculty) on campus for educationally and socially purposeful reasons. Those positive, supportive relations, in turn, provide the social bonds of trust, transparency, and mattering that foster sense of belonging. And this seems true for Black men, women, and gender-variant students regardless of campus racial composition, which is good news considering prior scholarship documenting the "Black male crisis" in higher education, racialized sexism faced by Black women at PWIs, and queer/transphobia at HBCUs (Coleman et al., 2020; Strayhorn, 2013).

A second contribution of this study is what it suggests about the "conditional effects" of LLCs on Black students' collegiate experiences. In this study, sense of belonging scores were higher on average for Black LLC students at HBCUs and PWIs, with the highest average scores for Black LLC participants at PWIs. So, it is not just that LLC participation is associated with stronger sense of belonging for all students (e.g., Inkelas et al., 2018) or for Black students at both campus types, but LLCs *may* produce slightly stronger gains for Black students at PWIs that can be culturally isolating, socially hostile, and unwelcoming (Patton et al., 2011).

Alternatively, results suggest that LLCs may even be effective in boosting Black students' belonging at HBCUs, where they generally represent a critical mass. That outcomes vary between Black students at HBCUs and PWIs is consistent with past research on smaller and locally constructed survey samples (Reeder & Schmitt, 2013). However, the fact that these differences emerged for Black students' sense of belonging across a large, multi-institutional sample underscores the importance of further understanding the structure, form, and scalability of residential learning communities at diverse colleges, HBCUs, and other MSIs.

Findings from this study supported Inkelas and Weisman's (2003) conclusion that "the living-learning effect is tangible and that it does add something unique and special to the college experiences of students who choose to participate" (p. 360), especially Black students at PWIs and HBCUs. Creating formal arrangements and residential programs that compel students to meet with faculty for academic (e.g., discussing coursework) and social (e.g., seeking advice on personal concerns) while also providing peer support and opportunities to discuss major social issues (e.g., human rights, global conflict) seems important and powerfully potent for boosting Black students' sense of belonging at PWIs and HBCUs. The "c" in LLC stands for *community*, which is built through shared experiences, language, and traditions, to name a few. Campus administrators and practitioners should consider these results when designing inclusive learning environments as part of larger belonging campaigns and by infusing LLC components throughout the student experience (e.g., cluster courses, cultural outings, lunch-and-learn events).

Results provide additional evidence affirming the importance of supportive learning environments like LLCs for Black students at both HBCUs and PWIs regardless of gender identity. Findings have several implications for practice. Housing professionals at both types of institutions might consider LLCs an effective strategy for nurturing Black and other under-represented racial/ethnic minority students' academic and social involvement, which, in turn, promotes college success. Provosts and chief administrative officers might consider these results when leading strategic planning efforts aimed at raising student retention rates. Because Black students in LLCs felt a higher sense of belonging in college, a remedy for low retention may be launching new LLCs or promoting Black students' participation in existing residential learning communities that provide controlled environments for academic and social engagement with equity-minded faculty and peers. Of course, prior research has shown that well-structured LLCs require considerable costs and logistics (Inkelas & Soldner, 2011). Private foundations and government agencies might consult these findings when identifying funding priorities. Launching campaigns to provide much-needed resources to MSIs like HBCUs to develop new or expand existing LLCs is one way to promote Black students' sense of belonging, which, in turn, is associated with raising Black student retention and persistence rates (Strayhorn, 2019).

Like all studies, this project has limitations. One limitation of this study is that it lacked a randomized controlled design. Students do not necessarily opt to participate in LLCs at random. Future researchers might consider addressing this issue in terms of design. Randomization is necessary to control for variations in participants' choices. Other limits include that the database does not permit comparison by LLC type (e.g., discipline- vs. service-focused) or discerning LCs from LLCs directly. Future researchers should develop indicators that allow such disaggregation.

In sum, the findings of this study suggest that LLCs may serve as an important complement to Black students' experiences in college regardless of gender identity, although the influence varies slightly by campus racial composition. This is the first study, to our knowledge, that compares LLC participation for Black students at HBCUs and PWIs. The study found a measurable advantage for those attending both campus types. These findings await additional empirical testing but hopefully inform immediate application, deliberate actions, as well as future policies, programs, and practices.

Correspondence concerning this article should be addressed to Terrell L. Strayhorn, Virginia Union University; tlstrayhorn@vuu.edu

REFERENCES

BrckaLorenz, A., Garvey, J. C., Hurtado, S. S., & Latopolski, K. (2017). High-impact practices and student-faculty interactions for gender-variant students. *Journal of Diversity in Higher Education, 10*(4), 350–365. https://doi.org/10.1037/dhe0000065

Caviglia-Harris, J. L. (2021). Community is key: Estimating the impact of living learning communities on college retention and GPA. *Education Economics, 30*(2), 173–190.

Coleman, R. D., Wallace, J. K., & Means, D. R. (2020). Questioning a single narrative: Multiple identities shaping Black queer and transgender student retention. *Journal of College Student Retention, 21*(4), 455–475. https://doi.org/10.1177/1521025119895516

Garvey, J. C., Arambula Ballysingh, T., Bowley Down, L., Howard, B. L., Ingram, A. N., & Carlson, M. (2020). Where I sleep: The relationship with residential environments and first-generation belongingness. *College Student Affairs Journal, 38*(1), 16–33.

Green, S. B., & Salkind, N. J. (2003). *Using SPSS for Windows and Macintosh: Analyzing and understanding data* (3rd ed.). Prentice Hall.

Hausmann, L. R. M., Schofield, J. W., & Woods, R. L. (2007). Sense of belonging as a predictor of intentions to persist among African American and White first-year college students. *Research in Higher Education, 48*(7), 803–839.

Hoffman, M., Richmond, J., Morrow, J., & Salomone, K. (2002). Investigating sense of belonging in first-year college students. *Journal of College Student Retention: Research, Theory & Practice, 4*(3), 227–256.

Inkelas, K. K., Daver, Z. E., Vogt, K. E., & Leonard, J. B. (2007). Living-learning programs and first-generation college students' academic and social transition to college. *Research in Higher Education, 48,* 403–434. https://doi.org/10.1007/s11162-006-9031-6

Inkelas, K. K., Jessup-Anger, J. E., Benjamin, M., & Wawrzynski, M. R. (2018). *Living-learning communities that work: A research-based model for design, delivery, and assessment.* Stylus.

Inkelas, K. K. & Soldner, M. (2011). Undergraduate living-learning programs and student outcomes. In J. C. Smart & M. B. Paulsen (Eds.), *Higher education: Handbook of theory and research, Vol. 26* (pp. 1–55). Springer.

Inkelas, K. K., Vogt, K. E., Longerbeam, S. D., Owen, J., & Johnson, D. (2006). Measuring outcomes of living-learning programs: Examining college environments and student learning and development. *The Journal of General Education, 55*(1), 40–76. https://doi.org/10.2307/27798036

Inkelas, K. K., & Weisman, J. (2003). Different by design: An examination of outcomes associated with three types of living-learning programs. *Journal of College Student Development, 44,* 335–368. https://doi.org/10.1353/csd.2003.0027

Jessup-Anger, J. E., Armstrong, M., Kerrick, E., & Siddiqui, N. (2019). Exploring students' perceptions of their experiences in a social justice living-learning community. *Journal of Student Affairs Research & Practice, 56*(2), 194–206.

Jessup-Anger, J. E., Johnson, B. N., & Wawrzynski, M. R. (2012). Exploring living-learning communities as a venue for men's identity construction. *Journal of College & University Housing, 39*(1), 162–175.

Johnson, D. R., Soldner, M., Leonard, J. B., Alvarez, P., Inkelas, K. K., Rowan-Kenyon, H., & Longerbeam, S. (2007). Examining sense of belonging among first-year undergraduates from different racial/ethnic groups. *Journal of College Student Development, 48*(5), 525–542.

Kuh, G. D., & O' Donnell, K. (2013). *Ensuring quality and taking high-impact practices to scale.* American Association of Colleges & Universities.

Kuh, G. D., O'Donnell, K., & Schneider, C. G. (2017). High-impact practices (HIPs) at ten. *Change: The Magazine of Higher Learning, 49*(5), 8–16. https://doi.org/10.1080/00091383.2017.1366805

Maestas, R., Vaquera, G. S., & Zehr, L. M. (2007). Factors impacting sense of belonging at a Hispanic-serving institution. *Journal of Hispanic Higher Education, 6*(3), 237–256.

Matthews, R. S., Smith, B. L., & MacGregor, J. (2012). The evolution of learning communities: A retrospective. In K. Buch & K. E. Barron (Eds.), *Discipline-centered learning communities: Creating connections among students, faculty, and curricula* (New Directions for Teaching and Learning, No. 132, pp. 99–111). Jossey-Bass.

Museus, S. D., & Chang, T. H. (2021). The impact of campus environments on sense of belonging for first-generation college students. *Journal of College Student Development, 62*(3), 367–372. https://doi.org/10.1353/csd.2021.0039

National Survey of Student Engagement (NSSE). (2021). *Engagement insights: Survey findings on the quality of undergraduate education—Annual Results 2020.* https://nsse.indiana.edu/research/annual-results/2021/index.html

Patton, L. D., Bridges, B. K., & Flowers, L. A. (2011). Effects of Greek affiliation on African American students' engagement: Differences by college racial composition. *College Student Affairs Journal, 29,* 113–123.

Reeder, M. C., & Schmitt, N. (2013). Motivational and judgment predictors of African American academic achievement at PWIs and HBCUs. *Journal of College Student Development, 54*(1), 29–42.

Rhee, B. (2008). Institutional climate and student departure: A multinomial multilevel modeling approach. *Review of Higher Education, 31*(2), 161–183.

Strayhorn, T. L. (2013). And their own received them not: Black gay male undergraduates' experiences with white racism, Black homophobia. In M. C. Brown, II, T. E. Dancy, III, & J. E. Davis (Eds.), *Educating African American males: Contexts for consideration, possibilities for practice* (pp. 105–119). Peter Lang.

Strayhorn, T. L. (2019). *College students' sense of belonging: A key to educational success for all students* (2nd ed.). Routledge.

Strayhorn, T. L. (2020a). Exploring the role of race in Black males' sense of belonging in medical school: A qualitative pilot study. *Medical Science Educator, 30,* 1383–1387. https://doi.org/10.1007/s40670-020-01103-y

Strayhorn, T. L. (2020b). Measuring the relation between sense of belonging, campus leadership, and academic achievement for African American students at historically Black colleges and universities (HBCUs): A 'gender equity' analysis. *Journal of Minority Achievement, Creativity & Leadership, 1*(1), 94–118. https://doi.org/10/5325/minoachicrealead.1.1.0094

Strayhorn, T. L. (2021). Analyzing the short-term impact of a brief web-based intervention on first-year students' sense of belonging at an HBCU: A quasi-experimental study. *Innovative Higher Education.* https://doi.org/10.1007/s10755-021-09559-5

Strayhorn, T. L., Williams, M. S., & Johnson, R. M. (Eds.). (in press). *Creating new possibilities for the future of HBCUs: From research to praxis.* Information Age Press.

U.S. Department of Education. (2020). *Condition of education, 2019.* National Center for Education Statistics.

Developing Low-income College Students' Sense of Belonging: The Role of Validation

Joseph A. Kitchen

Earning a college degree can be a transformational life experience for low-income students that breaks cycles of poverty and opens doors to rewarding career opportunities and increased quality of life (White House, 2014). The share of students from low-income backgrounds attending college has increased over the past few decades, and they make up a substantial proportion of today's college students (Fry & Cilluffo, 2019). However, they are much less likely to complete college compared with their higher-income counterparts (Cahalan et al., 2018, Fry & Cilluffo, 2019; NCES, 2018). Much attention has been paid to the financial factors that influence low-income students' college completion; however, low-income students face many cultural and social challenges in college that also have implications for their completion and are equally deserving of scholars' attention (Kezar, 2011). Developing a sense of belonging in culturally alienating college environments that privilege middle- and upper-class norms, values, language, and knowledge is one such challenge facing low-income students that has implications for their college success and completion (Hurst, 2010; Soria & Stebleton, 2013; see Strayhorn, 2019 for a comprehensive discussion of college sense of belonging).

Researchers have revealed a strong association between sense of belonging and students' social class and economic background (Bettencourt, 2021; Ostrove & Long, 2007; Soria & Bultmann, 2014). Notably, students from less advantaged economic and class backgrounds typically report a lower sense of belonging in college compared with their middle and upper-class peers (Bettencourt, 2021; Soria & Stebleton, 2013). They also face difficulty finding staff, faculty, and peers to connect with who share their social class backgrounds and experiences. To address gaps in college completion, educators (i.e., faculty, staff) bear responsibility for increasing low-income students' sense of belonging and identifying asset- and strengths-based practices that effectively promote low-income students' belonging (Colyar, 2011; Rendón & Muñoz, 2011). Validation is one such promising practice that focuses on *how* student support is delivered by staff and faculty rather than on *what* specific support offices and services are offered (Rendón & Muñoz, 2011.

Validation is a holistic process initiated by educators who (a) proactively reach out to students early on and consistently; (b) build genuine, caring relationships in and out of the classroom; (c) discover and affirm students' backgrounds and identities; (d) communicate to students that their backgrounds are valuable assets and have a critical role in their education; (e) reassure students of their innate capabilities and potential for success; and (f) actively connect students to support that is tailored to their

Joseph A. Kitchen is Assistant Research Professor, Pullias Center for Higher Education, University of Southern California.

backgrounds and identities to empower them to leverage their assets and achieve college success (Rendón & Muñoz, 2011). While still nascent, research has shown the promise of validation for promoting belonging among first-generation and community college students and as a practice that effectively mitigates the influence of discrimination on belonging (Baber, 2018; Hurtado et al., 2015; Museus & Chang, 2021).

Scholars have hypothesized that validating low-income students is a promising practice to increase their sense of belonging and success (Soria & Stebelton, 2013). To date, no robust quantitative research has focused on whether validation is associated with increased sense of belonging among low-income students explicitly, nor has research explored this relationship from a nuanced perspective that recognizes the many intersecting identities of low-income students. Accordingly, this study answers two research questions:

RQ1. What is the relationship between validation and low-income college students' sense of belonging in their first year?

RQ2. Does that link vary by low-income students' other characteristics (e.g., race, sex, GPA)?

STUDY CONTEXT

This study is part of a larger mixed-methods study of low-income student success at three campuses of the University of Nebraska system (Cole, Kitchen, & Kezar, 2019). The three campuses include the University of Nebraska, Kearney, a rural, regional, residential campus that began as a normal school; the University of Nebraska, Omaha, a metropolitan university that serves a racially, ethnically, and linguistically diverse student population; and the University of Nebraska, Lincoln, a Research 1 university and land grant institution. Each campus offers an ecology of support services to promote students' social, academic, and career development, such as student organizations and clubs, academic and career development offices, multicultural resource centers and programming, tutoring and study spaces, learning communities, and wellness support (e.g., counseling services, recreation opportunities). These support offices and services provide the staging where the process of validation from instructors, faculty, and staff (e.g., advisors, student affairs staff)—the variable of interest in this study—can occur. Prior qualitative evidence from the broader study suggested that validation provided by educators supports low-income student success (Hallett et al., 2020; Kitchen et al., 2021).

METHODS

Longitudinal surveys were administered to a cohort of college students attending the University of Nebraska system in 2016–2017 who applied for a scholarship for low-income students.[1] A baseline survey was administered early in the fall semester of 2016, and a follow-up survey was administered in late spring 2017. Data were collected that measured students' traits, frequency of socializing with peers, validation, and sense of belonging at the start and end of the first college year. I restricted the sample to students with complete background

---

[1] Data were drawn from a larger study of low-income student success (see https://pass.pullias.usc.edu/ for study details). I pooled our sample across low-income students who applied for the scholarship and subsequently received either (a) scholarship support, (b) scholarship and college transition program support, or (c) no additional support. There was no significant main effect nor moderating effects on the link between validation and belonging, so I pooled the low-income student sample. Scholarship and program support are controlled for in my analyses.

Table 1.
Variables, Descriptives, and Coding

Variables	*M*	*SD*	Description and coding	Rasch reliability	% variance explained
Sex	0.67	0.47	0 = Male; 1 = Female	—	—
Race/ethnicity	0.47	0.50	0 = White; 1 = Racially Minoritized	—	—
First-generation	0.71	0.45	0 = At least 1 parent has earned a 4–year degree; 1 = Neither parent has earned a 4–year degree	—	—
EFC	1345.95	1661.84	Expected family contribution (EFC) in dollars	—	—
ACT score	22.39	4.51	Composite score on the ACT standardized test with a possible range of 1 through 36	—	—
H.S. GPA	3.53	0.40	Continuous variable measuring high school GPA	—	—
Peer socializing	3.50	1.69	Hours spent socializing with friends each week; 1 = 0 hrs; 2 = 1–5 hrs; 3 = 6–10 hrs; 4 = 11–15 hrs; 5 = 16–20 hrs; 6 = 21–25 hrs; 7 = 26–30 hrs; 8 = More than 30 hrs	—	—
Belonging (Baseline)	4.34	0.94	1 (Strongly disagree) to 7 (Strongly agree)[a]	0.82	51.8
Validation	4.36	0.84	1 (Strongly disagree) to 7 (Strongly agree)[a]	0.88	55.7
Belonging (End of first year)	4.27	1.04	1 (Strongly disagree) to 7 (Strongly agree)[a]	0.84	53.2

[a]Participants were asked to rate the extent to which they agreed with scale statements.

information who completed both surveys. I defined low income as below the expected family contribution (EFC) cutoff for Pell eligibility (U.S. Department of Education, 2016). The final analytic sample was 687 students.

Table 1 presents variables and coding. Belonging was measured at baseline and the end of the first year using adapted 8-item scales (Willms, 2003). Validation was measured using an adapted 12-item scale (Hurtado et al., 2011) on the posttest that asked students to report validating support they received during the year. Table 2 shows sample scale items for validation and belonging. Controls were primarily selected based on factors that may impact belonging

(Strayhorn, 2019). Rasch modeling was used to generate estimates of individual scores relative to our psychosocial constructs (validation and belonging) because they are not directly measurable and because this approach is not sample dependent—which is useful for longitudinal studies (Granger, 2008). Rasch rating scale models were used to transform ordinal responses to interval scales, and psychometric functioning was evaluated using WINSTEPS (Linacre, 2018; Wright & Masters, 1982). Data showed good fit for the Rasch rating scale models; each variable measured one underlying latent trait, was reliable, and exhibited item fit scores within the acceptable range of 0.5 to 2

Table 2.
Sample Scale Items for Key Psychosocial Constructs

Psychosocial Variable	Sample Scale Items
Belonging (Baseline)	I will make friends easily. I will feel like I belong. I will feel like I am a member of the [campus] community. I expect other students will like me.
Validation	Faculty empower me to learn here. At least one staff member has taken an interest in my development. Faculty believe in my potential to succeed academically. Staff recognize my achievements. Instructors encouraged me to meet with them after or outside of class. I feel like my contributions were valued in class. Staff encourage me to get involved in campus activities.
Belonging (End of first year)	I feel like I belong. I make friends easily. I see myself as an important part of the [campus] community. I feel I am a member of the [campus].

mean-square (Wright & Linacre, 1994). Table 1 presents psychometrics, and a detailed psychometric report and full scales can be found at https://pass.pullias.usc.edu/.

Analytic Design

For RQ1, I computed hierarchical linear multiple regression models to estimate the relationship between validation and belonging among low-income students (accounting for controls) and to identify the amount of variance in belonging explained by validation above and beyond the variance explained by controls alone. For RQ2, I incorporated interaction effects to determine whether any of the control variables moderated the relationship between validation and belonging among low-income students (e.g., Race*Validation; Sex*Validation). My sample of low-income students was pooled across the three University of Nebraska campuses. Future research should extend the findings presented here to examine the potential role of institution type as it relates to the link between validation and belonging.

FINDINGS AND DISCUSSION

Table 1 presents descriptive statistics. Model 1 (controls only) accounted for 34% of the variance in belonging [Adj. R^2 = 0.34; $F(10, 676)$ = 36.83, $p < 0.001$)] (see Table 3). Model 2 measured the link between validation and belonging, accounting for controls, and explained 49% of the variance in low-income students' sense of belonging [Adj. R^2 = 0.49; $F(11, 675)$ = 60.46, $p < 0.001$)]. Validation uniquely explained an additional 14% of the variance in low-income students' sense of belonging, above and beyond controls. Validation was strongly and significantly associated with low-income students' sense of belonging (β = 0.41, $p < .001$)—the largest standardized coefficient estimate of all variables in the model. For RQ2, no interaction term was statistically significant at the $p < 0.05$ level, suggesting that the strong relationship between validation and belonging held true for low-income students across diverse characteristics (e.g., EFC, GPA, race, sex, first-generation status, ACT score, pretest levels of belonging).

Table 3.
Modeling the Relationship Between Validation
and Belonging Among Low-Income Students (*N* = 687)

	Model I		Model II	
	β	p-value	β	p-value
Sex	−0.06	n.s.	−0.04	n.s.
Race/Ethnicity	0.03	n.s.	−0.02	n.s.
First Generation	−0.01	n.s.	0.00	n.s.
EFC	0.06	n.s.	0.05	n.s.
ACT Score	−0.06	n.s.	−0.06	n.s.
H.S. GPA	0.14	***	0.10	**
Peer Socializing	0.14	***	0.11	***
Belonging (Baseline)	0.52	***	0.40	***
Validation	-	-	0.41	***
Adjusted R^2	0.34	***	0.49	***
R^2 –Change	-	-	0.14	***

Note. The dependent variable, sense of belonging, is reported at the end of students' first year of college. Standardized beta coefficients reported. No VIF was above 1.7, indicating multicollinearity was not an issue (Cohen et al., 2003). Scholarship and program support, while not the focus of this examination, are controlled for in the results shown above.

**$p < 0.01$. ***$p < 0.001$. n.s. = non-significant at $p < 0.05$ level.

I extended prior research on low-income student success by identifying the promise of validating support as an asset-based approach to increase sense of belonging in environments students may find culturally alienating and unfamiliar (Hurst, 2010; Kezar, 2011). Low-income students reported a higher sense of belonging when they experienced support from educators who built genuine, caring relationships with them; affirmed that their backgrounds and experiences are assets that have a place in their learning experience; and empowered them to succeed by connecting them to resources tailored to their needs (i.e., validating support; (Kezar et al., 2020; Rendon & Muñoz, 2011). In turn, an increased sense of belonging can potentially address disparities in the success of low-income college students. Moreover, I contribute to the literature by identifying a promising practice to boost belonging that works

equally well across many other low-income student characteristics (e.g., race, sex). This finding is important because low-income students are more likely to hold other marginalized identities (Engle & Tinto, 2008).

Because students' social class or socioeconomic status is often less visible or apparent to educators than other identities (e.g., race; Soria & Stableton, 2013), it will be vital for educators to initiate and normalize conversations around economic backgrounds and social class and to collaborate with students to discover and discuss the strengths they carry given their low-income backgrounds. Educators can incorporate structured opportunities to discuss social class in cocurricular activities, discuss the social class backgrounds of scholars who authored class readings, and get to know students in both academic and social settings. Moreover, scholars have previously suggested that receiving validation from educators across multiple college contexts immerses marginalized students in an affirming system of college support that promotes success (Kitchen et al., 2021)—including belonging, as we affirm in this study. College leaders are responsible for promoting and incentivizing the system-wide adoption of asset-oriented, validating approaches to support low-income students. Finally, validation, by definition, is a holistic process (Rendón & Muñoz, 2011). I found it was related to higher belonging across other low-income student identities (e.g., race, sex), but to reap the full benefits of validation on low-income students' belonging, educators should remain conscious of students' multiple identities and take the opportunity to recognize and affirm other identities that low-income students hold as well to engage in holistic validation and boost belonging.

In the past, the common approach to increasing low-income students' sense of belonging was to introduce myriad programs and interventions (e.g., TRIO, summer bridge; Tinto, 2012). This study pivots from that approach and suggests that *how* support is delivered by educators (i.e., validation), rather than *what* support is offered, is linked to low-income students' sense of belonging. Thus, it is likely possible to scale this approach to create a validating college support system, where educators across campus contexts (e.g., classroom, advising) engage low-income students in validating support and increase their belonging. Sustaining this validating system of support at scale in the long-term would likely require a broader shift in the cultural norms in higher education, given that most colleges are steeped in a culture of individualism and competition, and are task-oriented and managerial, focused strictly on delivery of a fixed set of services (Kezar et al., 2022; Kezar, 2011). However, outlined below are at least three ways to initiate this shift and begin to have a real impact on low-income students' sense of belonging in college.

First, train educators on how to validate low-income students. Such training should include context-specific (e.g., classroom, advising) illustrations or scenarios for educators on what validating support looks like in their context and how they can enable low-income student success. For instance, a faculty advising training scenario could present two versions of how an advisor might broach the topic of identifying a major and career path with a low-income student—one deficit-oriented and one validating (see Kitchen, 2021). The deficit-oriented scenario would focus on helping the student identify a major or career path with the goal of achieving social mobility. While seemingly benign, this approach implies the goal of college for low-income students should be to "move up" and leave their social class of origin, which can be invalidating and alienating (Ardoin & martinez, 2019). The validating scenario could showcase a faculty advisor who instead focuses on discussing with the student what life experiences (e.g., classes, jobs) they have had and communicating the value of those experiences to the student in helping them identify a good major or career fit, identifying the student's personal goals for college, and then describing how they as an advisor can leverage students' experiences and help them access resources to chart a path to achieve their goals (experienced as validating).

Second, appropriately configure hiring practices to identify and hire validating educators. Educators—the people who interface with students directly—serve a critical role in fostering a validating support system for low-income students and, in turn, increasing their belonging. To build and sustain that system, it is incumbent upon hiring managers and institutional leaders to identify and hire educators who believe in an approach to student support that is asset-oriented, holistic, and validating (Kitchen et al., 2021; Kezar et al., 2022). This orientation could be assessed through interview questions or performance tasks that gauge how educators respond to a common issue faced by low-income students navigating alienating college environments. That response might be evaluated based on whether it reflects an asset-oriented, validating approach and used to guide hiring decisions. Institutional leaders should also model validation for existing staff and faculty from diverse backgrounds (including low-income) to illustrate the power of this practice and embed validation in the broader institutional culture such that it becomes second nature for educators.

Third, identify promising offices and programs on campus that are already doing this work (i.e., validating students and cultivating belonging) that can serve as campus-specific models for other educators in the broader campus context. There are likely educators at your institution who are effectively serving low-income students by engaging in validating practices in welcoming spaces like multicultural centers, first-generation support offices, and TRIO. Leaders should identify those offices on campus that are effectively supporting low-income student success and belonging through validation as a resource and highlight the promising work of these educators in campus newsletters, town halls, and trainings to educate others on campus on their validating approaches to support. If asked to go beyond normal duties, educators in these offices should be duly compensated for their service to campus (e.g., money, recognition).

While I highlighted just a few practical examples here, other research, such as Kitchen and colleagues (2021) and Rendón and Muñoz (2011), has outlined several other concrete strategies for validating marginalized students (e.g., affirming the value of their participation in class and cocurricular settings, showing genuine interest in their development) that are relevant to supporting low-income students and, as I found, could, in turn, promote their sense of belonging and college success.

Correspondence concerning this manuscript should be directed to Joseph A Kitchen, University of Southern California; kitchenj@usc.edu

REFERENCES

Ardoin, S., & martinez, b. (2019). *Straddling class in the academy*. Stylus.

Baber, L. (2018). Validating experiences among urban community college students in a college transition program. *Community College Review, 46*(3), 316–340.

Bettencourt, G. (2021). Understanding working-class students' sense of belonging on campus. *Journal of Higher Education, 92*(5), 760–783.

Cahalan, M., Perna, L. W., Yamashita, M., Wright, J., & Santillan, S. (2018). *2018 indicators of higher education equity in the United States: Historical trend report*. The Pell Institute.

Cohen, J., Cohen, P., West, S., & Aiken, L. (2003). *Applied multiple regression/correlation analysis for the behavioral sciences*. Routledge.

Cole, D., Kitchen, J. A., & Kezar, A. (2019). Examining a comprehensive college transition program: An account of iterative mixed-methods longitudinal survey design. *Research in Higher Education, 60*(3), 392–413.

Colyar, J. (2011). Strangers in a strange land. In A. Kezar (Ed.), *Recognizing and serving low-income students in higher education* (pp. 121–138). Routledge.

Engle, J., & Tinto, V. (2008). *Moving beyond access: College success for low-income, first-generation students*. Pell Institute for the Study of Opportunity in Higher Education.

Fry, R., & Cilluffo, A. (2019). *A rising share of undergraduates are from poor families, especially at less selective colleges*. Pew Research Center.

Granger, C. (2008). Rasch analysis is important to understand and use for measurement. *Rasch Measurement, 21*(3), 1122–1123.

Hallett, R., Reason, R., Toccoli, J., Kitchen, J., & Perez, R. (2020). The process of academic validation within a comprehensive college transition program. *American Behavioral Scientist, 64*(3), 253–275.

Hurst, A. (2010). *The burden of academic success*. Rowman & Littlefield.

Hurtado, S., Alvarado, A., & Guillermo-Wann, C. (2015). Creating inclusive environments: The mediating effect of faculty and staff validation on the relationship of discrimination/bias to students' sense of belonging. *Journal Committed to Social Change on Race and Ethnicity, 1*(1), 60–81.

Hurtado, S., Cuellar, M., & Wann, C. G. (2011, Summer). Quantitative measures of students' sense of validation. *Enrollment Management Journal*, 53–71.

Kezar, A. (2011). *Recognizing and serving low-income students in higher education*. Routledge.

Kezar, A., Kitchen, J., Estes, H., Hallett, R., & Perez, R. (2020). Tailoring programs to best support low-income, first-generation, and racially minoritized college student success. *Journal of College Student Retention*. Advance online publication. https://doi.org/10.1177/1521025120971580

Kezar, A., Perez, R., Hallett, R., & Kitchen, J. (2022). Scaling success for low-income, first-generation, and/or racially minoritized students through a culture of ecological validation. *Journal of Diversity in Higher Education*. Advance online publication. https://doi.org/10.1037/dhe0000401

Kitchen, J. A. (2021). Promoting college students' major and career self-efficacy through validating support. *Journal of College Student Development, 62*(4), 422–437.

Kitchen, J. A., Perez, R., Hallett, R., Kezar, A., & Reason, R. (2021). Ecological validation model of student success: A new student support model for low-income, first-generation, and racially minoritized students. *Journal of College Student Development, 62*(6), 627–642.

Linacre, J. (2018). *WINSTEPS: Rasch measurement computer program*. Winsteps.com.

Museus, S., & Chang, T. (2021). Impact of campus environments on sense of belonging for first-generation college students. *Journal of College Student Development, 62*(3), 367–372.

NCES. (2018). Immediate college enrollment rate. *The Condition of Education*, 1–4. https://nces.ed.gov/programs/coe/pdf/Indicator_CPA/coe_cpa_2018_05.pdf

Ostrove, J., & Long, S. (2007). Social class and belonging: Implications for college adjustment. *The Review of Higher Education, 30*(4), 363–389.

Rendón, L., & Muñoz, S. (2011). Revisiting validation theory. *Enrollment Management, 5*(2), 12.

Strayhorn, T. (2019). *College students' sense of belonging* (2nd ed). Routledge.

Soria, K., & Bultmann, M. (2014). Supporting working-class students in higher education. *NACADA Journal, 34*(2), 51–62.

Soria, K., & Stebleton, M. (2013). Social capital, academic engagement, and sense of belonging among working-class college students. *College Student Affairs Journal, 31*(2), 139–153.

Tinto, V. (2012). *Completing college: Rethinking institutional action*. University of Chicago Press.

U.S. Department of Education. (2016). *Federal Pell Grant payment and disbursement schedules*.

White House. (2014). *Increasing college opportunity for low-income students*. Retrieved from https://obamawhitehouse.archives.gov/sites/default/files/docs/increasing_college_opportunity_for_low-income_students_report.pdf

Willms, J. (2003). *A sense of belonging and participation: Results from PISA 2000*. OECD.

Wright, B., & Linacre, J. (1994). Reasonable MNSQ fit values. *Rasch Measurement, 8*(3), 370–371.

Wright, B. D., & Masters, G. N. (1982). *Rating scale analysis: Rasch measurement*. MESA Press

Assessing Impact of Study Abroad on Graduation Rates of Underrepresented Students

Tory L. Brundage   Gayle Christensen   Anne K. Althauser   Sudha Sharma

EXPANDING INTERNATIONAL EDUCATION

Fueled by globalization, technological advances, and more accessible travel, the role of international education on college and university campuses has had a period of immense growth. According to the Institute of International Education's 2019 *Open Doors* report, just over 340,000 US students participated in a study abroad program for credit during the 2017–2018 academic year. The number of students choosing to study abroad has steadily increased over the past 25 years. Immediately prior to the COVID-19 global pandemic, 10.9% of all undergraduates in the US studied abroad at some point while pursuing their degree. This rapid expansion has largely been welcomed on college campuses due to globalization and the sense that such opportunities can be transformational for students. Consequently, there is interest among administrators, scholars, instructors, and policymakers to better understand the effects of study abroad on student learning and outcomes. Though the COVID-19 global pandemic caused an unprecedented decrease in international education, the enduring forces of globalization will likely yield a strong return

to study abroad programming when permitted and safe (Marginson, 2020). As such, it remains important to understand and assess outcomes related to study abroad participation at an institutional level.

ASSESSING STUDY ABROAD

The student success literature has evolved a substantial interest in understanding and implementing high-impact practices, aspects of the college student experience that positively influence college persistence and completion rates (Kuh, 2008). A promising supposition of Kuh's 2008 work was the notion that high-impact practices would not only increase student engagement and degree completion but that the effect would also be evident among historically underserved student populations. Additionally, the existing racial and ethnic disparities in higher education have led some to call for a more targeted focus on graduation rates across racial and ethnic student populations to identify the most impactful practices (Johnson & Stage, 2018; Stohs & Schutte, 2019). While multiple studies have examined the effect of studying abroad on graduation rates (Haupt et al. 2018), few have explored

Tory L. Brundage is a Doctoral Candidate in the College of Education, Gayle Christensen is the Associate Vice Provost for Global Affairs and an Affiliate Assistant Professor in the College of Education, Anne K. Althauser is an Institutional Analyst in the Office of Planning & Budgeting; Sudha Sharma is a Web Developer in the Office of Global Affairs, and all at the University of Washington, Seattle Campus.

how that effect may vary across student populations (Bell et al. 2021). Given that students of color have been consistently underrepresented in study abroad programs (International Institute of Education, 2019), there is a gap in the literature assessing study abroad for students of color as a high-impact practice. This inquiry aimed to (a) advance a common research model proposed in the literature for assessing study abroad and (b) use this model specifically to measure the impact of studying abroad on graduation rates for historically underserved student populations.

METHODS

This analysis used the Leveraging Education Abroad Participation for Graduation (GRAD LEAP) model (Haupt et al., 2018), which calls for a common approach to data analysis when exploring questions about the impact of education abroad on college student graduation rates.

Study Setting and Participants

This was a retrospective analysis of deidentified data accessed through an internal student database at a large, public research institution on the West Coast of the US. The campus has a formal Office of Study Abroad that supports students with selecting and participating in a wide range of international education programs offered by the institution. Additionally, the office has an adviser focused on equity and access, as well as a needs-based scholarship program for studying abroad. Furthermore, and relevant to this study, there are TRIO programs and Educational Opportunity Program offices that support students of color through a wide range of efforts, as well as race-conscious pipeline programs available in many academic pathways. The program offerings are similar to those offered at many large public institutions in the US.

The study included enrollment and student academic records from first-time, first-year,

and fully matriculated undergraduate enrollees during the 2012, 2013, and 2014 academic years. International students, defined as those studying on an F1 student visa, as well as students admitted through the transfer or post-baccalaureate application processes, were excluded. Using these criteria, a total of 15,620 unique records were included in the analysis. Within this overall population, 2,282 students who identified as Black, Latinx, Native American, and/or Pacific Islander (BLNP) were defined as historically underserved based on graduation rates consistently below the institutional average (see Table 1). Data from 2012 to 2014 were used to allow sufficient time to accurately measure the outcomes of interest: graduation rates at 4, 5, and 6 years. Roughly 9% of the data were missing one or more variables, but the missing indicator method was used to include all cases.

Measures

Independent variable. The independent variable was a flag in the student record indicating whether a student had ever participated in one of the university's international education programs (0 = *did not participate*, 1 = *did participate*). For this study, we did not consider program type, duration (i.e., short-term, full-year exchange), time of year (e.g., summer vs. academic year), or whether a student studied abroad more than once.

Dependent Variables. Graduation status (0 = *has not graduated*, 1 = *graduated*) was captured at the conclusion of each student's 4th, 5th, and 6th year of enrollment.

Matching Criteria. As per the GRAD LEAP model (Haupt et al., 2018), additional variables were selected to assess students' incoming characteristics and account for any selection bias that may predict study abroad participation. These variables included race, sex, first-generation status, high school GPA, SAT scores, area of study (STEM vs. non-STEM specifically), and first-year college GPA. Pell eligibility and cumulative GPA in the term prior to studying abroad are also recommended for inclusion in the GRAD LEAP model (Haupt et al., 2018) but were not available for this study. Due to student privacy concerns, high school location, free/reduced lunch percentage, and median household income by zip code were included as proxy variables for Pell eligibility. These variables are frequently used to measure the share of low-income students at colleges and universities (Delisle, 2017). We recognize that there are limitations with the available variables related to income but note that we only used them for matching purposes so that students with similar characteristics were matched for the analysis. Given the variability of timing and duration of study abroad programs, the GPA during the term prior to study abroad could not reliably be included in the analysis.

Data Analysis

An initial descriptive analysis yielded the means and standard deviations for each matching variable of interest, as well as the zero-order correlation between all matching criteria and the independent variable (see Appendix). Then, in line with advancing the GRAD LEAP model (Haupt et al., 2018), propensity score matching (PSM) was employed to directly account for the selection bias likely present between students who choose to study abroad as compared to those who do not. Additionally, PSM has been recommended as "particularly useful for examining the impact of programs and processes on student progress" (Liu & Borden, 2019, p.147). A PSM analysis in the context of this study allowed for estimating the average effect of study abroad participation on graduation rates. This analysis used nearest-neighbor (NN) matching, matched with all ties when identifying NN, and applied a probit model to predict student graduation rates.

FINDINGS

Descriptive statistics indicated that all students who studied abroad in this dataset graduated at higher rates across the four-, five-, and six-year marks as compared to their peers who did not study abroad (shown in Table 1). On average, students who studied abroad graduated at rates 15.65 percentage points higher than those who did not.

Furthermore, when focusing on the BLNP population of interest and matching across the GRAD LEAP model (Haupt et al., 2018) suggested covariates to account for selection bias, significantly higher graduation rates for those who studied abroad were still observed. In these data (shown in Table 2), the chance of a BLNP student having graduated in 4 years was higher by 8.41 percentage points for those who studied abroad compared to those who did not. Five- and six-year graduation rates were 11.81 percentage points higher for those who studied abroad compared to those who did not.

DISCUSSION

Using a recently proposed and standardized evaluation model, we demonstrated the positive impact of study abroad on BLNP student degree completion. In our findings, study abroad is associated with positive and substantive differences in four-, five-, and six-year graduation rates in the general student population and has a pronounced positive impact on graduation outcomes within the BLNP student population even after accounting for factors that may contribute to selection bias. As such, these results further affirm studying abroad as a high-impact practice and support the idea that studying abroad may be an intervention that can enhance student success, particularly for those who have historically lower persistence and degree completion rates. International education opportunities and study abroad have

Table 1.
Graduation Rates for Populations of Interest (*N* = 15,620)

	4-year	5-year	6-year
All Students	66.92%	82.07%	84.12%
Student population by SA participation:			
Studied Abroad	79.12%	94.81%	96.53%
No Study Abroad	63.49%	78.48%	80.63%
Student population by race/ethnicity:			
White	69.58%	82.57%	84.26%
Asian	67.62%	84.75%	86.99%
Latinx	57.87%	75.62%	78.66%
Black	46.80%	71.36%	76.21%
Native	42.86%	57.14%	62.86%
Pacific Islander	46.48%	73.24%	76.06%

Note. N = 15,620 total students

Table 2.
Study Abroad PSM Results for BLNP Students

Graduated in	ATTβ	(SE)	ᵶ	95% CI
4 years	.084	(.033)	2.55*	[.019, .149]
5 years	.118	(.025)	4.72**	[.069, .167]
6 years	.118	(.024)	4.94**	[.071, .165]

Note. ATT = average treatment effect on treated.
*$p < .05$. **$p < .01$.

long been cited as potential catalysts for greater student engagement, persistence, and, consequently, degree completion (Kuh, 2008). This study adds to the literature by using a recently proposed and standardized model for evaluating study abroad (Haupt et al., 2018). Additionally, it answers the call to focus on graduation rates for historically underserved students (Stohs & Schutte, 2019) and yields evidence that the benefits of studying abroad are seen by BLNP students specifically.

A particular strength of this study is its use of the GRAD LEAP model (Haupt et al., 2018), which allows for findings to be compared with similar studies, and thus contributes

to broadened understanding of studying abroad as a high-impact practice. These findings build on a recent study by Bell et al. (2021), which made use of the GRAD LEAP model (Haupt et al., 2018) to examine the information from multiple institutions to better understand education abroad outcomes for BLNP students. Our study bolsters their findings that BLNP students who study abroad graduate in higher numbers at the four-, five-, and six-year mark. A potential limitation of this study is that it includes data only from a single institution and may not be generalizable. Additionally, we note that while we were able to align our study very closely with the GRAD LEAP model (Haupt et al., 2018), we were not able to include each variable as suggested due to data restrictions. Future research should make use of the GRAD LEAP model to further adapt and validate the model to consistently assess the impact of studying abroad across institutions and over time. In addition, deeper inquiry into how studying abroad may influence intercultural competencies or student engagement and how these concepts relate to academic success is warranted.

Support for students of color is multifactorial and varies widely across institutional contexts. The results of this study have prompted our own institution to consider how students of color are supported in their academic endeavors and provide background to assist with the prioritization of study abroad within these efforts. For example, the race-conscious pipeline and cohort programs on this campus have acted as a catalyst for BLNP students to participate in study abroad through individualized advising and developing relationships with particular study abroad programs. In interpreting our findings, other sites may also find it useful to consider the environment of student support services that can help students access high-impact opportunities generally and study abroad specifically.

CONCLUSION

Given the positive retention and graduation outcomes associated with studying abroad, it is critical to expand access and integrate international education programming into the broader higher education curriculum. Short-term study abroad programs may be particularly useful when supporting certain student populations in that they are both more accessible and replicate the community or cohort-building efforts that may already happen at an institutional level to support certain student populations. Additional recommendations include training for academic advisers on how students may best include study abroad opportunities in their course of study, commitment to partnerships between offices of minority affairs and study abroad to ensure that students have the necessary support to enable participation in study abroad, and financial aid and scholarship programming for study abroad. It is also important to share information about the role studying abroad can play in enhancing graduation widely in the higher education community. Across institutions and in the higher education literature, it continues to be important to diligently assess and examine the benefits of studying abroad through various methods and models, such as the GRAD LEAP model (Haupt et al., 2018). These efforts, especially for students who have been historically marginalized and underserved, may be even more important at a time when the world is reopening after the unprecedented educational disruption of the COVID-19 pandemic.

Correspondence concerning this article should be addressed to Tory Brundage, University of Washington; toryb@uw .edu

REFERENCES

Bell, A., Bhatt, R., Rubin, D. L., & Shiflet, C. (2021). Effects of education abroad on indices of student success among racial–ethnic minority college students. *Journal of Diversity in Higher Education.* Advance online publication. https://doi .org/10.1037/dhe0000327

Delisle, J. (2017). *The Pell Grant proxy: A ubiquitous but flawed measure of low-income student enrollment.* Brookings Institution Reports.

Haupt, J., Ogden, A. C., & Rubin, D. (2018). Toward a common research model: Leveraging education abroad participation to enhance college graduation rates. *Journal of Studies in International Education, 22*(2), 91–107. https://doi.org/10.1177 /1028315318762519

Institute of International Education. (2019). *Open doors 2019 report on international educational exchange.* https://p.widencdn .net/6tpaeo/Open-Doors-Annual-Data-Release-2019-11-17 -Print

Johnson, S. R., & Stage, F. K. (2018). Academic engagement and student success: Do high-impact practices mean higher graduation rates? *The Journal of Higher Education, 89*(5), 753–781. https://doi.org/10.1080/00221546.2018.1441107

Kuh, G. D. (2008). *High-impact educational practices: What they are, who has access to them, and why they matter.* Association of American Colleges and Universities.

Liu, X. & Borden, V. (2019). Addressing self-selection and endogeneity in higher education research. In J. Huisman & M. Tight (Eds.), *Theory and method in higher education research, Vol. 5* (pp. 129–151). Emerald Publishing Limited. https://doi.org/10.1108/S2056375220190-000005009

Marginson, S. (2020). *COVID-19 and the market model of higher education: Something has to give, and it won't be the pandemic.* Centre for Global Higher Education. https://www.researchcghe.org/blog/2020-07-20-covid-19-and-the-market-model-of-higher-education-something-has-to-give-and-it-wont-be-the-pandemic/

Stohs, M. H., & Schutte, J. G. (2019). The graduation rate myth and the equity gap. Journal of *Applied Social Science, 13*(2), 94–114. https://doi.org/10.1177/1936724419876677

APPENDIX
Descriptive Statistics and Correlations for Study Variables (*N* = 15,621)

Measure	M	(SD)	1.	2.	3.	4.	5.	6.	7.	8.	9.	10.	11.	12.	13.	14.
Independent variable																
1. Studied abroad	.22	(.41)	—													
Matching criteria																
2. Sex (Female: 1)	.52	(.50)	.21**	—												
3. White	.50	(.50)	.08**	-.04**	—											
4. Asian	.29	(.45)	-.10**	.01	-.64**	—										
5. Latino	.08	(.28)	.04**	.04**	-.30**	-.19**	—									
6. Black	.03	(.16)	.02*	.02**	-.16**	-.10**	-.05**	—								
7. Native	.01	(.07)	-.01	.01	-.07**	-.04**	-.02*	-.01	—							
8. Pacific Islander	.01	(.07)	.00	.01	-.07**	-.04**	-.02*	-.01	-.01	—						
9. STEM major	.53	(.50)	-.18**	-.19**	-.03**	.06**	-.02**	-.03**	.00	.00	—					
10. 1st generation	.29	(.46)	-.04**	.06**	-.22**	.10**	.19**	.12**	.03**	.04**	-.03**	—				
11. HS GPA	3.75	(.21)	.04**	.11**	.10**	.04**	-.11**	.18**	-.04**	-.03**	.08**	-.12**	—			
12. SAT composite	1239	(159)	-.01	-.18**	.17**	.01	-.20**	-.20**	-.05**	-.06**	.18**	-.39**	.25**	—		
13. 1st year GPA	3.25	(.44)	.16**	.07**	.16**	-.05**	-.13**	-.09**	-.04**	-.05**	-.08**	-.22**	.38**	.36**	—	
14. FRL %	34.02	(21.84)	-.02*	.03**	-.17**	.04**	.16**	.10**	.03**	.03**	-.00	.34**	-.01	-.30**	-.17**	—
15. H. Income	90750	(32613)	.03**	-.03**	.07**	.04**	-.12**	-.08**	-.03**	-.03**	.01	-.30**	-.04**	.26**	.13**	-.69**

Note. Pearson's *r* reported.

*$p < .05$. **$p < .01$.

Artificial Goods: Credentialism and Student Affairs Professional Development

Laila I. McCloud   Niki Messmore

Because of ongoing pessimism and frustration with the increased work expectations that do not correlate with increased financial compensation, student affairs professionals are left wondering what the future of student affairs is (21st Century Task Force, 2020). Graduate preparation programs and professional associations that have maintained their position as significant socialization agents for the field (Duran & Allen, 2020; Perez, 2016) are also wrestling with this question. Many student affairs professionals spend several years in graduate school being socialized into ways of being, thinking, and doing that often perpetuate whiteness. This socialization shows up in the classroom where faculty position graduate Students of Color as the experts on race-related issues (Harris & Linder, 2018) while failing to encourage racial identity development among white graduate students (Briscoe & Jones, 2022). This socialization continues as educators become enmeshed in their institution's culture. When these graduate students transition into full-time employment, the positioning of particular groups of people as experts on certain issues will follow them. The presumption of expertise on certain topics (e.g., anything diversity related) carries over into the availability of professional development opportunities.

In recent years, opportunities for student affairs educators to pursue professional development have increased. These opportunities include pursuing additional degrees (e.g., a master's or doctoral degree or certificates) or learning experiences sponsored by professional associations (e.g., conferences, C.E.Us., or certificates). However, these opportunities come with physical and financial costs that need to be collectively assessed and evaluated by professionals and faculty compared to their effectiveness in enhancing student affairs practice and improving the quality of life for student affairs educators. Graduate preparation programs and professional associations have pushed practitioners and faculty to think about the role of credentialism in perpetuating whiteness, neoliberalism, and labor inequity that fuel our current evolution.

THE ROLE OF ARTIFICIAL GOODS

For this conversation, we understand credentials as any formal education deemed necessary or helpful for career advancement and social mobility. Credentialism perpetuates inequality in that individuals in senior-level positions operate as gatekeepers by controlling who has access based upon what Collins (2019) referred to as an "artificial good" (p. 243). Certificates

Laila I. McCloud is Assistant Professor of Higher Education at Grand Valley State University. Niki Messmore is Director of Medical Service Learning at Indiana University School of Medicine.

become an artificial good as they are used to demonstrate that a student affairs professional has more education, not that they are more skilled or knowledgeable. In this case, the increasing call for more skilled workers pushes student affairs educators to obtain additional educational currencies in a highly stratified labor market. Student affairs professionals are also in a unique position because their place of employment is both a site and guarantor of information production (Walters, 2004). We exist in a system that promotes credentialism while also seeing it as tied to our own success and credibility. We will explore these credentialing initiatives from our perspectives as a Black woman faculty member in a higher education and student affairs (HESA) graduate program and a White woman, mid-level student affairs professional.

WHO'S CREDENTIAL IS IT?

Contemporary social issues have pulled our attention to how whiteness dictates the entry into and movement within the student affairs profession. For example, the COVID-19 pandemic prompted many highly rejective graduate programs to eliminate their reliance on standardized testing to grant admission. The question remains whether the decision to eliminate the testing requirements was about disrupting whiteness or a response to limited opportunities to complete the test. Once students are enrolled in the program, faculty spend a significant amount of time assuaging students' concerns about their professional futures. Graduate students receive messages that they should know the functional area they want to work in for the rest of their careers. However, students who are racially marginalized often comment that they worry about having future career opportunities limited if they pursue certain functional areas. This worry is exacerbated by students' social locations and the organizational structure of

student affairs divisions, which promote siloing of student identity and development. Two issues arise from this siloing as it relates to credentialing. First, the presence of certificates for particular functional areas perpetuates the idea that there is a particular way of doing the work and that it can be taught. Second, the absence of certificates for a functional area assumes that the work cannot or does not need to be taught. Together these assumptions perpetuate whiteness by giving value to certain types of student affairs work.

The value of student affairs certificates is cemented in the belief that they will address a distressed labor market and provide a pathway for advancement. We believe that this push for certificates is another manifestation of neoliberalism within higher education. In this context, we understand neoliberalism as promoting the personal benefits of professional development in the name of social mobility and distinction. These certificates push past traditional means of professional development (e.g., attending professional conferences) to offer an individualized and quantifiable measure of expertise. In this instance, student affairs professionals become consumers seeking additional ways to differentiate themselves in the field. Many who already possess a graduate degree are expected to pay private entities anywhere from $200 to almost $3,000 for a certificate in hopes of furthering their careers. The rise of this model has the potential to increase the competition and inequality that already exists among student affairs professionals.

As previously mentioned, the value of student affairs certificates rests on preparing professionals to transition into or advance in a particular functional area. Given these certifications' financial and time costs, the outcome exacerbates inequality within our field. We also cannot forget that not every functional area, multicultural student affairs, to name one, has been included in this certification process. The fact that a significant number of professionals who are racially marginalized work in functional areas without certificates highlights yet another way student affairs practices reinforce boundaries around entry and advancement.

Scholars have argued that student affairs is a "one size does not fit all" or a low consensus field (Manning et al., 2013; Torres et al., 2019). These arguments acknowledge the diversity in how student affairs divisions are organized and how our work is practiced in relation to campus and societal dynamics. However, we do agree that there is a basic level of knowledge required to successfully support student development. Distilling this information into a single exam on which mid-level professionals will be evaluated is puzzling. The standardized exams associated with certificates perpetuate this idea of "testing for whiteness" (Au, 2020) rather than understanding whether the professional has a deep and critical understanding of student affairs theory, policies, and practices.

LOOKING OUT FOR EACH OTHER: COLLABORATION BETWEEN GRADUATE PREPARATION PROGRAMS AND STUDENT AFFAIRS DIVISIONS

We would like to offer one starting point for student affairs divisions to collaborate with HESA graduate preparation programs to address disrupting the individualized and consumer-driven nature of specialty certifications. If we wish to make our case to university colleagues that student affairs is a field of study and practice, we must become better storytellers. To have better stories to tell, we have to prioritize collaboration. The current collaboration model between many HESA programs and student affairs divisions is simply a labor exchange. HESA programs rely on student affairs programs to provide practical work experiences and compensation in the form of tuition remission or stipends. Student affairs divisions rely on HESA programs to equip emerging professionals with foundational knowledge about the field. The transactional nature of this relationship must be remedied. Campus-based professional development opportunities can be held in collaboration with HESA programs. This collaboration ensures that program faculty and student affairs professionals are leveraging our collective content and pedagogical knowledge to facilitate the conversations.

Student affairs is in a precarious place that certifications will not solve. Certifications will not address the underemployment, low compensation, and burnout that professionals experience (21st Century Task Force, 2022). Labor inequity alongside long hours, ineffective supervision, toxic workplaces, and exorbitant student loan debt has led some professionals to seek opportunities outside academia. The field must address the root causes of labor inequity if they want to protect the recruitment and retention of staff.

The arguments for and against credentialism are two sides of the same coin. Ultimately, we all are working to combat the problem of supporting the professional development of student affairs professionals. Yet, we believe that the current pathway toward credentialism will perpetuate whiteness, neoliberalism, and labor inequity.

Correspondence concerning this article should be addressed to Laila I. McCloud, Grand Valley State University; mcclolai@gvsu.edu

REFERENCES

21st Century Task Force. (2022). Report on 21st Century Employment in Higher Education. ACPA College Student Educators International.

Au, W. (2020). Testing for whiteness? How high-stakes, standardized tests promote racism, undercut diversity, and undermine multicultural education. In H. P. Baptiste & J. J. Writer (Eds.), Visioning multicultural education (pp. 99–113). Routledge.

Briscoe, K. L., & Jones, V. A. (2022). "Whiteness here, whiteness everywhere": How student affairs professionals experience whiteness at predominantly White institutions. Journal of College Student Development, 63(6), 661–676. https://doi.org/10.1353/csd.2022.0054

Collins, R. (2019). The credential society: An historical sociology of education and stratification. Columbia University Press.

Duran, A., & Allen, E. (2020). Exploring how professional associations socialize student affairs graduate students and new professionals. Journal of Student Affairs Research and Practice, 57(2), 132–147.

Harris, J. C., & Linder, C. (2018). The racialized experiences of students of color in higher education and student affairs graduate preparation programs. Journal of College Student Development, 59(2), 141–158.

Manning, K., Kinzie, J., & Schuh, J. (2012). One size does not fit all: Traditional and innovative models of student affairs practice. Routledge.

Perez, R. J. (2016). A conceptual model of professional socialization within student affairs graduate preparation programs. Journal for the Study of Postsecondary and Tertiary Education, 1, 35–52.

Torres, V., Jones, S. R., & Renn, K. (2019). Student affairs as a low-consensus field and the evolution of student development theory as foundational knowledge. Journal of College Student Development, 60(6), 645–658.

Walters, D. (2004). The Relationship between postsecondary education and skill: Comparing credentialism with human capital theory. Canadian Journal of Higher Education, 34(2), 97–124.

Investing in the Educational Success of Black Women and Girls

Lori D. Patton, Venus E. Evans-Winters, and Charlotte E. Jacobs (Editors)

Sterling, VA: Stylus, 2022, 312 pages, $37.50 (softcover)

Reviewed by Emerald Templeton, St. Mary's College of California

In her seminal work, *Black Feminist Thought: Knowledge, Consciousness, and the Politics of Empowerment*, Hill Collins (2000) described the "hidden space of Black women's consciousness" (p. 98) that includes self-definition; self-determination; and resistance to racism, sexism, classism, and white supremacy. Lori D. Patton, Venus E. Evans-Winters, and Charlotte E. Jacobs's work is an embodiment of this consciousness. Much like how Hill Collins designed *Black Feminist Thought*, the editors of this volume created an accessible text grounded in Black women and girls' experiences, knowledges, and existence. As a Black woman scholar whose research underscores the experiences of Black women in higher education while uncovering the logics of valuing diversity, I recognize the authority of this work and find that it aligns with and informs my scholarly interests. As a former Black girl who has trudged through misogynoir throughout my educational experiences, I feel incredibly affirmed, seen, and celebrated through this work. Written from the vantage point of women and girls across the spectrum of Black womanhood and girlhood, the authors of this edited volume artfully describe how we navigate the American system of education while maintaining our meanings and intonating our expressions (Hill Collins, 2000). This text is organized into four sections: (a) Mattering for Black Women and Girls in

Schooling Contexts, (b) Naming and Challenging the Violence and Criminalization of Black Women and Girls, (c) Navigating Politics and the Politicization of Black Women and Girls in Higher Education, and (d) Still We Rise: Black Women and Girls Lifting and Loving Black Women and Girls. The chapters in these sections provide the reader with context, discussion questions, further reading, and additional resources. These sections weave together narratives that illustrate the depth, breadth, and rigor of scholarship about Black women and girls. Each section sheds light on multiple experiences and voices, which I will describe below.

In the first section, Mattering for Black Women and Girls in Schooling Contexts, Patton et al. set the tone for this volume and lay a foundation for understanding the ways of knowing (epistemologies), being (ontologies), and thinking (ideologies) that influence Black women and girls' efficacy in school. Chapter 1, "Mid-Twerk and Mid-Laugh," uncovers how Black girls' ability to express themselves through laughter and dancing in culturally situated ways is stifled and criminalized. Further, the author posits that this level of expressiveness provides an opportunity for learning that schools can engage for transformation. In Chapter 2, readers are presented with ways to enact the Black girls' literacy framework, which allows schools to expand learning and literacy beyond simply reading and writing to a nuanced practice that situates learning in sociopolitical, historical, and cultural contexts. Similarly, Chapters 3 and 4 discuss the ways myths and stereotypes depict Black girls as older than they are, disrespectful, and underachieving. Such myths must be dispelled so that Black girls can find belonging and safety in spaces that were not intended for them. Together, these chapters encompass why

Black girls matter and how schools can begin to embrace that fact.

The second section, Naming and Challenging the Violence and Criminalization of Black Women and Girls, begins by situating the education of Black women and girls within a political context that surveils, polices, and arrests them. Chapters 5 and 6 detail the ways in which schools are failing Black girls—pushing them out and deeming them "nobodies"—by highlighting compelling cases and data related to their involvement with school discipline and the legal system. Further, the ways in which a lack of care and value for Black women and girls persist through higher education are explicated in Chapters 7 and 8. The authors herein urge educators and administrators to challenge their biases about gender and race and interrogate how the intersection of those identities reveals the ways they characterize and value Black women and girls. By naming and challenging the misrepresentation, unwarranted sanctions, and violence they experience, institutional actors can begin to explore how to enact policies and practices that support, care for, and value Black women and girls.

The authors in section 3, Navigating Politics and the Politicization of Black Women and Girls in Higher Education, discuss the rules, norms, and expectations that Black women learn to maneuver in postsecondary settings. The authors in Chapter 9 introduced the idea of Black women "struggling successfully" in college, meaning that they have found ways to achieve their goals despite a lack of investment from the college or its actors. From hair to mental health to disability, Chapters 10, 11, and 12, respectively, identify the negative assumptions about appearance, strength, and vulnerability unique to gendered, raced, and disabled bodies and describe the pathologizing of disabilities. Using an intersectional approach and incorporating a number of lenses, including social comparison theory and Black feminist thought (Chapter

10), critical discourse analysis (Chapter 11), and critical race theory (Chapter 12), the authors help readers analyze how Black women and girls are situated with respect to power in educational institutions. The discourse around navigating disabilities and identity is a welcome and necessary addition that needs further refinement and unpacking throughout the educational pipeline. Finally, Chapter 13 explores the author's family history with colonization and misogynoir and theorizes about how to use the "master's tools" (Audre Lorde) to advance the educational needs of Black women and girls.

The fourth and final section, Still We Rise: Black Women and Girls Lifting and Loving Black Women and Girls, leaves us with uplift, inspiration, and hope. Chapter 14 describes a transformative, rather than restorative, justice approach to education wherein educators cultivate care for and relationships with Black women and girls. Highlighting the understudied and underrecognized area of Black women's pedagogical practices, Chapter 15 includes Black women students' narratives about the deep care and "badassery," or resistance to oppressive systems, they experienced from Black women teachers. A step further, the authors in Chapter 16 describe the ways in which Black women and girls have supported and retained one another through the use of social media and digital platforms. With the broad reach online tools afford, Black women are using these connections to locate educational resources, provide encouragement to others, demystify and navigate the academy, and build cultural capital. Chapter 17 ties a nice bow on this volume with a liberatory vision for Black women and girls wherein they are seen, valued, and their assets recognized. This edited collection ends with an overwhelming call for an ethic of love—a radical approach to education and a necessary investment in Black women and girls.

Overall, this text presents an impressive and vital contribution to the field of education, particularly as related to interlocking systems of oppression (i.e., race, gender, class, disability) and how Black women and girls navigate them. Similar works from Evans-Winters and Love (2015) and Perlow and colleagues (2018) have described the ways in which Black women in education use Black feminisms and liberatory practices, respectively, to resist and sustain themselves. Likewise, Patton, Evans-Winters, and Jacobs offer an alternative lens to dominant white ideologies from which to teach, research, legislate, or practice in education. With an understanding of and appreciation for political, social, and historical norms culturally relevant to a group (i.e., Black women and girls), institutions can engage in more equitable and just practices that avoid stereotyping, misnaming, and oppressing that group.

What this book does well is provide strategies for educational institutions to employ that will center and affirm Black women and girls, thereby transforming the schooling and learning experiences to include everyone. Each chapter is embedded with lived experiences, narratives,

and compelling data that demonstrate the strength of scholarship while being useful to inform teaching, research, policy, and practice. Not short on citing up-and-coming Black women scholars, as well as noting seminal works from literary greats such as Patricia Hill Collins, Audre Lorde, bell hooks, and Cynthia Dillard, this text is engaging and thought-provoking. This text can be used as a training tool and guide for creating a culture of belonging and respect for others' humanity. Shedding light on the ways in which institutional policies and practices are often rooted in values that marginalize, the narratives herein offer historical context and a barometer by which to measure equity and inclusion efforts and the policies that support them. Further, this text situates a burgeoning area of study and inquiry at the center of a call to action and reimagining of an educational system that benefits everyone. We have all been offered an invitation to invest in a new way of thinking and doing that centers the experiences of Black women and girls and has the potential to transform the world.

REFERENCES

Hill Collins, P. (2000). *Black feminist thought knowledge, consciousness, and the politics of empowerment*. Routledge.

Evans-Winters, V., & Love, B. L. (2015). *Black feminism in education: Black women speak back, up, and out* (Black Studies and Critical Thinking). Peter Lang.

Perlow, O. N., Wheeler, D. I., Bethea, S. L., & Scott, B. M. (2018). *Black women's liberatory pedagogies: Resistance, transformation, and healing within and beyond the academy*. Springer Nature.